Multiculturalism

Canada and India

Comparative Studies

Multiculturalism

Canada and India

edited by

R.K. Dhawan ✦ D.K. Pabby

Prestige

an international publishing house

Published by
Prestige Books
3/28, East Patel Nagar
New Delhi 110 008
Ph. 9818755529

ISBN: 81-7551-166-4

Printed at Chaman Offset Press, New Delhi 110 002

Contents

WOMAN'S QUESTION

UNITY IN DIVERSITY: CANADA AND INDIA

CREATIVE WRITING

A New Diversity: Canada and India

R.K. DHAWAN and D.K. PABBY

Culture is an integral part of a nation. To begin with, we are confronted with the question: what is culture? The Oxford English Dictionary defines culture as "a particular form or type of intellectual development in a society generated by its distinctive customs, achievements and outlook." Broadly speaking, culture is taken as constituting the way of life of an entire society and includes codes of manners, dress, language, rituals, social customs and folklore of a nation.

Every nation has a distinct culture of its own. But when an independent country becomes a colony, the native culture undergoes a radical change. This is true of countries like Kenya, Nigeria and India. When these countries came into contact with Western culture, a process of change was initiated, and this process, in the course of time, destroyed their traditional cultures. While Indian literature had cross-cultural encounters with English studies, Canada has been undergoing a cultural metamorphosis with the mix of second races and people, from all over the world.

II

Immigrant literature, native writing and cross-cultural studies are the burgeoning areas of contemporary Canadian writing, and these truly represent the face of multicultural Canada. The rich diversity of Canada has great similarity to the cultural scenario in India, a country which constitutes several regions and languages. The issue of multiculturalism has acquired importance and urgency in view of the problems inherent in a mix of people with different ethnicities and religions, living together. The present volume, with its interesting collection of contributions, will help create greater awareness of the way Canada and

India, two important countries of the Commonwealth, are emerging as vibrant multicultural societies.

III

Both Canada and India are former colonies of the British empire and are now important members of the Commonwealth. But one can easily perceive the distinct ways in which Europe in general and England in particular had their impact on the social, political, cultural and literary milieu of the two countries. The major part of Canada is peopled by immigrant Europeans who settled down in its vast land by waging a fierce struggle against the hostile landscape. Then there are immigrants from other countries such as Japan, China, Africa, India, Sri Lanka, Pakistan and other south Asian countries, though their number may be much smaller as compared to the European settlers. The Canadian society also has minority settlements of the natives who have become exiles in their own land. Canada has two official languages, English and French, and the Federal Government proclaimed the policy of Multiculturalism within a bilingual framework in October 1971. The question of equality of status of women in all walks of life vis-à-vis the patriarchal mode has been bought into the main focus by strong feminist movements and dynamic activists and their organizations. Canada is far ahead of India in the field of socio-economic, technological and industrial advancements. It is, in fact, economically, educationally and technologically, one of the frontline developed countries of the world. But this immigrants' nation has its own share of problems and tensions which are exhibited through its long-continuing question for national identity especially at the cultural and literary level. It is so because the natives there had hardly any established and resilient literary tradition of their own except in some folk forms—legends, myths, set of beliefs, songs etc. and these too were not given their due by the 'master-immigrants.' Aldous Huxley wrote in "Text and Contexts": "Nations are to a large extent invented by their poets and novelists."[1]

IV

In the context of its varied problematic, the process of inventing the Canadian nation has been an ongoing process that began in the nineteenth century and these issues are alive even today. Writers like Margaret Atwood, Robert Kroetsch, Margaret Laurence (died 1987), Rudy Wiebe, and a host of other contemporary writers, through their writings—in themes, characters, narrative modes and strategies—are trying to highlight this quest for national identity by defining, redefining, analyzing and exploring it from all possible angles. The identity crisis of the protagonists in Laurence's fiction is a microcosm of the problematic of complex Canadian identity at the national level. In this connection, Laurence's views reinforce the dilemma of the complexity of this psycho-social and psycho-cultural Canadian construct:

> If our upsurge of so-called nationalism seems odd or irrelevant to outsiders, and even to some of our own people (what's all the fuss about?), they might try and understand that for many years we valued ourselves insufficiently, living as we did under the huge shadows of two dominating figures, Uncle Sam and Britannia. We have only just begun to recognize ourselves, our land, our abilities. We have only just begun to recognize our legends and to give shape to our myths.[2]

In the case of India also, the quest for identity has been a significant issue at the social, cultural, literary, emotional and psychological levels. Like Canada, the long spell of colonial rule, though it initiated the process of modernization and industrialization, also set in motion the process of deculturation of its rich heritage and the whole phenomenon was geared to provide all kinds of benefits to the rulers and exploitation of the ruled. The resultant phenomena are too glaring to be ignored. With political freedom came the trauma of 'partition' from whose ill-effects India has not been able to recover even today. Modernization having degenerated into 'blatant aping of the West,' the edifice of our traditional value system that has all along been oriented towards the spirit of self-denial, self-sacrifice, limiting of worldly desires, etc. has started developing cracks. Materialistic and consumerist tendencies are developing fast, generating a dialectical relation between tradition and modernity. Then there are new tensions and new demands with reference to the joint family system, norms of morality, gender-bias, generation gap, urbanization, marital maladjustments, phenomenal increase in employment opportunities for women and its overt and covert impact on male psyche, persistence of colonial discourse as a hangover of the British rule, etc. Moreover, casteist and communal politics, lip-service to the concept of secularism, criminalization of politics, acceptance of 'corruption' as a component of the widespread but inevitable social malady, lure of getting rich almost overnight even through questionable means, saying goodbye to the Gandhian values but swearing by Gandhian ethics and codes, sectarian and secessionist tendencies gaining impetus, violence and sexism eating into the vitals of the society, population problem acquiring titanic proportions, religious and linguistic minorities, cultural and ethnic diversities, regional disparities and increasing aspirations of 'the Dalits' and 'the backwards,' etc., are redefining and interrogating the relevance and role of societal norms, patterns of behaviour at the psycho-social and psycho-cultural level. Like Dalit literature in India, the emergence of native writers is making itself felt in the literary areas of contemporary Canadian literature. The native women writers write about human dignity and emotional sensitivity of black women, giving expression to the whole experience of a female culture.

V

Perceptive Indian English writers are taking due note of all these emerging trends in the social, cultural, political and literary life of the country and are re-visioning the complex phenomena through their writings. As the empire is writing back, most of these inversions, for obvious reasons, relate to the urban sensibility in the case of Indian English writings though the rural scenario is also being portrayed by a miniscule minority like Kamala Markandaya.

Anita Desai, Shashi Deshpande and Arundhati Roy are essentially articulators of the middle-class and upper middle-class psyche in the main and of the urban elite sensibility upto an extent, particularly with reference to the emerging phenomenon of gender-discrimination and assertion of female identity vis-a-vis the patriarchal character of the Indian mindset. They use modernist narrative strategies and techniques, experimenting with the form of the novel and the art of characterization in the Anglo-American tradition of the psychological novel, thus exploiting the potential of the narrative to mirror the confounding and at times perplexing reality depicting the society in turmoil and transition through the identity-crisis of the protagonists in their novels.

VI

Like India's own complex literary heritage, Canadian literature is written in more than one language. It reflects a regionally diverse and multicultural society. The wide variety of literatures in both the countries—Canada and India—fosters the growth of a unique composite identity in each case. Canada today is a complete world in microcosm because it has various distinctive ethnocultural groups and communities. Diversity of cultures has given rise to the emergence of varied literatures, the most noteworthy being Indian-Canadian literature. It constitutes the works of those writers who show a marked Indian sensibility or maintain a distinct South Asian identity. The last decades of the twentieth century saw the emergence of this new generation of writers—poets, dramatists and novelists—who have achieved their separate and distinct identities both in subject matter and style of their works. Notable amongst them are Rohinton Mistry, Bharati Mukherjee, Uma Parameswaran, Himani Bannerji, Shauna Singh Baldwin, Anita Rau Badami, Rahul Varma and Rana Bose.

VII

The most recent area of western literature that has affected both Canada and India is the emergence of queer studies, i.e., alternative sexualities. There is a growing interest in the issue of alternative sexualities across the world, both in the academia and among the lay readership. As marginalized groups, lesbians, homosexuals and hijras have been the most intensely oppressed. In the liberalized, postmodern cultural environment, there is a growing sensitivity to understand lesbians, homosexuals and hijras. We have to examine the problems they face at the workplace and in the neighbourhood, the life-styles they adopt and their struggle for survival.

In America and Western Europe, large publishing houses have begun to publish works on lesbian and homosexual writing. Several universities in Canada have established the departments of Gay and Lesbian Studies. In India, there is a great deal of response to lesbian and gay studies. Like Western publishing houses, Indian publishing companies like Penguin, Kali for Women and Women's Press have brought out literature on queer studies. Same-sex love has become a hot topic in day-to-day life, T.V., films and creative writing.

As is evident from the foregoing discussion, multiculturalism is both a social fact and the prevailing ideology both in Canada and India. It is undoubtedly the most distinctive feature of postcolonial Canada's national self-image. In many ways, the Canadian scenario is largely akin to one in India. A comparative study yields rich dividends. Hence this volume. We cannot close this introductory discussion on the subject without expressing our gratitude to those who have inspired and extended their cooperation in the preparation of the present project, especially Dr. Chandra Mohan (IACS), Professor Jameela Begum (Thiruvananthapuram), Professor D. Parameswari (Madurai), Professor Harish Narang (J.N.U.), Dr. Subhash Chandra and Dr. Suman Bala (Delhi) and Dr. S.S. Sharma (IGNOU).

NOTES

1. Frank Birbalsingh, "National Identity and the Canadian Novel," *Journal of Canadian Fiction*, 1.1 (Winter 1972), p. 57.
2. Margaret Laurence, *Heart of a Stranger* (Toronto: McClelland and Stewart, 1976), p. 217.

Canadian Multicultural Mosaic*

SUBHASH CHANDRA
S.B.S. College, University of Delhi

There is hardly a country in the industrialized world today where one can find an ethnically homogenous population. The aftermath of colonialism, the creation of refugees—often the result of ethnic conflicts—and the movement of peoples in search of greater economic, political or social opportunities have contributed to the worldwide mix of peoples. "Canada is in the forefront of countries affected by this growing diversity; it is also a country that has known ethnic diversity right from its inception." (Schwartz 10)

Canada chose the pattern of mosaic for its multicultural society as against the concept of melting pot, adopted by the United States of America. However, multiculturalism has been a fraught issue in Canada, ever since it was adopted in 1971.While on the one hand Pierre Trudeau, the then Prime Minister of Canada, has been hailed as a visionary statesman, who had the prescience to foresee that Canada's progress, peace and stability inhered in multiculturalism, on the other, he has been seen as a shrewd politician who, with a deft political move, strategically won over the sympathies and votes of the immigrant minorities and strengthened his party and government. There have been suggestions to initiate public debate on the policy and reconsider it. Richard Gwynn, a noted columnist, suggested in *The Vancouver Sun* in 1994 (A 8) in his column, headlined: "Multiculturalism

---

* *I am grateful to the Department of Foreign Affairs and International Trade, Canada and the Shastri Indo-Canadian Institute, New Delhi, for the award of Faculty Research Fellowship which enabled me to visit Canada during June-July 2002 and collect the materials for this article.*

Needs New Owners" that there should be an open public discussion on the issue to re-evaluate it. "A Letter to the Editor" in *The Toronto Star* (2001: A 27) proposed that "Canada's Brand of Multiculturalism Needs Rethinking" And as if in response to these suggestions, the policy of multiculturalism, continued to be under assessment till as late as September 2001, as reported by *The Toronto Star*, under the caption "Trudeau's Legacy is Still under Assessment." (2001: A 21) The present paper will consider:

(i) Official/governmental attitude towards and efforts for making the concept of multiculturalism workable,
(ii) The role of the print media
(iii) Whether the policy of multiculturalism has been a success

The "impetus to Canada's multicultural policy lay in the negative response of immigrant ethnic minorities to the mandate of the Royal Commission on Bilingualism and Biculturalism (B and B. Commission, as it came to be known) in the 1960s.

"Reacting against a policy that would relegate non-English and non-French Canadians to the status of second-class citizens, spokespersons for the immigrant ethnic collectives demanded equal treatment." (Kallen 165) However, volume IV of the Report of the Royal Commission contained observations on the question of ethnic and cultural pluralism and the status of various cultures and languages. Seizing on those recommendations, Trudeau announced the policy of multiculturalism within the bilingual framework in the House of Commons on Friday, October 8, 1971 with the following words: "It was the view of the royal commission, shared by the government and, I am sure, by all Canadians, that there cannot be one cultural policy for Canadians of British and French origin, another for the original peoples and yet a third for all others. For although there are two official languages, there is no official culture, nor does any ethnic group take precedence over any other. No citizen or group of citizens is other than Canadian, and all should be treated fairly" (*House of Commons Debates* 8545).

The royal commission was guided by the belief that "adherence to one's ethnic group is influenced not so much by one's origin or mother tongue as by one's sense of belonging to the group and by what the commission calls the group's 'collective will to exist.' The government shares this belief." (*House of Commons Debates* 8545)

The Federal policy of multiculturalism, thus, is a process of appreciating cultural diversity and enabling the visible minorities to attain equity and social justice. It encourages different ethnic groups to preserve their ethno-cultural identity within the overall Canadian values of Respect, Equality and Diversity, by sustaining their religious and cultural beliefs and rituals, and lifestyles comprising food habits, dress codes, belief systems. The policy of multiculturalism helps evolve a pattern of social life in which diversity and tolerance of multiple ethnic groups are accommodated besides providing state support to visible minorities in matters of employment and social security for building a strong, secular, peaceful and progressive Canada. Multiculturalism is for all Canadians; it is a part of the Canadian identity, part of the nation-building process. "No ethnic should feel out of the mainstream, because multiculturalism is the mainstream."

Some critical voices have emerged during the past few years, publicly questioning, and assailing multiculturalism as social ideology. A survey by the *Toronto Globe and Mail* and *CBC News* reported that "nearly half of Canadians believe the country accepts too many immigrants, including too many refugees who abuse tax laws" (*Letherbridge Herald* A3). There are some negative perceptions of multiculturalism: far from uniting Canada in diversity, it is being seen as divisive. It creates ethnic ghettoes that are out of tune with the kind of Canada the policy describes. Multiculturalism is seen as a policy for the ethnic minorities that has little to do with the mainstream Canadians. Some of the academics have begun to think the policy has eroded national and communal social goals and values; multiculturalism has come to be termed as "mosaic madness." And from the perspective of ethnic academics like Neil Bissoondath and Arnold Itwaru, beneath the surface of the ideal and practice of multiculturalism, lie its failures, the case of Donald Marshall Jr., who was falsely implicated and imprisoned on murder charges, being one of the several relevant examples.

It is noteworthy, however, that significant measures have been taken by the Canadian Federal Government/Provincial Governments to make multiculturalism policy a success since the Multiculturalism policy was adopted. For example, Canada ratified in the seventies three important United Nations Conventions: i) on elimination of racial discrimination, ii) on civil and political rights, and iii) on social economic and cultural rights. The Canadian Human Rights Act of 1977 gave Canadians legal protection from and recourse against individual discrimination. The Charter of Rights and Freedoms in the 1982 Constitution recognized multiculturalism for the first time in federal legislation, calling for the whole charter to be interpreted in a way that "preserves and enhances the multicultural heritage of Canada." (Greg 9) It also guaranteed equal protection and equal benefit of the law, free from discrimination on the basis of race, national or ethnic origin, colour and religion. In 1985, following the "Equality Now! Report" and the "Abella Report" on employment equity, federal employment-equity legislation and programmes were introduced, targeting visible minorities and Aboriginal Canadians as well as women and disabled persons. Article 3 (1) of Canadian Multiculturalism Act of 1988 (Statutes of Canada, 35-36-37 Elizabeth II, Chapter 31, Assented to 21 July 1988) reiterates that "multiculturalism reflects the cultural and racial diversity of Canadian society and acknowledges the freedoms of all members of Canadian society to preserve, enhance and share their cultural heritage" and "provides an invaluable resource in the shaping of Canada's future" (Brou and Waiser 637) The Broadcasting Act was passed in 1991 (assented to on February 1, 1991). It lays down, inter alia, in Article 3 (1) (d) (iii) that the State through its programming and employment opportunities arising out of its operations serves the needs and interests, and reflects the circumstances and aspirations, of Canadian men, women and children, including equal rights, the linguistic duality, and multicultural and multiracial nature of Canadian society and the special place of aboriginal peoples within that society." (3) The Employment Equity Act was passed in 1995 which aimed at achieving equality at the workplace. A significant example of the steps being taken to make the policy of multiculturalism authentic and effective is a court ruling that "allows jurors to be screened for racial prejudice" (*The Toronto Star*: 1993, A 10). Yet another law to curb racism in Canada was passed in 1994, which stipulated that "Race-related Crimes May Carry Longer Jail Terms" (*The Toronto Star*: 1994, A 3). I will like to mention another example of the fair intentions of the ruling machinery: Non-White creative writers held a conference on the theme "Writing Thru Race: A Conference for First Nations Writers and Writers of Color" on 30 June-3 July 1994. Interestingly, White writers were barred from participating in it. However, the Federal Canada Council and Ontario Culture Ministry funded the sessions, much against sharp public criticism, of course from the Whites, who argued that tax collected from all sections of society was being used to promote the interests of a particular segment and that the Conference was exclusionary and discriminatory in nature.

Ethnic publications are encouraged and even partly or fully funded by the Federal government in order to preserve and enhance the cultural heritage of ethnic categories. Some of the examples of these ethnic publications are *Namaste Canada* in Hindi, *Nagara* in Punjabi and *Hamdard* in Urdu.

Even at the Provincial level, laws have been passed and measures have been taken with a view to making the practice of multiculturalism strike deep roots. The government of Ontario some years back limited the competition in the matter of hiring and promotion process to the designated groups. The Employment Equity Legislation Bill 79 applies similar requirements to private companies to ensure that every employer's workforce, in all occupational categories and at all levels of employment, shall reflect the representation of Aboriginal people, people with disabilities, members of racial minorities and women in the community." University of Ottawa Law School designed an "Education Equity Program" under which certain categories (on grounds of illness, religious holidays, physical disabilities, single parenthood and racial background of minorities) would be provided "examination accommodation," meaning they would be given double the time for writing the exam. These measures by Ontario and Ottawa came in for criticism for bringing about discrimination in reverse. But here, what is important to note is the official anxiety to promote multiculturalism.

It could, therefore, be argued that multiculturalism policy has met with reasonable success in as much as nine of the ten provinces of Canada which have adopted formal multiculturalism policies that reflect the broader approach to multiculturalism taken at the federal level. Other governments, particularly from Western and Eastern European countries faced with European unification and with changing populations have been evincing interest and making enquiries from the Canadian federal government. The use of the concept of multiculturalism "spread from Canada to many countries, notably Australia" (*Canadian Encyclopedia* 1535). The Economic Council of Canada released a report called "New Faces in the Crowd," following a two-year study of the economic and social benefits of immigration: they looked at some length at multiculturalism and concluded that as an approach for managing ethnic differences, "it fits the best theory." They found that the multiculturalism strategy has "already registered some modest success in reducing the amount of intolerance in Canadian society." (*New Faces in the Crowd: Economic and Social Impacts of Immigration*)

Coming to the role of the print media vis-à-vis multiculturalism and ethnicity, the scenario is not quite bright. The print media not only reflects but also constructs ideas and attitudes through reporting (headlines, placement of news stories, the space devoted to them—it is difficult to measure the space because the page size in printouts is shorter), advertisements and adopting an ideological stance through the editorials and columnists' contributions. Before analysing the response of some of the major English dailies to ethnic events/situations/issues, it would be pertinent to point out that the major English newspapers are owned by cartels of white Canadians (consisting of few wealthy families). It is not that the print media is blatantly racist: there are instances of issues being responded to, by and large, in unbiased manner. For example, *The Toronto Star* published a story on top of the front page, with a photograph, covering five columns horizontally, with the headline "Sikhs Mark 295th Anniversary" (1994, 1, with a detailed report on page A 6). Similarly, the same paper published a report about Buddha Jayanti, with the headline "Buddha's Birthday Celebrated: Thousands of Metro Residents Mark Wesak" and "Celebrating Buddha's Life" (1994: A 6: 6 May, middle of the page and Sunday: 8 May 1994, top left, respectively), the latter report covering four columns horizontally.

The present paper will take up two events and examine the response of the print media to them to explore, if there has been a bias in tackling them. I will also comment on the advertisements, appearing in two major English dailies, *The Globe and Mail* and *The Toronto Star* to analyse the featuring of ethnics in those ads.

The Hijab Case, as it came to be known, involved a Muslim woman, Mousselyne who was ordered out of the courtroom, for wearing Hijab, head-cover, prescribed by Islam for women. The case was extensively reported. *The Montreal Gazette* carried the story on the first page, with the photograph of the woman, with the headline: "Muslim Woman Expelled by Judge for Wearing Head Scarf in Court" (2 December, 1993: 1 and 2) and again on 3 December 1993 on the first page, on top, spanning four columns, with the headline: "Judge Draws Fire for Expelling Woman from Court," and yet again on 8 January 1994—headline: "Muslim Woman Faces Grilling Over Religion." The same newspaper continued its interest in the issue and reported again on Saturday, 8 January 1994, with the headline "JUDGE: His Lawyer Says Use of Hijab Might Have Been Legal Tactic (A2—spanning four columns) and on 13 April 1994, with the headline "Judge in 'Hijab Case' Declares an Abiding Admiration for Muslims" (B3—spanning four columns). The judge concerned made the clarificatory statement at a social gathering of Muslims. It is indeed creditable for this newspaper to report the issue prominently and not lose interest in the case even after four/five months. It is clear that the pressure built by the print media made the Judge clarify his position and attempt to remove the hurt suffered by Muslims. In another case, known as the Legion case, in November 1993 a legion branch of the Royal Canadian Legion in British Columbia barred a group of Sikh veterans from entering after a Remembrance Day parade on account of their wearing turbans. The print media took up the case and covered it extensively. *The Globe and Mail, The Toronto Star, The Winnipeg Free Press* and the *Montreal Gazette* carried the stories. *The Globe and Mail*, a major English daily, went to the extent of coming out with a sympathetic editorial and castigated Whites for their racial bias. The result was the Legion Headquarters in Ottawa not only reversed the ruling of the British Columbia Legion Branch Office, but apologized for the humiliation suffered by the Sikh veterans.

However, there have been instances of bias. For example the death of a white police officer in an encounter with Mohawks, an Aboriginal tribe in Oka, Quebec, over the acquisition of land, belonging to the Natives Reserve for the purpose of turning it into a golf course, was reported as the first lead story on the first page of *The Toronto Star* (incidentally this paper is located in Toronto). The headline read: "Officer Dies as Mohawks Battle Police." (*The Toronto Star*, Thursday, 12 July 1990). The photographs accompanying the news make the bias against Mohawks obvious: the first photograph on top right, shows a Mohawk, waiting behind a machine gun. The second photograph underneath the first one shows a triumphant Mohawk standing on an overturned police van. *The Vancouver Sun* also carried this news as the first lead, with the headline "Quebec Officer Shot Dead in Mohawk Showdown" (Wednesday, 11 July 1990). But the killings of Blacks, Sikhs and Natives in racist violence generally merit only a small space on pages other than the first one.

There have been persistent reports that the mainstream media misrepresent the Native issues. *The Toronto Star* of Sunday, 29 May 1994 carried the headline: "Natives Assail Bias in Reports Dealing with Indian Issues" (A 12). Similarly, the Blacks have often railed against the stereotyping that the print media does when it comes to them. They are associated with violence and crime generally, which makes their lives difficult in the Canadian society. The Black students remain alienated and the Blacks in general find it comparatively difficult to land jobs.

No doubt, the print media is accused of creating stereotypes of Blacks, but it is also true that it is the print media which has highlighted the plight of Blacks. Here are some of the stories published in *The Toronto Star*. I will give only the headlines: (i) "Young Blacks Brace for Crime's Aftermath" (April 9, 1994 top left three columns page A 6). (ii) "We're All Targets, Black Students Say (April 14, 1994 top extreme left, two columns, together with photograph spanning three columns. (iii) "Father Tells What It's Like for Black Kids in Metro" (April 15, 1994, three columns top left with photograph). (iv) "Blacks Speak Out: Anyone Listening?" (April 16, 1994, letter of the Week B 3) and most important (v) an editorial headline: "Young Black Males" (May 15, 1994). I would like to quote the concluding words of the editorial: "It behoves bosses everywhere—in the private sector, in all government departments and the broader public sector, especially the police to ensure that their staff are not peddling private prejudices on office time. The rest of us, too need to listen to the voices of our Black youth. They have a message for us all."

An analysis of one week's editions of *The Globe and Mail* and *The Toronto Star*, the two major English dailies, reveals that approximately ninety six percent of the advertisements, featuring human models, feature only the Whites, whether they are males, females or children. Even though a range of products like cars, furniture and shampoos are used by the ethnics, one does not find them as models in the ads. Occasionally, a Black or a Native Canadian can be seen in them, but other ethnics are conspicuously absent.

On the strength of the several measures taken by the Federal and Provincial governments, and taking into account the by and large fair and unbiased attitude of the print media, it can be said that Canada remains a country where immigrants are treated with dignity, and where they are able to preserve their diverse ethnic cultures without let or hindrance from the governmental machinery. Canada is a country where racism is not entirely absent, but it is a country which is the least racist among the nations of the world. In Canada, there exists a citizenship of civility between all residents regardless of who they are and where they come from. A landed immigrant in Canada enjoys full equality from the day of setting foot on the Canadian soil and of being granted landed immigrant status.

No doubt, the media needs to be further sensitised towards the ethnic minorities. But compared to other multicultural countries across the globe, Canada does present a space to ethnic minorities where the official machinery is constantly busy trying to ensure an environment which is politically and economically equitable and socially and culturally protective of their individual/group cultural identities.

Bibliography

Brou, Dave De and Waiser B, Bill. 1992. *Documenting Canada: A History of Modern Canada in Documents: Saskatchewan.* Fifth House Publishers.

Canadian Encyclopedia: Year 2000. 1999. McClelland and Stewart, Toronto: Ontario.

Gwynn, Richard. 1994. *The Vancouver Sun.* A 8: 4 January.

Greg, Gauld. 1992. "Multiculturalism: The Real Thing," *Twenty Years of Multiculturalism: Successes and Failures*, ed. Stella Hryniuk. Manitoba: St. John's College Press.

House of Commons Debates. 1971. Vol. VIII, pp. 8545-48.

Kallen, E. 1982. *Ethnicity and Human Rights in Canada*: Toronto: Gage.

Letter to the Editor. 2001. *The Toronto Star.* A 27: Wednesday 26 Sept.

Letherbridge Herald (5 November 1991), A 3. Source credit is given to the *Vancouver Sun* and Peterson.

New Faces in the Crowd: Economic and Social Impacts of Immigration. Report. 1991.

Schwartz, Mildred A. 1991. "Introduction" *International Journal of Canadian Studies*, Spring, Vol. 3.

The Toronto Star. 1993 A 10: Friday 3 December; 1994. A 6 Monday 25 April; 1994 A 12: Sunday 29 May; 1994 A 3: 30 May 1994; 2001 A 21: 28 September 2001.

How Do We Say and See the Word: Spoken, Written, Sung and Drawn: A Personal Essay

CYRIL DABYDEEN
University of Ottawa, Canada

Saying and *seeing* the word (emphasis mine) spoken, written, sung and drawn are somewhat symbiotic; there are also semiotic implications because of the images we construe stemming from constructions inherent in "saying" and "seeing". And for a creative writer like myself "word" also suggests "world," inevitably, because of my being and working in the diaspora. No doubt, this latter takes on its own dynamic: the way it impacts on the numinous self, as things become crystallized through the alchemy of the imagination. Thus Guyana, land of my birth, also includes the Caribbean, and the Americas, Europe, Africa and Asia with memories being continually resonant and echoic. Maybe George Lamming summarizes it best what I am alluding to: "I do not think there has been anything in human history quite like the meeting of Africa, Asia and Europe in this American archipelago we call the Caribbean."

Discourses about deconstruction: how words truly resonate and become worlds of meaning and consciousness also come into play. Here I invoke philosopher Wittgenstein: "My language makes up the boundaries of my world"; in my case, I feel everything is reflected in my poems, stories, novels, personal essays and reviews that I have written over the years.

It is worth mentioning that I've been living in Canada for the past three decades. I recall late Caribbean-born novelist Sam Selvon once telling me that he preferred living in Canada (in his Calgary base, before he passed away) instead of England because Canada is part of the Americas where he felt closer to his native Trinidad. Contiguity of geographical space and the spirit of the place also become symbiotic; and I may add that it is significant for me to be here at this Symposium in New York City—indeed the Americas. I thank the organizers for making it happen, and for generating a real context for how one *says* and *sees* the word as a creative writer.

Diaspora—mentioned above—I am inclined to see in terms of old diasporas and new diasporas. Jewish people have gone through their own epochal movement from one place to another place, and ultimately to Israel, to mention one example. New diasporas include peoples moving from Guyana and the Caribbean, and from other parts of the world; within recent times—to the so-called metropole; all are engaged in what economists refer to the push-and-pull factors seen in immigration dynamics. The sense of exile, self-imposed or not, not unexpectedly, also comes into the picture.

Underneath all these factors at play is the longing for identity—it is essentially why we write; it is also how we see the nation, Guyana, or some place else (Canada), because of cultural memory, leading essentially to a reconfiguring of identity as we consciously or unconsciously merge the past self, so to speak, with the present situation. Indeed I often reflect on my formative years in Guyana, my having been born and raised in a sugar plantation (Rose Hall), and then being an active creative writer from a young age (I'd won the country's highest poetry prize in 1964, the Sandbach Parker Gold Medal); and history's markers have remained with me because of the colonial experience; and, therefore, how I view history often comes into play in my work as I "plumb the bottomless pool of origins" (Wilson Harris). It's why too, I think, one critic in Canada described my work thus: "Dabydeen frequently works back through consciousness or history to describe an original condition of unfragmented wholeness" (*The Fiddlehead*, University of New Brunswick).

Indeed Canada is also my space, as I try to infuse it with sensibilities of my Guyanese and Caribbean background, aligned with the sense of the vast country that Canada is, famously inspiring awe and beauty. Significantly, how we use language is closely integrated to how we say and see the word in this context and how we interpret past experiences overall. Often fractured experiences come into play because of the residues of colonialism that linger (mentioned before). The life in Canada is now integral with other current issues relating to human rights and the discourses associated with multiculturalism. For me everything is problematised: concerns about how we live—how we truly say and see the word.

Realism is what I try to capture—my way of presenting humanism in my work without fancy image-making for its own sake, I will argue. Thus, language-use becomes crucial as I bear in mind what novelist Jan Carew urges writers to do, if subversively: "to mash up the language." Thus, *saying* the word is engaging in writing a two-toned English, with dialectal and sprung rhythm elements always at work. Orality, as it is called, is embraced: it is very much part and parcel of the overall dynamic of expression. Not unexpectedly then, as T.S. Eliot exhorts: the aim of the poet (the writer) is to "purify the dialect of the tribe," which is particularly relevant for me because of my own distinctive Guyanese experiences.

Overall, how I see and define literature is also relevant. Usually at readings in Canada and elsewhere I quote Eldredge Cleaver as an introductory comment that "literature is the combination of the alphabet with volatile elements of the soul." It is nothing less but how we truly say and see the word.

II

Stephen Spender has said that a writer must mythologize the ground on which he walks; and I do walk in the Americas, in my being here in Canada: the Great White North. The notion of the "idea of the North" (Margaret Atwood) is very much with me, even as we also hear about the tropicalization of Canada, and Toronto being described as the "Caribbean of the North." The same description can no doubt be applied to New York City or South Florida.

But the polarities with respect to Canada also enter the picture. I recall the South African writer Ezekiel Mphalele—almost 80 years old—when he first came to Canada, expressed the view to me that he felt he was coming "to the Arctic." That says a lot; then too, I recall being told at the University of Miami a few years back that to be considered a writer in Canada one has to write about the Franklin Expedition . . . in seeking, if only metaphorically, the Northwest Passage.

The proposition, therefore, is that geography is sometimes destiny; and I have lived my seminal years in Canada in the Lake Superior region—I'd planted trees in my student days—a fortuitous way of bringing Canada closer to me: the flora and fauna, if nothing else, which I would later extend to mean "the landscape of the imagination" (mentioned in my anthology *A Shapely Fire: Changing the Literary Landscape*, 1987). But ethnicity is also destiny, as has been said: in my case, because of my racial background (and being involved in activism at the community level to bolster human rights and multiculturalism. Note: my most frequently anthologized poem is called "Multiculturalism".

What I am trying to say most of all is that writing about Guyana or any other place as geographical reality is aimed at not just capturing the zeitgeist, or writing about an "imaginary homeland" a la Salman Rushdie. Memory is indeed the mother of the muses; memory is the imagination (James Joyce); and artist Salvador Dali emphasized "the persistence of memory"; for me it's everything that crystallizes in the act of creating. More than often, "the past is a condition of the present," as Scottish-Canadian novelist Alistair McLeod suggests.

My definitive view is that one writes best about Guyana (or Canada) by being away from it, not unlike James Joyce writing about his native Ireland in his classic work, *Ulysses,* while living in Europe. Thus from my Canada base, where I am at, things are distilled in the imagination as the right alchemy occurs, enabling me to produce worthwhile art. Like all other unconscious acts, tropical and temperate zones merge with metaphors functioning as contrasts, and help to shape irony seen in my work. It is not surprising then that one of my books is entitled *North of the Equator*.

Carl Jung said that anything psychic is "Janus-faced . . . it looks forwards and backwards"; and maybe I am a better writer for being aware of more than one place. Guyana becomes distilled as I see my own experiences in terms of binaries; and it determines how I am inclined to truly *say* and *see* the word.

Therefore, too, it is not unnatural that I would write a poem entitled "Sir James Douglas: Father of British Columbia"—for Douglas was born in British Guiana (Scottish background) and came to Canada via the Hudson Bay Company, reflective of my inchoate historical sense. Or, living in Ottawa makes me conscious of the fact that one of the more well-known hotels here is the *Lord Elgin*—also the name of one of the ships that brought indentured labourers (like my forebears) from India to Guyana.

III

Saying and seeing the word relates to one's sense of finding an enduring identity; and it is significant that as a writer I see myself engaged in self-exploration: in who I am, and who I am becoming; and maybe it's true about what was said of me at the inaugural meeting of the American Association of Commonwealth Language and Literature Studies Conference held in Rhode Island a few years ago: that I am "one of the most hybrid writers around"—if being one often grappling with the sense of home and homelessness. As critic George Steiner puts it, we indeed become extraterritorial: we move around many cultures, many homelands; and a "multilingual matrix" is at work.

I will keep being interested in contradictions and paradoxes—the way artists do—and try to maintain integrity in order to tell the truth while at the same time explore all the possibilities that writing affords and simultaneously capture the quality of emotion in each experience as best as I possibly can. With Derek Walcott no doubt, I can say too that the only country I am really loyal to is 'the country of the imagination.'

And if Guyanese and West Indians are wanderers, as has been said, then we are truly "nomads of the imagination" (Wole Soyinka) in expressing the word; and the only tribe as a wanderer that I belong to is the tribe of the imagination. In this context, a Carl Jung reference is apropos: art is "nothing but a tremendous intuition striving for expression."

This paper (a draft) was delivered at Columbia University, New York City, on Sept. 3, 2004 at the Guyana Folkfest Symposium. Cyril Dabydeen was the only Canadian who presented a paper at this event.

Against the Grain: The Canadian Desert

BEVERLEY CURRAN
Aichi Shukutoku University, Nagoya

The desert is a landscape seldom foregrounded; it is, as Nicole Brossard describes it, a landscape "*sises à l'arrière-plan de nos pensées*" (177), situated in the background of our thoughts. In *West of Everything*, Jane Tomkins calls the desert of the popular imagination the classic Western landscape: "Fertility, abundance, softness, fluidity, many-layeredness are at a discount here" (74), but this desert is an imaginary landscape which conflates local landforms of prairie and range with a biblical land of severe conditions and extreme temptations. And just as Edward W. Said has observed cinematic representations of Palestine that portray "a Promised land conveniently empty of any inhabitants" (159), so the American desert has required the removal of natives from view, and the slaughter of animals before it could become the available site for the cowboy legend (Egan 21) in which the solitary hero (usually male) proves capable of overcoming any hardship the landscape may offer. This erasure is an initial chapter in how "colonial discourse turns empty space into inhabited place through the discourse of mapping and naming" (Ashcroft 128), marking the desert as a geographical object of desire. Thus were the deserts of Australia legally designated *terra nullius* in order to initiate the British Imperial project (Bordo 13), and it is the idea of a void, too, perhaps, that allows the United States to conduct nuclear tests in the southwestern deserts of its own land, out of sight.

At the same time that the desert has excited the Western imagination, it has also eluded it. If traditional Western narrative unfolds over time and the desert is a considered timeless landscape, then it would appear foreign and even hostile to that process. The desert's elusive and attractive qualities overlap in the Western imagination with an undifferentiated and generic East as a "space of otherness" along with a similar belief in its inscrutability and "imperviousness to change" (Schick 70). It is this conflation with the East that also renders the desert as a sexualized imagined geography: dancing boys and belly dancers are part of its erotic edge, intensified by the desert's links to temptations, and where the practise of self denial can be a richly erotic form of self-indulgence. While the "emptied" desert is rendered as space rather than place, some deserts exist as names that evoke the frisson of the unknown in spite of their familiarity. There is, for example, the Sahara "the schoolboy's desert" as George Bachelard calls it, the "immense horizon of sand found in every school atlas" (204), inaccessible in both geographic and temporal terms. The allure of the desert begins by poring over a map or page of a book, and imagining the romance of danger, the discovery of the ancient and forgotten, and of stories usurped from a culture hidden behind some "foreign" language. In Canada, there is no desert, at least in English, although there is a precedent for the French classical usage of "désert" to render the wilderness (Bordo 17). Configurations of land, however, have been frequent tropes in Canadian writing, and as W.H. New explains in *Land Sliding: Imagining Space, Presence, and Power in Canadian Writing*, "landscape is a place, but also it is a body of attitudes in time, couched in the manner of speech and asking to be read in its own terms" (New 130). New's study of land-based metaphors in Canadian writing is preoccupied with features of the Canadian geography, althogh the author admits an impatience with "the barren land snowscape" that has been repeatedly evoked in writing, and the European and American assumptions about that image that have proved so influential on Canadian culture. Is it only to resist "the snowscape mindset" (Ice Crystals online) that a Canadian writer, steeped in winter, imagines the desert, or are there other reasons to choose that landscape as a setting for a story, or as a verbal trope? Margaret Atwood wryly refers to the limited appeal of the Canadian landscape in *Strange*

Things: The Malevolent North in Canadian Literature (1995) from the colonial perspective: Canada's geography and its lack of "the exoticism of Africa, the strange fauna of Australia, or the romance of India," locate it on "the bottom rung on the status ladder of ex-British colonies" (2), another landscape joining the desert in a forgotten corner of the imagination. In spite (or because of) that dismissal, Canadians have always valued the "wilderness" over the city as a reflection of themselves. At the same time, in response to the need for an identity distinct from the United States, Canada "developed essentialist and geographical fictions to stress its innate difference," and with it, a resistance to "the interrogation of discursive systems and the intersections of knowledge, language and power" (Brydon and Tiffin 66). Over the past couple of decades, some Canadian writers, including Atwood, have interrogated these intersections, specifically linking, for example, Canada and the desert to make space for a narrative that is more ecological than developmental, that re-reads the "emptiness" as a place great with life. The desert then is an appropriate site for authors complicating the notion of nation and of self to include a more "densely textured understanding of who we are" (Niranjana 186). In this paper, I would like to look at how some Canadian writers imagine the desert, and how their choice of this site for their stories—particularly as a site for stories of translation, of love and war—goes against the grain of the dry clarity and air-tight arguments of historical narrative and critical positions, to make an unlikely space for writers and readers to swim with words and memory. In the examples that follow from Margaret Atwood's *The Blind Assassin*, Nicole Brossard's *Le désert mauve/Mauve Desert*, and Michael Ondaatje's *The English Patient* and *Anil's Ghost*, the notion of the "desert" will function in different accents and registers as a site of narration.

I will begin with evidence of how this re-siting in Canadian writing changes the "timeless" desert found in Atwood's latest novel, *The Blind Assassin*. While the desert is not the setting for the novel, it hovers about Ontario like a mirage, skewing our versions of both. Atwood begins the novel with a fictional reconsideration of where one might locate a story, a quest, with a number of possibilities: "dinner jackets and romance, or shipwrecks on a barren coast? You can have your pick: jungles, tropical islands, mountains. Or another dimension of space." (9) The collocation of these geographies suggests they are all viewed as extra-terrestrial. But the listener prefers another setting: a desert, with date palms and an oasis. The storyteller balks, evoking the landscape as sterile ground for the imagination unless there are props suggestive of ancient mysteries or erotic possibilities:

> Not much scope, with deserts. Not many features, unless you add some tombs. Then you could have a pack of nude women who've been dead for three thousand years, with lithe, curvaceous figures, ruby-red lips, azure hair in a foam of tumbled curls, and eyes like snake-filled pits. (9)

If, as the storyteller asserts, deserts then have no intrinsic sex appeal, they do conjure a particular version of romance. The romance of the desert through reading books about Egypt and longing to see the pyramids is an attraction not to the geography but to the props of a romance, of a "luxurious, ambitious, relentless vanished life"; where the desert is the unobtrusive white space surrounding stories of the restless rich, hardy adventurers, or perhaps, of missionaries. In *The Blind Assassin*, pulp fiction makes the desert part and parcel of a mysterious but very sexy East, as heady as Xanadu, as arousing as a belly dance. In Atwood's novel, Toronto costume balls in the late 30s abound with free translations of the idea of the Eastern desert manifest in (women's) costumes consisting of boleros, bare midriffs, and harem pants with nose veils. At roughly the same time, members of the Group of Seven (a group of artists clumped together in the same way we conflate deserts) are creating specifically Canadian wilderness icons that are landscapes devoid of human and animal presence, an imaginary ideal that became accepted as the "distinctive visual paradigm of modern Canada" (New 142). And in another neck of the woods in the 20s and the 30s, uranium is being used indiscriminately as radium in medicines or in luminous paint (Roff 55) and causing bone cancer and leukemia, even before it becomes a component of nuclear weapons and its taint a further dimension of the Western desert. Thus the sands of the desert wilderness shift to simultaneously accommodate a Western story and a stage setting of the erotic East. There is desire in this desert, but also danger in its seductive nature: "You can see how people are drawn to it, but like waterfalls or deep lakes, deserts are "places of no return." (473) As Atwood's novel progresses, the desert of the East is replaced by the desert of Back East in Toronto, arguably the cultural heartland of anglophone Canada, reversing the predictable Canadian pattern which views the West as the wilderness frontier and the East as the site of settlement and power. The desert's timelessness is downgraded to ageing and decay and sexual fever is replaced by aridity as the seasons turn on their hinges, "the earth swings farther from the light" (222) and the air dries out, "preparing us for the Sahara of centrally heated winter. Already the ends of my thumbs are fissuring, my face withering further." (222) The seasons revolve and blur, the signs of ageing, like earlier signs of sex, are like indecipherable hieroglyphics, or a secret code; the skin is like desert sand, like winter snow: "written on, rewritten, smoothed over." (371) Evidently we have not escaped the "snowscape mindset" here, but translated the desert into it. The desert in Awood's novel did not leave Canada, remaining an imagined place, a kitsch reproduction, which was more a comment on the lack of authentic "culture" that Canada lacked when (inevitably) compared with the grand civilizations of Europe, specifically England. But what Terry Goldie has identified as Atwood's "assertive maple leafishness" grows increasingly rare as Canadian acts of narration move away from nationalism as an essential component of a writer's consciousness. 'Where is here' is no longer a question confined to locations above the Medicine Line/49th parallel and probably never has been.

The desert in Québécoise writer Nicole Brossard's novel *Le désert mauve/Mauve Desert* is equally fictional, being in fact, the title of a book that a woman finds in a secondhand bookstore; in the process of reading it, she falls in love with it and decides to translate it. In short, the desert in *Le désert mauve* is a landscape of desire. "*Le désert est indiscriptible*/The desert is indescribable," begins the novel, *Le désert mauve* (1987), twinning the landscape and the lesbian as conceptual impossibilities. In a manner reminiscent of what Bill Ashcroft describes as the "sense of dislocation between the environment and the imported language" used to describe it that marks the tension between language and the experience of colonized place (Ashcroft 153), Brossard finds both desert and lesbian *désir* to be excluded Others in the dominant cultural tradition. Her project is to open that gap and, in the lapse of language, queer it in a process that will translate a desert marked by nuclear contamination and male violence into a landscape of lesbian desire. In describing the process of writing *Le désert mauve*, Brossard has said that "before the idea of the novel had definitely shaped itself," she knew that it would be in a "hot place, where the weather, *la température*, would be almost unbearable; people would be sweating; the light would be difficult" (*Mauve Desert*: A CD ROM translation). That site became the American southwestern desert of Arizona and New Mexico because of its contradictions: its beauty and danger, its timelessness and history; and its decadence, the traces of Western civilization in the litter of old bottles and the abandoned, rusting cars. Marking a trajectory that is north-south in her version of the desert, Brossard links the heat and light of the desert with the cold and harsh reflective glare of sunlit snow in wintry Montreal, subjecting "the misleading reflections" of the desert's white light to a translator's gaze. This story of the desert sparks in the instant formed by a single symbol: light, but that light is translated into the blinding glare of the sun, the blinking neon of motel signs, the restless movement of headlights, or the instantaneous flash of a gun or a bomb. Meanings ricochet off each other, prompting the novel's narrator, Mélanie, to wonder, "*La réalité avait un sens, mais lequel?* (28)/ Reality had a meaning, but which one?" (25), and the translator to rephrase that question as, "*La réalité avait un sens. Comment*?" (198)/ "Reality had a meaning. How?" (15), and inviting us to wonder what makes the desert so "natural" that it draws helicopters full of tourists bent on enjoying its ecological exoticism.

In writing her novel, Brossard imagined the desert through the images and words of books she read about the desert, appropriating the flowers and cacti that excited her through their names, through language. The novel's translator, that is, the character Maude Laures, the translator within the novel, finds the desert as a dimension of her reading, and, like the process of translation, a space, a landscape, an enigma entered with each reading." (133) *Le désert mauve* was an attempt by Brossard to translate from French to French, but her descriptions of the desert landscape the saguaro, senita, ocotillos, and arroyo show Spanish to be a language of the desert, as well as one of colonialism. The translator, Maude Laures, increases the code switching in her version of the novel, adding more Spanish phrases to her text, and Japanese, too, to magnify the echo of nuclear destruction that resonates in *l'homme long's* beautiful equations and his poetic recitations in the "dead" language of Sanskrit. Linking the desert through language with nuclear testing gives it a "semantic density," as Nicholas Entrikin calls it, that extends far beyond the geographical location to recognize the events embedded in that space through associative memory. *L'homme long*/ longman is certainly linked through language to J. Robert Oppenheimer, the director of the original atomic bomb project at Los Alamos, New Mexico. Maude Laures re-reads both *l'homme long* and his words. She renders him more substantial, calling him *l'homme oblong*/o'blongman to increases his menace, and changes his words, "I/am/become/Death-*maintenant nous sommes tous des fils de chiennes*" (17)/ I/am become/Death now we are all sons of bitches" (173), borrowed from Oppenheimer, who was himself making reference to the *Bhagavad Gita*, by absorbing the English into French to acknowledge Western complicity with the insidious use of nuclear technology, while at the same time clearly making gender distinctions and rejecting inclusion in the category of sons of bitches'. Thus she writes, "*La mort Je/ suis/la mortJe suis un enfant d'chienne*" (187)/ "Death/I/am/ death I am a sonofabitch." (173)

Even though the American desert is found in a country where a war has not been fought on its own soil for seven generations, the desert is still a site of struggle between the past and the future, "with the popular imagination constructing a past largely evacuated of machinery and a future utterly filled with it" (Detweiler 221). As Jane Detweiler points out in her essay, "Landscaping the Final Frontier," technology was a crucial factor in the settlement of the empty "deserted" spaces of the West by "centralizing such phenomena as the building of transcontinental railroads and telegraph communications, as well as the electrification of the western states." (224) Brossard peoples her desert with geometricians and scientists, and lesbian mechanics living under poisonous clouds of smoke that stop time, in a desert "pockmarked by decades of nuclear detonations" (Detweiler 218); and when she asks, "What then is the desert?" (138), it is erased of the human, traced by the human, a site simultaneously ancient, essential, and postmodern, "a site of the conjunction of the beautiful and the toxic" (Frow 1): To erase human traces, to fascinate with these same traces, derision, the approximate calculation of the life expectancy of a tin can, of a car wreck half-buried in sand, of a traffic sign at a crossroads. Of disappearance, traces, traces amassed. The exact calculation of languages that have ended up in space like an explosion (138). In the desert, fear can be exact, too: "beaks, fangs, stingers, forked tongue" (178), but there is another kind of fear found in the images of the motel, television, "a fear that frightens on the screen as in thought." (179) Perhaps it is the exactness of the desert that attracts the English, famous for their own "precise behaviour" as we read in Michael Ondaatje's *The English Patient*; and perhaps it is the uneasiness of technology so easily camouflaged by sand and deceit, on sites at the background of our thoughts that currently constitute "the secret of deserts from Unweinat to Hiroshima." (295)

The desert holds the secrets of the English patient's identity in Ondaatje's novel, and never relinquishes them. The titular English patient is, in fact, a character-site of the desert, a man whose intimate geography has been burnt to anonymity. Lying, dying, fixed on his bed in a room in a Tuscan ruin, the English patient occupies the dead centre of Ondaatje's narrative, and recalling the desert in terms of his own seared somatic state and through his memory, as he mediates between the nurse, thief, and sapper that share the provisional space of the abandoned villa. Brossard's interest in the desert was as a landscape of desire; her fascination in the process of translation was in the merging of tongues those of language, yes, but those of the woman reading and the woman writing, desiring each other, giving each other ideas. While the desert is still the site of a love story and of translation, it is located in the past and reached only by drifting on a raft of morphine. The English patient is a reservoir of information and a pool of memory, "a translated subject, a liminal figure," not someone who has "gone native" but someone whose identity has become terminally displaced through cross cultural experience" (Jay 421); and his stories of the desert are fragments of an immense and fluid interweave of narrative that no longer fits snugly together in an assured and sturdy way. This is a sabotaged narrative contained neither by genre nor nation state, a communal production of an epistemic community with transnational allegiances (Pease 2). It would mark a maple leaf waving narrative such as Atwood's as an anachronism; for Ondaatje's purpose, the national terrain of the Canadian narrative is, like the English patient, not dead exactly, but in the process of a radical translation. The novel reminds us that the desert experienced an averting of Western eyes for hundreds of years after Herodotus, from 425 BC to the beginning of the twentieth century (133): The nineteenth century was an age of river seekers. And then in the 1920s there is a sweet postscript history on this pocket of earth, made mostly by privately funded expeditions and followed by modest lectures given at the Geographical Society in London. (133)

Love and war and endless emotion charge the explorations, but in the name of scientific objectivity, these are erased in the process of writing, much in the way that "the truth of lived communal (or personal) experience has often been totally sublimated in official narratives, institutions, and ideologies" (Said 147), or technology airbrushed out of the wilderness in order to differentiate between the corruption of Civilization and the purity of Nature. The English patient had entered the Libyan desert as an explorer "between the wars" in 1930, and gradually become nationless, nameless. For him, the desert "could not be claimed or own edit was a piece of cloth carried by winds, never held down by stones, and given a hundred shifting names long before Canterbury existed, long before battles and treaties quilted Europe and the East." (138-39) As an explorer, he thought he was acting alone, or in concert with a group of men who cared only for the land, although one wanted a sand dune named after him, another a village. In the reports delivered to the Royal Geographic Society, "all human and financial behaviour [lay] on the far side of the issue being discussed which [was] the earth's surface and its interesting geographical problems.'" (134) Thus his eye fooled, for even as it registered the brightness and faith and colour" (261) of a desert illuminated by the communal book of moonlight, he misread the implications of European presence there: The ends of the earth are never the points on the map that colonists push against, enlarging their sphere of influence. On one side servants and slaves and tides of power and correspondence with the Geographical Society. On the other the first step by a white man across a great river, the first sight (by a white eye) of a mountain that has been there forever. (141) As in Atwood and Brossard, the desert here is a destination reached by reading, and indicates how "history enters us" through maps and language. The English patient knew the desert before he had ever been there, "knew when Alexander had traversed it in an earlier age, for this cause or that greed." (18) In the wake of his seduction in and by the desert, the attraction to that geography is in the re-reading, turning the pages backwards and "retreat[ing] from the grand storystumbl[ing] accidentally upon a luxury, one of those underground pools where we can sit still. Those moments, those few pages in a book we can go back and forth over" (*Skin of a Lion* 148); in the English patient's case, the story of his illicit love for a married woman. But like a book, the desert is also "crowded with the world" (285), and with the aid of books in code to guide spies and armies across it, the desert has been "raped by war and shelled as if it were just sand." (257) Caravaggio, the thief, sums it up: "The trouble with us is we are all where we shouldn't be." (122) "Europe is fighting wars in the "vast and silent pocket[s]" (134) of the Libyan Desert; Kip, a Sikh, is in Italy, is fighting English wars. The British army teaches him the skills and the Americans teach him further skills and the team of sappers are given lectures, are decorated and set off into the rich hills. "You are being used, boyo Get the hell out of Dodge City." (121) As much as the desert in *The English Patient* consists of fragments of stories drifting on a raft of morphine speaks of a "classical" European colonialism and military presence, it also evokes in its "hypnotic unreality" a remote imperial power using technology to keep its distance from the realities it seeks to control (Said 160). It is a desert then ineluctably troped with technology. Along with linguistic translation, there is the translation of guns by touch; the mechanical aptitude of the English patient, like the Sikh sapper Kip's cultural "affinity" with machines; and the radio, the hearing aid, the equipment that will become miniaturized and more sophisticated surveillance weapons for all kinds of later wars. And, as David Williams reminds us in "The Politics of Cyborg Communications," Marshall McLuhan wrote in 1964 that "all technology, including language as a means of processing experience, [is] a means of storing and speeding information. . . . In such a situation all technology can be plausibly regarded as weapons" (31), which lie adjacent to the extreme actions of civilization such as the bombing of Hiroshima.

In *Anil's Ghost*, Ondaatje strips the desert narrative of its hypnotic density, melding desert and island geography to further his exploration of violence, specifically that of the civil war in Sri Lanka. Anil Tissera, a forensic anthropologist, arrives in Colombo "directly from working in sparse high-tech desert towns of the American Southwest. Although her last location, Borrego Springs, hadn't seemed, at the start, enough of a real desert to satisfy her" (148): Too many cappuccino bars and clothing shops on the main street. But after a week she was comfortable in what was really a narrow strip of civilization, a few mid-twentieth-century luxuries surrounded by the starkness of the desert. The beauty of the place was subtle. In the south-weastern deserts you need to look twice at emptiness, you needed to take your time, the air like ether, where things grew only with difficulty. On the island of her childhood she could spit on the ground and a bush would leap up. (148) She had been sent by a human rights group based in Geneva to try and unearth the source of ongoing murders which have made fear endemic. The desert is sited in the background of this story, but never forgotten, offering a geographic counterpart to the amygdala, the somatic location for fear in "the dark aspect of the brain," and offsetting the isolated image of the island by providing an echo of its pattern in the manner of "those nineteenth century novels where brothers and sisters in different cities could feel the same pains, have the same fears." (135) Her lover is left in the desert as she was in *The English Patient*, while Anil attempts to open another container of secrets. The novel also echoes Brossard's desert, in the lesbian of Anil and Leaf Niedecker, their "high speed driving in the desert, swerving back and forth in the night" 236). In Sri Lanka, Anil remembers the desert like a story: once upon a time in the West. Like a movie. But her partner, Leaf, wanders in the desert of the southwest, losing her memory as she succumbs to Alzheimer's. The Western story, like a cowboy with a willed version of Alzeimer's, forgets history and denies the communal nature of consciousness, letting wars fester beyond its borders, and profiting from the sale of weapons or other multi-use technologies; letting waste be disposed of somewhere where nobody cannot see it, somewhere where "we" do not live. Technology allows the domination from a distance in a way that translates "classical" European colonialism into a remote imperial power that does not occupy the land so much as preoccupy the mind and recolonize the soul. The desert here is no longer indescribable for it adheres to a familiar plot of controlling turf and trade. As I said, quoting Nicole Brossard at the beginning of this paper, the desert is a location situated in the background of our thoughts, except for those whose lives are inextricably part of that geography, like the Aboriginal Australians living alongside the uranium mines and Maralinga and Emu Field test sights;

the Navajo, Lakota and Hopi of the Four Corners (Arizona, New Mexico, Colorado and Utah) downwind of the Nevada Test Site; the Inuit, Ojibway nation and Dene Indians of Canada caught between the US's Alaska test site and the old Soviet sites of Novaya Zemlya and Semipalantinsk (Roff 55). Foregrounding the desert and making its geography intimate rather than remote is a way to protest how secrets are "hidden" in locations emptied of meaningful life and written out of histories. Without boundaries the land knits us together in a communal fate that cannot be escaped, no matter how the cowboy story has insisted. There is no point in going off to the desert and living in isolation, seeing civilization as corrupt and wilderness as pure and no one can ride off into the sunset: the desert offers no demarcations that give us our bearings or leave us solitary readers.

Works Cited

Ashcroft, Bill. *Postcolonial Transformations*. New York, London: Routledge, 2001.

Atwood, Margaret. *The Blind Assassin*. London: Bloomsbury, 2000.

Bachelard, Gaston. *The Poetics of Space* (1958). Trans Maria Jolas. Boston: Beacon Press, 1964.

Bordo, Jonathan. "The Terra Nullius of Wilderness Colonialist Landscape Art (Canada and Australia) and the So-Called Claim to American Exception." *International Journal of Canadian Studies/ Revue internationale d'études canadiennes*. 15, 1997: 13-36.

Brossard, Nicole. *Le désert mauve*. Montréal: l'Hexagone, 1987.

_____. *Mauve Desert*. Trans. Susanne Lotbinière-Harwood. Toronto: Coach House Press, 1990.

Brydon, Diana, and Helen Tiffin. *Decolonizing Fictions*. Sydney: Dangaroo Press, 1993.

Detweiler, Jane. "Landscaping the Final Frontier." *Western Futures*. Ed. Stephen Tchudi. Reno, Las Vegas: Nevada Humanities Committee, 2000. 217-44.

Egan, Ken, Jr. "Montana Apocalypse." *Western Futures*. 17-30.

Frow, John. *What Was Post-Modernism?* Sydney: Local Consumption, 1991.

Haraway, Donna. *Simian, Cyborgs, and Women: The Reinvention of Nature*. New York: Routledge, 1989.

Haynes, Roslynn D. *Seeking the Centre: The Australian Desert in Literature, Art and Film*. Cambridge: Cambridge UP, 1998.

Jay, Paul. "Translation, Invention, Resistance: Rewriting the Conquest in Carlos Fuentes's *The Two Shores*.'" *Modern Fiction Studies*, 43 (2) Summer 1997: 405-31.

Jenik, Adriene. *Mauve Desert: A CD-ROM Translation*. Los Angeles: Shifting Horizon Productions, 1997.

New, W.H. *Land Sliding: Imagining Space, Presence, and Power in Canadian Writing*. Toronto: University of Toronto Press, 1997.

_____. "Ice Crystals." *Journal of Modern Literature*, 23(3/4): 565-73.

Niranjana, Tejaswini. *Siting Translation: History, Post-Structuralism, and the Colonial Context*. Berkeley: University of California Press, 1992.

Ondaatje, Michael. *In the Skin of a Lion*. London: Picador, 1987.

_____. *The English Patient*. Toronto: Vintage Books Canada, 1993.

_____. *Anil's Ghost*. Toronto: McClelland and Stewart, 2000.

Pease, Donald E. "National Narratives, Postnational Narration." *Modern Fiction Studies*, 43(1) Spring 1997: 1-26.

Roff, Sue Rabbitt. "Let Them Eat Yellowcake." *Western Futures*, 55-72.

Said, Edward W. *Reflections on Exile and Other Essays*. Cambridge, MA: Harvard University Press, 2000.

What is Writing?
Native Canadian Women Speak

SUNEETHA RANI
University of Hyderabad

Native literatures construct their histories and deconstruct colonial hegemony. The politics of native literatures is to release the native life imprisoned by white colonialism. For native writers, literature is not a leisure time activity or pleasure writing. Writing for them is liberation, healing and medicine. It is not only a medicine for the long-suffering, culturally-eliminated and identity-deprived indigenous people, but also a healing tool for the ailing and racially discriminating white society.

Speaking on the subject of the importance and effect of stories, Lenore Keeshing Topias highlights the need to study and interpret life stories: "Stories, you see, are not just entertainment. Stories are power. They reflect the deepest, the most intimate perceptions, relationships and attitudes of a people. Stories show how a people, a culture, thinks."[1] Native Canadian women's stories hold a mirror to a people, a culture and their thoughts. They depict a displaced culture, disowned people and thoughts in crisis. Life stories of Native Canadian women function as community stories, for they present community experience and collective history. It is with the aim of sharing and conveying this common memory of the culture that Native Canadian women write. With a heritage of thousands of years of oral tradition, Native Canadians switch over to written literature in English to exercise their power of articulation and narration.

Stories are power because, as Topias says, stories reflect the deepest, the most intimate perceptions, relationships and attitudes of a people. But, the question is, when these stories of victimisation are narrated in the language (English) and form of the victimiser, is the victimised really using the stories as negotiations of power? As Native Canadian writing repeatedly reveals, there is an attempt to record the glorious past before the advent of the colonisers and the days of colonisation by the Native writers. It is Native Canadian history in making where Natives write about Native experiences from their point of view. This is also an attempt to condemn "the other" who is "othering" the Native Canadians in their own country, and to prove the lack of credibility in white narratives of Native Canada.

The burden of the coloniser's language becomes a torment for them. But they have no other choice except to write in English if they want to reach as many readers as possible in their as well as the white communities. They can write in their languages only to experiment or to show the remnants of their nearly extinct languages. But, if they want to use their stories as narratives of power they have to narrate and share "l'anguish,"[2] an ordeal of the colonial language. Maria Campbell explains her struggle with English and how she emerged victorious: "For a long time I couldn't write anything, because I didn't know how to use English. . . . When I was writing I always found that English *manipulated* me . . . then I was able to manipulate English, and once I was able to manipulate English, I felt that was personal liberation."[3]

In this context, the concept of *wordarrows*[4] describes the situation. Words function as arrows attacking the imperialist and discriminationist attitudes of a racist society. It is not a mere record of the past but an ongoing battle in which Natives counter the attitude of white society and literature towards Natives. While using writing as *wordarrows*, Native Canadian women not only write their stories but also contemplate about the art of writing. Storytelling has always been part of their tradition and their life because that was a way of sharing experiences and thus educating and warning the young and the inexperienced. Contemporary Native Canadian women's writing also aims to educate their own people as well as other sections, especially the politically dominant ones about Native experience and Native history. Thus, writing for them is educating. It is an education about identities as well.

Patricia Monture Angus says, "Growing up 'Indian' in this country is very much about not having the power to define yourself or your own reality. It is being denied the right to say, 'I am!'—instead, always finding yourself saying, 'I am not.'"[5] This represents the predicament as well as the literary commitments of the Native Canadian woman writer. This is a situation where justification of what she is not comes before the assertion of who she is. It is her identity constructed by the other that the Native Canadian woman writer deconstructs. It is precisely at this point that the need for and the longing of the Native Canadian women writers to define themselves begin. In order to define themselves, they have to shatter the image already created by the other. Before they construct their identity, they have to free themselves from the impositions and expectations of the other. And hence the discourse starts at "I am not" rather than at "I am." In such a situation where Native Canadian women writers write to prove themselves and disprove "the other," how do their narratives function as stories of power when they are written in English in the supposedly western literary tradition?

The metaphor of "blanket" that Cheechum uses while talking about the Native predicament in Maria Campbell's *Half-Breed* is very relevant in the Native Canadian situation. It is this blanket of identity that is thrust on the women writers by the dominant section of the society as well as by the State. It is the Native women's constant struggle to tear the blanket and come out to prove what they are that we come across in their writing. It is like the blankets that were distributed among the Australian Aborigines in the early colonial times by the British. They were the blankets used by people who were suffering from and died of dreadful diseases in England in the "shelter" of which Aborigines perished in great numbers. These blankets of identity distributed to Native Canadians in the name of preservation and protection became an unbearable burden for the natives under the weight of which their physical as well as psychological self suffered a great calamity. The words of Cheechum comparing their identity to the blanket are very insightful and put the native situation in a nutshell very effectively: "when the government gives you something, they take all that you have in return—your pride, your dignity, all the things that make you a living soul. When they are sure they have everything, they give you a blanket to cover your shame."[6]

It is from this identity crisis and a longing to define one's own identity that Beth Brant's concept of identity emerges. Even before she explains her title *Writing as Witness*, she describes her identity. Her identity locates her in the context of Canadian writing as well as Native Canadian writing. It also indicates the purpose of Beth Brant's writing which is one of the important points that she takes up for discussion in her book. She projects herself only as a contributor to Native Canadian women's writing, but not as a creator, pioneer, initiator of a literature or a literary tradition. She identifies herself as a lesbian, mixed-blood, urban, not educated in western tradition and makes it clear that she is not the spokesperson for the Mohawk nation or any nation. She also expresses her wish to convey the message that words are sacred. This serves as a foundation for her argument that begins by calling Pauline Johnson the spiritual grandmother of the First Nations women writers. She defines Native women's writing as follows:

> I look on Native women's writing as a gift, a give-away of the truest meaning. Our spirit, our sweat, our tears, our laughter, our love, our anger, our bodies are distilled into words that we bead together to make power. Not power *over* anything. Power. Power that speaks to hearts as well as to minds.[7]

No wonder she says that Native women's writing is the Good Medicine that can heal them as a people. She identifies the major difference between Aboriginal writing and European-based "literature" as the collective experience expressed in native writing. They write as members of an ancient, cultural consciousness and their muse is "us," their muse is ancestors, their muse is their people, earth and nature. Deep connections with female elders and ancestors manifest as respect for female wisdom in their lives and writing. We are also reminded of the words of Topias here. It is to exercise this power over minds and hearts that she writes. They do not have political and social power. However, their cultural heritage gives them spirituality as legacy on which Native Canadian writers have a complete hold. It is to share their spirituality that she writes.

It is from this effort to heal that Beth Brant's concept of "recovery-writing" emerges. It is a recovery from the age-old colonisation, discrimination and exploitation. It is also a recovery of their literary tradition which was drastically affected by colonisation and implementation of English language. Recovery-writing is writing that is recovering and also writing which helps native people recover. Beth Brant identifies Recovery-writing as another component in the movement of Native women writers. Let us see how she describes recovery-writing:

> Recovery from substance abuse, as well as racism, sexism and homophobia. . . . Highly charged with anger, this recovery-writing is, at the same time, gentle with the knowing of how difficult the path is toward the Good Red Road. There is empathy and comparison in the telling of our people's struggle to stay clean and sober, there is rage against the State that employed *and* employs addiction to attempt our cultural annihilation. (18)

Thus native literature stands for the Native Canadian situation symbolically as well as literally. While even Native Canadian identity and existence become political, how can Native literature remain untouched by politics? This is the question that Beth Brant poses. In response to the criticism that Native literature is too political, she asserts the political aspect of their literature and questions, when was it not political: "our very survival *is* a political act." (46)

It seems, literature with a purpose, coming from the marginalised sections is often labeled as too political. It is accused of lack of literary aesthetics and of repetition. Probably being overtly political, according to the canon makers, makes native literatures too political and thus non-literary. Refusal to conform also makes Native Canadian literature invalid for literary scrutiny. Beth Brant takes up the charge levelled by the critics and throws it back with the same vehemence at them. She aims a series of questions at the white critics:

> our work is said to have no plots! If we won't conform, how can these conformist reviewers write reviews?! Perhaps the questions should be: why are critics so unimaginative in *their* writing? Why are they ignorant of what is being written by my sisters? Why is a white-European standard still being held up as the criteria for all writing? Why is racism still so rampant in the arts? (11)

This raises the basic questions about the definitions of writing and the criteria for deciding why a particular writing is literature. While the Native literatures are considered to be too autobiographical, repetitive, coarse, raw and nonliterary, Beth Brant attacks the white critics for their unimaginativeness thus subverting the charges against their writing. Racism in arts is being challenged by Beth Brant. She gives a new definition to writing by questioning the white literary tradition and also deconstructing the same. While she explains the reasons and purposes of her writing, a new literary theory and a new literary tradition take birth. Let us examine how she does that. But, before going to Beth Brant's contention of her role as a writer, let us see what Ruby Langford Ginibi, an Australian Aboriginal writer, says about Aboriginal literature: "Most of our writing up until recently has not been defined as 'real' literature. Pray tell, what is literature? In the dictionary, it states it's a form of the written word, though, over the last ten years, there has been a revolution in Aboriginal writing."[8] This shows how white literary tradition has been judgemental about native literatures.

It is interesting that Beth Brant, who asserts herself as a lesbian also mentions that her native society itself does not tolerate the "two spirit" people. Feminism and feminists are not out of her scope as well. Experiencing her gender consciousness does not stop her from differentiating between Native women and the white feminists. It is here that we are reminded of an Australian Aboriginal writer Jackie Huggins. Jackie Huggins looks at writing as liberation, But for her this liberation has to be a freeing from white feminists as well, because, gender did not prevent white women from colonising the Aboriginal women. White feminists are no less than the missionaries who showed the zeal to reform the "uncivilised." On the other hand, white feminists' attempts to assimilate Aboriginal women into the movement will hamper Aboriginal movement by giving more importance to gender than race and by creating divisions between Aboriginal men and women.[9] In a similar manner, Beth Brant articulates the native dimensions of feminism:

> Some of us may have been uncomfortable with the word, but not the force behind the word. . . . I think it's time we realize that feminism is not just about white women, it is about all of us. Writers like Lee Maracle, Betty Bell, Kate Shanley, argue for a feminism that encompasses sovereignty, children, earth, class, race, sexuality, and all the varied and exciting aspects that make community possible. We are changing the face of feminism. It is no longer a middle-class, white movement for acknowledgement and better pay—it is about uranium in our drinking water, fetal alcohol syndrome, family violence, a life for the generation to come. We are writing about this in passionate and poetic language. We are not afraid to bring "family secrets" into the open air of this new day. The "secrets" belong to all of us. (39)

These family secrets are the consequences of the marginalised situation that the natives have been placed in. By bringing these family secrets into the public, Native Canadian women's writing widens the scope of feminism beyond gender issues to the social, political, historical and economic issues which decide the status of gender in the society.

Beth Brant also states that issues of race and class have to be discussed apart from gender. She reiterates that these issues have to be discussed not on "their terms." Identification with gender issues and moving away from the conventional by declaring her lesbian inclinations, Beth Brant establishes a unique identity for herself. But this does not alienate her from her racial identity, racial predicament and racial commitments. She remains a Mohawk lesbian and reinforces the race and gender aspects of her identity which are the crucial decisive factors in her native existence. Her political agenda is not to take arms but use literature as a weapon. Her political strategy is to neither assimilate nor alienate, but demand for an equal status protecting her unique identity.

The political stand of native women writers decides the form, content and tone of the text, where writer herself becomes the subject as well as the object. Beth Brant's stand, though rooted deep in community consciousness, her identity as a Mohawk lesbian compels her to counter the charges and assaults and charges from her own as well as the white society.

Beth Brant contemplates making bread as her writing is not going well. Both these creative activities follow the western model, leaving no chance for the native way of life. In fact, writing itself challenges the native oral tradition. Using paper to write challenges the ecological balance as paper is considered the flesh of trees and using the computer challenges the natural lifestyle of the natives. As she is making bread, she is writing in her mind. She is contemplating, formulating her thoughts and debating the activity of writing from a Native perspective. Making bread in an oven and writing on a computer—both are western concepts or reflect the western lifestyle. These two may be linked thus erasing the boundary between art and craft.

But, somewhere in the whole description something sounds striking. One is reminded of her description of her identity as one who is not educated in the western tradition. With this "distance" that she creates between herself and the western education, where does her writing on computer fit in? It is not the much debated question of authenticity of native experience or what is "Native" in a changed scenario. But, it is the issue of Beth Brant, consciously and deliberately, using the analogy of making bread and writing on computer, thus bringing the question of her Native identity for discussion once again. Here, Beth Brant stands as a representative of the Natives who are subjected to forcible acculturation, though they have never been able to get an acceptance into the society which is proposing reconciliation and assimilation.

This comparison also takes us to her statement that memory is like a drum. One tap and the sound reverberates. If memory is a drum, the reverberation is Native literature. Note the obvious difference between the analogies of bread making, computer writing and the drum tapping. While memory is represented by the traditional drum, writing is represented by machines and mechanisation. This may lead us to the very activity of writing or written literary tradition which is alien to Native oral tradition. Brant says, "My people are an oral people. This means that our stories, our history, our value-systems, our spirituality have been given to us by the spoken, not the written word." (49) That is why, while her drum and the reverberation go through no change and remain intact, writing on computer becomes "alchemy." This could be the mixture of two identities leading to an identity crisis or mixture of two literary traditions which contributes to written, replacing the oral.

Brant taps the drum of memory to extract truth, to spread truth and replace untruth, thus cleansing herself as well as the community memory, white or black, which is fed on untruth. It is an experience of unlearning falsehood and learning truth:

> I feel a personal responsibility and a strong desire to tell the truth. Sometimes that desire is a physical craving as I sit in front of my machine, sweating, hurting, struggling with a contra language to conceive new words. I desire to make rage a living testament. I desire to heal. I desire to make beauty out of circumstances that are not beautiful. I desire truth. (53)

Brant states that she wants to speak the truth. According to her, there are no multiple truths as the white world says. There is only one truth, the ultimate truth. That is the truth that she wants to speak through her writings. But, what is that truth? Can there be an ultimate, sole truth? Is it the Native experience that she is describing as the ultimate truth? If so, which Native experience? Obviously, Native experience before the advent of the colonisers has become a fact of the past now. For the contemporary Native Canadian it does not hold any relevance except to know the past. Is this the truth about the bitter fact of colonisation and the aftermath? If so, does she look at other Native writers who also have been writing this truth? In any case, who is she talking to?

Who is she sharing this truth with? Natives or whites? With those who know the truth or unaware of the truth? As a Native historian, she tries to throw light on the distorted facts and deceiving fictions about Native Canadians woven by the whites. Probably the best example is about Princess Pocahontas. It is exactly these hidden truths that Brant tries to speak about. Her accounts of Pocahontas reveal the amazing side of the story of Pocahontas and put the white version in a questionable position. This questions the historicity of white narratives.[10] But, it still remains a question as to what were the sources for Beth Brant, oral literature or white narratives? How far were they not influenced and distorted by various influences involved in a colonised-coloniser discourse?

It is also interesting to note the way Beth Brant connects the oral tradition with recovery-writing and healing. She says that oral tradition requires a telling and a listening that is intense and intentional. Giving-receiving-giving is a complete circle of truth. Native writing gives the gift of love which is the overwhelming instinct in their spirit. She also complains that love is a word that is abused and made empty. She feels a deep spiritual bonding with the people, Carrier, Menominee, Cree, Cherokee, Lakota, Inuit, Abenaki and many others whom she identifies as the threads of a weaving: "Writing is an act that can take place in physical isolation, but the memory of history, of culture, of land, of Nation, is always present—like another being. That is how we create. Writing with all our senses, and with the ones that have not been names or colonized, we create." (20) They write from that sacred place which has not been stained or touched by imperialism or hatred. Writing is a mysterious and magical act that brings possibility of transformation: "Writing helps me to let go. The spirits of writing bring comfort, assurance, righteous anger, deliverance." (118) She continues:

> I was able to use writing to heal a wound that was very deep and festering. I was angry—writing brought me calm. I was obsessing about the past—writing gave me insight into the future. I was in pain—writing cooled the pain, brought me out of that condition. Writing was/is medicine. It is the only thing I know that brings

> complete wholeness while it is making a visitation. Making love comes close—orgasm, like writing, is a spiritual communication. (119)

Like all Native writers, she exclaims that they are alive and they have survived and will survive in spite of all the atrocities that are imposed on them: "the thieves who wished to eradicate all memory of us, who wished to eradicate *our* memory. I believe that memory is like the drum, one tap and the sound resonates and reverberates into our very soul. One poem, one story, one painting, and our hearts and bodies respond to the message—we are here. We remember." (36) Saying that a long and honourable tradition of their culture is telling truth, she states that they write about being human.

Writing for her is spiritual communication. Like orgasm, it is the ultimate in creation. By bringing in this analogy, she raises the veil on the debate on spirituality and sexuality. Writing is spirituality for her. Spirituality is one with sexuality. Thus, writing, spirituality and sexuality come under one group. All the three support each other, give birth to one another and lead to one another. Even here, largely western tradition interferes by separating spirituality and sexuality thus alienating writing or by compelling it to choose either spirituality or sexuality. While her argument about spirituality and sexuality sounds convincing and seems a new dimension to the art of writing, Lee Maracle's contention about sexuality comes to mind. Lee Maracle, a Native Canadian woman, draws our attention towards the sexuality and sexual life of Native Canadians. Her refusal to be a yes girl itself is an attempt to rewrite the native Canadian woman's identity created by the whites.

Her description of the identity of the native women expresses her contempt for the stereotypical images created by the colonisers as well as her concern for the predicament of the native women:

> We are the females of species: 'Native,' undesirable, non-sensuous beings that never go away. Our wombs bear fruit but are not sweet. For us intercourse is not marked by white, middle-class, patriarchal dominant-submissive tenderness. It is more a physical release from

> the pressure and pain of colonialism—mutual rape. Sex becomes one more of the horrors of enslavement, driving us to celibacy.[11]

Thus, Lee Maracle carves out an image of the native Canadian woman, who is a victim of centuries of colonisation. But this native Canadian woman is not just a creation of the whites. She is an individual in her own right, with a community identity and cultural heritage. She is not recognised as a woman, as a desirable person by the whites. When she says that man-woman relationships among Native Canadians are not submissive tenderness but mutual rape and a release from the pressure and pain of colonisation, Lee Maracle not only sums up the native Canadian situation but also hits hard at the white attitudes and the white stereotypes. In all this, she does not forget to examine her own privileged position from other's point of view. Although she identifies herself with her people, she is also conscious of her own unique identity as a woman who can speak and as a successful writer.

It is amazing to read these two interpretations of sexuality of Native life. While one equates sexuality with spirituality and with the act of writing, thus emphasising sex as celebration of creation or the capacity to procreate, the other looks at sex as violence between the subjugated sections. While for Beth Brant it is sharing, for Lee Maracle it is taking revenge and pouring out frustration. While Brant glorifies her lesbian relationships, Maracle criticises society for not viewing Native women as "women" and for not respecting their sexuality. In both cases, woman's body becomes the site of desire. But, Brant says that sex, especially orgasm, makes sure that everything in the world is in balance and thus thanks the creator, whereas Lee Maracle attacks the racial and gender discriminating society for looking at Native woman as the object of desire but with no respect for her sexuality, liberty and identity.

Brant reiterates that Native literature is not only about sexuality and eroticism. As it is not a mere reactionary writing, it is also not merely about sexuality and sex. It is also about love, love for nature, for earth, for living beings, for life, for creation.

Beth Brant claims, "much of Native lesbian writing celebrates Earth as woman, as lover, as companion. Woman, lover, companion celebrated as earth." (15) Homophobia is the eldest son of racism, they work in concert with each other, whether externally or internally and Native lesbian writing identifies these two evils that cause destruction to Native people. Native lesbian writing is not only about sex and sexuality but these "two-spirit" writers merge the selves that colonialism splits apart. That is when eroticism comes into the picture, as the power of procreation. Kateri Akiwenzie-Damm says: "in a broad sense Indigenous erotica speaks about the healing nature of love, about love that celebrates us as whole people, about love that is openly sexual, sensual, emotional and spiritual. Love, and the expression of it, is a medicine to heal the pain of oppression, hatred, lovelessness, and colonization. It is a way for indigenous writers and other artists to freely express themselves and their ideas about love and sexuality, without being constrained by imposed moral codes of definitions."[12]

Separating sexuality and spirituality means to place these two words in competition with each other, to deny the power of sex and spirit: "Our sexuality has been colonized, sterilized, whitewashed. Our sense of spirit has been sterilized, colonized, made over to pander to a growing consumer need for quick and easy redemption" (Brant 60). The political motives and nature of the Native writing surface once again when Akiwenzie-Damm says, "I see very clearly that this is a huge political statement. To reclaim and express our sexuality is part of the larger path to decolonization and freedom. And so the work continues because I believe passionately that when indigenous people de-colonize ourselves we'll not only free our minds, we'll free our bodies, our spirits, our whole selves." (151)

These are only some of the preliminary questions regarding the autobiographies of Native Canadian women which demand interdisciplinary knowledge as well as an awareness of a wide range of issues. Every question leads to a set of similar and different questions. Together they produce a very stimulating discussion on the issue of identity in Native Canadian women's writing. To sum up, in the words of Emma LaRoque in her "Preface," "Here Are Our Voices—Who Will Hear":

> To discuss Native literature is to tangle with a myriad of issues: voicelessness, accessibility, stereotypes, appropriation, ghettoization, linguistic, cultural, sexual and colonial roots of experience, and, therefore, of self-expression—all issues that bang at the door of conventional notions about Canada and about literature. (xvi)

NOTES

1. Penny Petrone, *Native Literature in Canada: From the Oral Tradition to the Present* (Toronto: O.U.P., 1990), p. 121.
2. Nourbese Philip's "l'anguish" is used in conjunction with language owing to the experience of anguish absorbed from growing up in the language of the coloniser (1998), cited in Laura Ann Cranmer, "Exploring Voice and Silence in the Poetry of Beth Cuthand, Louise Halfe and Marlene Nourbese Philip," *(Ad)dressing Our Words: Aboriginal Perspectives on Aboriginal Literature*, ed. Armand Garnet Ruffo (Penticton: Theytus, 2001).
3. Maria Campbell, "Strategies for Survival," *Kelley*, 1992, pp. 9-10.
4. Gerald Vizenor coined this term meaning words are like arrows that can be aimed at the narratives of colonial power, cited in Neal McLeod, "Coming Home through Stories," in Ruffo.
5. Patricia Monture Angus, *Thunder is My Soul: A Mohawk Woman Speaks* (Halifax: Fernwood, 1995), p. 3.
6. Campbell, p. 159.
7. Beth Brant, *Writing as Witness: essay and talk* (Toronto: Women's Press, 1994), p. 8.
8. Ruby Langford Ginibi, "My Mob, My Self," Kerry Reed-Gilbert, (compiled), *The Strength of Us as Women: Black Women Speak* (Charnwood: Ginninderra Press, 2000), p. 18.
9. Jackie Huggins, *Sister Girl: The Writings of Aboriginal Activist and Historian* (St. Lucia: University of Queensland Press, 1998).
10. "But this story is old and familiar. Take strong Nationalist women and turn them into pale myth. Make *our own people* believe the 'ies. This is what oppression is—the enforcement of amnesia—to make us forget the glory and story of our own history." (Brant 98).
11. Maracle (1996), pp. 20-21.
12. Kateri Akiwenzie-Damm, "Erotica, Indigenous Style," Ruffo, p. 149.

Enough is Enough': Re-writing of History by Jeanette Armstrong in *Slash* and Lee Maracle in *Sundogs*

ADITI VAHIA
M.S. University of Baroda.

While discussing the colonial history, Coomi Vevaina in *Intersexions: Issues of Race and Gender in Canadian Women's Writing* writes, "Infused with the feeling that they are divinely ordained to rule over other human beings and Nature, White imperialists travelled far-off lands, gave the indigenous people one hard push and merely said: "Move over!" (55) Consequently, twentieth century has witnessed many changes in the cultural scenario of different countries all over the world. Colonization by the whites has caused stagnation of cultural development in some societies while a complete death of culture in others. However, the decline of colonialism in the latter part of the century gave new dimensions to the postcolonial writing and along with others, writings on Native Canadian culture came into limelight.

The study of the vast and rich body of literature of the Native people of Canada had been too long neglected and ignored due to several reasons such as European cultural arrogance, their belief that the Indian was a vanishing race, etc. However, since the 1950s Canadians have become more aware of contemporary Native concerns, because of the changes in public attitudes due to the official policy of multiculturalism. In 1982 Canada's new constitution gave formal recognition to the Native people. Thus the Native Canadian literature, which till now had a suppressed voice due to its state of what Albert Memmi refers to as historical catalepsy during colonial rule, now has started voicing their feelings in a bolder manner. Young educated native Indians have taken up the task of leading their people to demand hard-earned and long-needed reforms. Native Canadian writers thus are celebrating the fall of colonialism by carving their own space in Canadian literature.

Uncle Luther, a character in Louis Owen's *The Sharpest Sight,* comments on the way history should be dealt with. He says, "a man's got to know the stories of his people, and then, he's got to make his own story, too . . . we got to be aware of the stories they're making about us, and the way they change the stories we already know." (91) Just as one can fight words with words, one can also fight history with history. Thus there was a need to re-write the already established history in its black and white form instead of using a variety of colours (ignoring the true picture).

In the 1980s emerged a younger generation of university trained writers who had a singular sense of purpose and a commitment. They began producing original and conscious works. This has resulted in a breed of Native writers all across the country who are imbued with a feeling of optimism and dedication. The issues which they discussed are related to Native Canadian people and their general position in their present Canadian nation i.e. their historical background, their miseries during colonial rule, their position in the postcolonial world, their complaints against their fellow Canadians and their strong desire to be regarded simply as Canadians without any particular aspect such as 'Indianness' highlighted which finally shows their faith in global harmony.

Describing the present condition of the Native Indians in Canada, Penny Petrone writes,

> Indian life in Canada is changing more and more. Indians are moving from the reserves to the cities and this change is reflected in their literature. Native writers continue to be concerned with their social, political and economic history, attempting to distinguish once and for all, right from the wrong, truth from fiction, to set the record straight. But now the problem that cities engender, because of skin colour and self-fulfilling stereotypes, have become

> the new subject of their literature. Understanding themselves in this challenging social context is their task. (139)

For fulfilling this particular task, the method which Jeannette Armstrong and Lee Maracle have chosen is re-writing of the history of Native Indians of Canada.

A common feature found in both these novels is that the writers of both mediate between two worlds: European and Native or modern and traditional in postcolonial situation, and are thus heirs to two cultures. However, driven by the wish to participate in the nation-building process and urge to establish their individual identity, they decided to remind native people of not only their tradition, but also their struggle to keep this tradition alive. This led them to keep history at the centre of their novels. As discussed by Juneja in *Post Colonial Novel: Narratives of Colonial Consciousness*, there are three ways found in dealing with history in fiction. "(a) Against History: mostly in the realistic novels (b) Dis/Mantling narrative in the novel using post-modern techniques and (c) Re-writing a tradition in the novel which appropriates indigenous narratological traditions." (106) *Slash* and *Sundogs* fall in the category where they have a different perspective on history. When the writer adopts the approach of rewriting history in his novel, he keeps the entire community in focus in spite of having one character being a hero or a heroine. Since it is tradition and history that he/she wishes to propagate, the novel presents a particular view where one comes across a strong feeling of community and also there is absence of an individual voice. This is to say that the voice of the protagonist is that of the entire community. Both Slash and Marianne represent the emotions felt by their respective clans. Moreover, they can be any Native Indian who is conscious of his/her position. Involvement of a common native in the mass movement allows the writer to convey that one does not have to be a legendary figure to influence or affect a fellow sufferer. One does not have to be John Kennedy who, upon being killed, caused "all them black people . . . burning cities all over the United States" (Armstrong, 31) or Elijah Harper with a firm 'No' for the Meech

Lake Accord. Instead, one can very well be a common person like Mardi, Maeg or Chuck in *Slash* who helped Thomas Kelasket to understand and react against the racial discrimination, or Lacey or Dorry who directly and indirectly encouraged Marianne to join the Run.

Jeannette Armstrong, an Okanagan writer, is not only aware of the position of her people in today's postcolonial world, but also realizes her responsibility as a writer. In a paper prepared for Saskatchewan Writer's Guild 1990, she voices the opinion of her community:

> Out of the belly of Christopher's ship
> a mob bursts
> Running in all directions
> Pulling furs off animals
> Shooting buffalo
> Shooting each other
> Left and right . . .
> Somewhere among the remains
> Of skinless animals
> Is the termination
> To a long journey
> And unholy search
> For the power
> Glimpsed in a garden
> Forever closed
> Forever lost. (202-3)

Armstrong feels that their task as Natives is two-fold: to examine the past and culturally affirm toward a new vision for all native people in the future, arising out of the powerful and positive support structure that are inherent in the principles of co-operation. There is an absence of an individual voice and the voice of a few characters is the voice of the entire community.

In *Slash* Armstrong gives the Native perspective on the North American Indian protest movement of the Sixties to the Eighties for a contemporary social studies unit for grade eight to eleven. Being actively involved in these movements herself, in this novel she tries to eradicate misconceptions and to recount the historical details clearly.

When the novel begins, Thomas Kelasket also known as Slash, appears as a sensitive boy studying in grade VI belonging to a happy stable family living a traditional life on a good reserve. From the discussions of his elders, he is quite aware that there is some tension in his community which is related with their being Indians. Before going to the town school, he is also warned by his father about the discrimination that they might face. However, his real troubles begin when he actually enters the school. Although he does not realize it initially, he and his Indian friends face obvious racial discrimination. Slash is confronted with a cultural shock because while he was instructed to be proud about being an Indian, that very Indianness was mocked at and came in their way in making friends and playing with other kids in the school. The principal says, "you Indians are lucky to be here. We'll get along fine as long as you don't steal from other kids." (23) Slash tries to understand these words for he knows that while stealing is considered bad among the white it is sinful for the Indians. The period which follows makes him realize that such racial prejudice is not limited only to words but is turned into actual discrimination when he witnesses incidents such as abuses hurled by the white boy Humphrey on Indians without any reason. Unable to take the insult of lying low, an Indian boy kicks him. Much to the surprise of Slash, "Monty didn't come back to school after that. We heard that the principal kicked him out for good, but Humphrey who started everything didn't even get detention." (24)

The sensitive child that he is, while trying to come to grips with the racial prejudice, Slash begins to question and think. He ends up becoming a troubled teenager. He doesn't know who is right anymore. He gives voice to his feelings of a confused Indian teenager in front of Uncle Joe. "We don't seem to be able to find answers or fit in anywhere. We don't seem to be able to live like you guys either." (55) He is also aware that in spite of changing their lifestyle completely, Indians will never be accepted as equals by the whites. "What it's all about . . . is that those things really mean help Indians become more middle class whites." (56)

His confusion gets added with frustration and hardships of his trial in the court and imprisonment. This ultimately leads him to the final awareness of the naked reality of racial discrimination. And his stay in the jail proves to be his learning period. After battling with the feelings of shame and helpless rage, he finally realizes his position and decides to react against it. His experiences in white school teach him to be ashamed of everything Native, his more realistic experiences in jail take him back to origins and teach him to be proud of his Indianness. This is in line with the position of the entire Indian community which is now ready to be an example of pride and power in being Indian. And as Mardi writes to Slash that their people were awake from their long sleep, the Indianness for which they were earlier instructed to be proud, is now felt and loved by people like Slash.

As the novel continues, Slash gets involved in the political and ideological world of the militant period of the American Indian movement where he meets people of his own kind and observes that a strong feeling of unity persists among the people. Nobody questions which band or which tribe a person belongs to; everybody was Indian. As Petrone states, "Slash indulges in all the passionate and tense restlessness of the period when oppressed and powerless people, moving together, changed themselves and their country profoundly and permanently." (14) He joins in protest rallies, caravans and demonstrations; participates in discussions, only to realize that there can never any agreement, one tidy solution.

Finally after two decades of educational experience marked by frustration, confusion and pain, Slash emerges as the archetypal hero in search of truth. His experiences make him stronger and wiser and he chooses to return home in the reserves. Now he realizes that his old Chief had said the same things that he heard from the Elders of the different tribes he visited across North America: "I thought about how much farther ahead I would have been if had listened to my own parents teach me those things while I was growing up. Instead it hadn't been good enough. I had to look for other solutions. I realized that there were people like me who had all that teaching right at home and had completely missed the point." Now he has a better understanding of the Indian rights movement and is glad to settle down in the hope that the next generation would gain some advantages. So he tells his son: "You are an Indian of a special generation. Your world will be hard but you will grow up proud to be an Indian."

Slash, thus, presents the details of the scattered events of an extraordinary period. Armstrong tries to illuminate the protest movement's structures and dynamics and in the process honours the past and present, and there is a hero who suffers due to his choices during his own pilgrimage from innocence to experience.

While Slash is concerned about the condition of the Natives even as a child and also throughout the novel, Marianne, the heroine in *Sundogs,* appears as an indifferent individual when the novel begins. She fails to understand her mother's anger towards the Premier which is displayed by the former's vehement quarrels with the T.V. She fails to understand why she is so sad about the people she has never met. She does have a realization that "despite a number of attempts by a dozen Native political organizations to be included in the constitutional talks over the last ten years, so far we are not considered a part of this momentous attempt to carve out a constitution uniquely Canadian. No one has been concerned until now." (1992, 48) She is also aware of her individual status in the whole drama: "I intrude on a private ceremony between our elders and the world." (49)

A very significant feature of the novel is that it makes one aware of how major events touch the lives of everyday people. It is remarkable to see how the historical events of Elijah Harper's symbolic blockage of the Meech Lake Accord changes the entire being of a twenty-year-old woman, the youngest in a large family, who is always considered a baby and a social non-entity to the extent that she herself had almost started believing it. It is only when Saul, the union of B.C. chiefs talks about Ellijah Harper "who said no to something or the other," (63) that Marianne suddenly becomes aware of herself as a native. The entry of Elijah wakes her into the hard reality of the gradual dying of the Native culture. She is shaken by her long passiveness for she is now able to identity herself with the rest of the community:

> I don't know why but I want to weep. I feel so consumed by the magic of it all, the absolute irony of it, the greatness and the simplicity of it, that I want to roll over the floor and wail. The plot. The physical, the murder of our whole people, is being documented by a man who sat in the House of Commons in Manitoba, silent for two years. (68)

The speech of Elijah penetrates her very being and she starts hating even the language of the whites: "I loathe English, feel imprisoned in its dry and cold delivery of pain and truth. I never realized this until I saw Elijah speak." (68)

Elijah's ideals wake her into an awareness of her domestic and social environment. She is able to comprehend her mother's fierce reactions: "I look at Momma and see her heroism. I see her fight day in and day out all of her life . . . the struggle for personal and psychological survival of Momma and all our old women."

Just as Slash comes into a prideful realization of his native self in jail, Marianne tattains this pride while watching Elijah on T.V. with her family: "I shed hot tears of shame, cooling tears of pride, sweet tears of recognition, tears of joyful truth. . . . I am not wiser about the raw facts of Elijah's actions but I understand his significance." (69)

The newly acquired awareness also leads to self-realization. She bleeds ancient wounds and wants to repair those inflicted on her family and tradition by wanting to have her brother who left them back in the family. She says,

> everyday that Elijah talks about the process of Nation Building . . . every day he stands alone, guarding our heritage validating our entire history as men and women, my betrayal of all that my mother and Aunty Mary hold precious hammers at my heart and turns my mind inside out. If Elijah upset Canada, he upset me a great deal more. (77)

She says that 'that Elijah,' meaning his ideals, affect her more than his person. The man does not matter as a public figure but changes her entire life. His beliefs that Canada has failed to learn from its old tradition, makes Marianne feel "I have lived twenty years on this earth making faces at my mother's sense of justice . and you stand there Elijah and affirm everything I know is dangerous to think, feel or believe." (77)

This consciousness finally leads her to join the Okanagan Peace Run. Maracle's discussion of the Peace Run reminds one of the statement made by Daniel David Moses that Native people have a sense of larger responsibility for th. planet. Marianne joins as a representative of Okanagan Nation, although unaware of what it means since she has not heard of that nation in her geography studies. She knows that there is such a nation and she also feels a sense of belonging, but her geography studies do not include this nation as if it is not significant. She nevertheless wants to join the race, for "this is not a race against human beings; it is a race against time, against the army." (170) Because she feels that the run is for a common cause, she is surprised that they stop only at Native communities. Although the run is abandoned in Ottawa, Marianne has acquired a deep satisfaction for she feels that the run recreated each of them. She feels that she had "acquired a vision of a different world. A world rich with peace. A world in which we are not invisible. A world in which we are not always running from behind, denied future." (197) Thus during this run, Marianne finds a moment of peace from the confusion and disunity in her own life.

Slash and *Sundogs* thus revive some historical events concerning the Indian communities, involving their respective protagonists. In the process they not only glorify these political movements, giving a realistic picture of the same, but they also tell how these movements changed the very beings of some people, elevating the significance of their lives in their own eyes. In both the novels, then, one finds a new bolder voice of the Aboriginal people confirming a very important idea that instead of being concerned with good or bad, Native people are concerned with peace and harmony and it is this belief, which if shared by one and all, will lead to a better world.

Works Cited

Armstrong, Jeannette. *Slash* Penticton, B.C.: Theytus (1985) 1992.

Currie, Noel E. "Jeanette Armstrong and the Colonial Legacy." *Native Writers and Canadian Writing*, ed. W.H. New. Vancouver B.C.: UBC Press, 1990.

Juneja, O.P. *Post-Colonial Novel: Narratives of Colonial Consciousness*. New Delhi: Creative, 1995.

Maracle, Lee. *Sundogs* Penlycton, B.C.Theytus. 1992.

. *I Am Woman*. Vancouver B.C.: Press Gang, 1996.

You will Flow Back to Your Beginnings: Problems of Identity and Aesthetics in Canadian Literature of Indian Diaspora

HARISH NARANG
J.N.U., New Delhi

Let me begin with an anecdote. In fact, I have only this anecdote to narrate in this presentation—well, almost. Some time ago, I was invited to be a penalist in a discussion on the occasion of a book-launch. The book was a novel—*Shahnaz*—by Hiro Boga, a woman writer based in Canada who traces her ethnic identity to the Parsi community in India. This was her debutant novel and the Canadian High Commission in India had invited a select audience that was a mix of scholars, teachers, media-persons and educated elite at large.

After the usuals of a book-launch, the writer was invited to read from the book. She read a passage here and an excerpt there—bits and pieces that she thought would arouse the curiosity of the potential readers of the book. Thereafter, both penalists were asked to present their initial responses to the book. More was expected to come out through the discussion that followed. The members of the audience then began to make their observations and ask questions—these were based primarily on the excerpts they had just heard or on the responses of the members on the discussion penal.

While my fellow-penalist handled a couple of queries addressed to her, I sat there wondering as to how much time would there be before the question I anticipated to be a must in such situations got asked. I would be surprised, nay very disappointed, if it gave us a go by this time. I had been in a number of similar discussions about writings by Canadian authors of Indian diaspora where the question always cropped up—sooner than later.

While I debated all this within myself, the question must have crept in quietly for soon it raised its head—I almost said 'hood' instead—in the form of a hand from a member of the audience. This was a familiar face—an old Canada hand, if one could transfer the register from diplomacy to literary evaluation.

"Madam," he began, "it's all fine—all this Parsi business in the novel, I mean Shahnaz and Shahrukh and their life here in Bombay and abroad, it's all very nice but where is Canada in this book?"

A smile spread across my face. So there it was—the big I question. The question of identity—no, not of Canada, nor of Canadians, although such questions still came up for discussion even after nearly a century and a half of Canadian existence as an independent nation. What, however, was being questioned at the moment was a more mundane identity—that of Canadian literature, particularly of a sub-genre namely Canadian literature of Indian diaspora.

As I observed above, I had been there before. This question of Canada being present in a book—a story, a novel, a poem or a play—by a writer who happened to be a Canadian. And the person asking the question appeared to be winning—at least nominally—since *Shahnaz* was the story of a young girl born and brought up in a wealthy Parsi family in India who is 'tortured by the hardships of living with her mentally ill mother' and who 'gains a new lease of life' when she and her husband Shahrukh—no there is no Khan in the name—are offered a life abroad. What follows are details—at times very depressing—of the travails of settling abroad, marital discord and her coming to terms with her painful past and finally her courage to set out 'to achieve a life she can truly call her own.'

What must have disappointed the scholar asking the question about the presence/absence of Canada in the book, was the fact that when the author sent her principal character abroad, it was not to some place in Canada but to Oregon in the United States of America. In fact, it must have been the unkindest cut of all to this most loyal advocate of Canadian identity in Canlit as Canadian Literature is sometimes referred to. So near and yet so far. In North America but not in Canada!

But then haven't these questions been asked before? From Vassanji, for instance, when his book *The Gunny Sack* was published. There was no Canada in that book either—well, almost. Of course, one of the principal characters of the book—Jibai—died in Canada while visiting one of her grand nephews. But that was about all about Canada in the book. The rest was all Africa or India—or somewhere in between. But then someone could have stood up and given the author a benefit of doubt—of sorts—by observing that the book had not been published in Canada. Ditto for his book of short stories—*Uhuru Street*—except that, it had been published in Canada.

And what about that other major writer—Rohinton Mistry? Does his collection of stories—*Tales from Ferozsha Baag*—have any Canadian presence? Well, he is certainly better than his other Parsi counterpart—Hiro Boga—since he packs one of his characters—Kersi Boyce, who is present in more than one story—to Toronto where he becomes—like the author who created him—a writer of short stories. Incidentally, in one of the stories in *Tales from Ferozsha Baag*, "Swimming Lessons," there is a whole discussion about the presence/absence of Canada in the stories written by Kersi. After the parents of Kersi who stay in Bombay, have read some of the stories in the collection published by Kersi, a copy of which he has sent to them from Toronto, they both discover that most stories are about the Parsi life in Bombay and there is hardly any presence of Canada or Toronto in the stories: "My hope is, father said, that there will be some story based on his Canadian experience, that way we will know something about our son's life there, if not through his letters then in his stories." (245)

Like his father, his mother too is puzzled about the absence of life in Toronto from his stories: "and Mother said that she would also enjoy some stories about Toronto and the people there; it puzzles me, she said, why he writes nothing about it, especially since you say that writers use their own experience to make stories out of." (246)

So while Kersi's parents discuss the reasons for the absence of Canada and Toronto from his writings, our scholar friend present in Hiro Boga's book launch could draw solace from the fact that the more well known Canadian writer of Parsi origins—Rohinton Mistry—had at least created some Canada connection in his books.

But then another name springs to my mind: Ashis Gupta. Now Ashis Gupta, as some of us know since he has been to India and to these parts of the country, is Calgary based Canadian who traces his Indian connection to West Bengal. Ashis Gupta has written a novel—*The Toymaker from Wiesbaden*—which too does not have any Canada in it. When I say 'no Canada,' I mean no mention of Canada at all. The principal character of the novel—Hans Schroeder—is a German who had joined the German army in the early days of World War II and he had been captured by the Russians when serving as an officer in a SS Panzer division and sent to Siberia. After spending seven years in Siberia when Hans returned to Wiesbaden, his hometown, he went to work in a toyshop. There he met Eva, fell in love with her and moved to Massachusetts with her to make a new beginning. After working hard to become a professional and what the text of the blurb calls 'a good, solid citizen,' Hans is charged with the murder of his wife Eva and their daughter Katarina. Well I won't go further with my Hans Schroeder story—I don't need to—and spoil your appetite for reading the book by revealing whether Hans got convicted or not. But what I do wish to emphasize is the fact that there is no Canada in the novel.

Another novelist, another text. The writer—Cyril Dabydeen. The text—*Wizard Swamy*. There is no Canada in this text too. The location is the Caribbeans and the characters primarily of Indian origin—descendents of those indentured labourers whom the British brought from India in the nineteenth century to work on sugarcane plantations. There are graphic details of the hard life that people of Indian origin belonging to the lower strata lead; then there is the description of crude attempts by people of Indian origin to save and promote their cultural heritage and finally there are the intrigues of dominating the Indian community by those Indians who have struck it rich. All this is there but there is no mention of Canada whatsoever.

Let me now return to the question raised by our scholar friend—Where is Canada in the book? I want to ask him—although I did not at that point of time and it does not matter that he is not here—if he ever asked such a question about those Canadian writers who are considered 'mainstream.' I wonder if he has read any of the Margaret Laurence books located in Africa. And these have no Canada in them either. Does it make Margaret Laurence less of a Canadian writer? If not, why pick on Hiro Boga or Moyez Vassanji or Rohinton Mistry or Nalini Warior or Lakshmi Gill or Ashis Gupta or Cyril Dabydeen?

So much for the Canadian part of the identity of writers of Indian diaspora. Let me return to *The Toymaker of Wiesbaden* to discuss another identity problem. If there is no Canada in the text, there is no India either. The whole text is so 'sanitised' of links with India that if it were not for the name of the author printed on the cover of the book—both Ashis and Gupta as names are so very Indian that it is difficult to mistake them for any other identity—it would be difficult to recognize any authorial connection with India—even by Indian readers of the book. If this be so, does the book cease to fit the bill of what I may like to call Canadian writings of Indian diasporic origin. Or, if Ashis Gupta were a single book author—luckily he is not—would he have been considered a member of the same writers' club as Vassanji and Mistry, for instance? The question I am asking is that a la Canadian identity of a writer depending on the Canadian input into a book, does his or her identity—diasporic identity vis-a-vis India—depend upon the Indian input into it. I don't know if my scholar friend raising the Canada question in Hiro Boga's *Shahnaz,* ever asked Ashis Gupta—Where is India in your book? What I do know is that when Ashis Gupta was here, he did visit a number of departments and centres of Canadian Studies and was introduced as a Canadian writer of Indian origin—whatever that expression means.

The Indian identity question of Canadian writers is not so simple. There are identities within identities. While it is simple with writers like Rohinton Mistry and Hiro Boga who fulfil the conditions of a 'continuous passage'—as was once demanded of the very first immigrants—there are others like Moyez Vassanji, Yasmin Ladha, and Ian Iqbal Rashid who acquired another identity en route—African. Similarly, Cyril Dabydeen, Neil Bisoondath and Ramabai Espinet had a Caribbean cruise before ending up in Canada. Lakshmi Gill is perhaps one of a class having come via the Philippines. Then there is Reshard Gul whose Indian origins were mediated twice—his people went to South Africa from India but he was born and brought up in England. Then there are those who came to Canada, saw and left—Bharati Mukherjee and Suniti Namjoshi, for instance.

Then there are identities that are acknowledged and identities that are not acknowledged. Vassanji, for instance, has always felt proud of his identity as a writer of the African reality—his African reality: "My contribution to literature about Africa is not negligible and has been recognized. I am a voice of the region of Africa I was born in and many people, not only African-Asians, respect me more for that. . . . An Asian high school student called me up recently and thanked me so profoundly for having changed her life, her writing, because finally she read someone in school who spoke to her; in Kenya and Tanzania people have thanked me, opened their family albums for me, given me their family histories because they believe I represent them." (Presentation at a Conference, unpublished)

And he has been equally proud of his Canadian Identity: "And yet I have also written about, contributed to Canada and the region there in which I live, Toronto. I have benefitted from the secure environment of that country and the generosity of its progressive elements. I am protected by its constitution and have demanded rights there, and opposed discrimination there. I have represented that country abroad at an official level." (Presentation at a Conference, unpublished)

In contrast is the bizarre case of Yasmin Ladha—Canadian writer of African origin who too—like Vassanji—traces her ancestry to India. This is what she has to observe about her identity in her book—*Women Dancing on Rooftops: Bring Your Belly Close* when she went to Chonju in South Korea:

> "On a light and dark green Chonju city bus, it's a given I ain't Canadian. My thighs jangle from stares, my breasts inflate into DD cups and my upper lip twitches neural, like first time electrolysis. . . . I wanna go home!"
>
> "Where are you from?" Chonjuites don't hear "Canada." They hear, "Calcutta"
>
> "Anyo, Anyo," I shake my head, "Ca-na-da," and begin an ever-demonstration: I put my left hand on my lap and say "America." Then I layer my right hand gently on top, "Ca-na-da." But Chonju folk just stare and point logically, "Indo-Indo." Only I don't want the baggage of plague, mantras or even Mother Teresa, but the affluence of my Canadian passport."

Such desperation to shed her Indian identity and to acknowledge the Canadian one! But the South Koreans would have none of it. Poor Yasmin!

For Chonjuites, Yasmin Ladha 'ain't Canadian' simply because her outward appearance does not match the stereotypical images of Canadians in their minds which are primarily of whites with light-coloured hair and blue eyes.

However, prejudice of a different kind was perceptible in another anecdote that a Canadian scholar friend of mine narrated to me recently when he came to India to participate in an international conference on religions. My friend who is a Professor of Philosophy of Religions in a premier Canadian university had spoken on, among others, the concept of Hindutva. Apparently impressed by his presentation, a participant approached him to congratulate him. He, however, could not help observing that the word 'Khan' in his name was incongruous with his competent presentation on a subject like Hindutva. My friend told me that he merely smiled but did not tell the person that his presentation flowed from the entry he had written on the subject for an *Encyclopedia on Religions of the World*, whose compilers did not care about his Muslim identity.

The relationship between identity and the kind of things one writes—or is expected to write, to be more precise—is equally true of creative writing as well. This also came up for discussion during the book-launch *of Shahnaz* that I have spoken about in the beginning of this presentation. After we had gotten out of the 'Canada-in-the book' tangle, another scholar got up to ask—the question was directed at the writer—if it was wise on her part to have written negative things about India in her novel. The reference to an episode in the book wherein the maidservant in the family tells Shahnaz how her daughter had been burnt by her in-laws, for not fulfilling their greed for more dowry. In her response, when the author—Hiro Boga—asked the scholar—in a kind of retort question—if such bride-burnings were not a part of the contemporary Indian socio-culture reality, the scholar observed that while that was true, there was no need to highlight them in books written by diasporic writers of Indian origin. "What would Canadians think of us," he observed before sitting down—apparently unconvinced totally with the author's explanation. Bride-burning was a shame but putting it in books to be read by foreign readers was a greater shame.

By a sheer coincidence, there is a discussion about the content of stories by Canadian writers of Indian origin in that story—"Swimming Lessons"—by Rohinton Mistry that I have referred to above. After having read a few of the stories in the collection sent to them by their son Kersi, the father observes:

> In the stories that he'd read so far Father said that all the Parsi families were poor or middle-class, but that was okay; nor did he mind that the seeds for the stories were picked from the sufferings of their own lives; but there should also have been something positive about Parsis, there was so much to be proud of: the great Tatas and their contribution to the steel industry, or Sir Dinshaw Petit in the textile industry who made Bombay the Manchester of the East, or Dadabhai Naoroji in the freedom movement, where he was the first to use the word swaraj, and the first to be elected to the British Parliament where he carried on his campaign; he should have found some way to bring some of these wonderful facts into his stories, what would people reading these stories think, those who did not know about Parsis—that the whole community was full of cranky, bigoted people; and in reality it was the richest, most advanced and philanthropic community in India, and he did

> not need to tell his own son that Parsis had a reputation for being generous and family-oriented. (245)

While my scholar friend asking the question about Hiro Boga's sense of propriety in including the 'bride-burning' episode in her novel could draw a consolation from the above-quoted observations of Rohinton Mistry expressed through the persona of Kersi's father, there is a big difference between the two. What Mistry's character is speaking about is the balance in one's portrayal of a community or a nation, my friend was laying emphasis squarely on 'sanitising' the portrayal by excluding whatever was hurtful to the positive image of the community—or the nation. This, he thought, was particularly true of writers writing from abroad. Indian writers writing from locations abroad had to be more loyal than Indian writers writing here. Faced with similar criticism—dilemma would be more appropriate, I think—Vassanji observes, in the presentation referred to above: "Am I a traitor to my origins, or a two- or multi-faced immigrant who will not denounce his past and pound his chest proudly with patriotic fervor and say he lives in the best country in the world."

I could not, at that time, help recalling the punishment meted out to a Canadian scholar of Sikh religious studies who had been summoned to the Akal Takht and punished for saying in his book certain things about the *Guru Granth Sahib* that the religious body did not like. Similarly, I cannot help recalling at this juncture what happened to Bhandarkar Institute at the hands of Shiv Sainiks for the help they rendered to a foreign scholar in writing a biography of Shivaji which contained some observations that the Sainiks did not like.

What I wish to state is that this relationship between the identity of a writer and content of his/her writing is full of trappings—for not just the writer but the community/nation in question as well.

Finally, before I close, a couple of observations about the aesthetics of such writings by Canadian writers of Indian origin. Not only is Canada missing from some of these writings but the aesthetics governing some of these writings is also very different from what may underlie generally so-called Canadian mainstream writing. For instance, this is what Moyez Vassanji has to observe about the sustenance of cultural heritage of these writings: "The experiences related by these new writers, the world described by them, the literary characters and personalities introduced by them were different and alien to those that Canadian literature had been used to. Bombay, Dar es Salaam—in my case—were sold in the bookstores of the country, vying with the prairies, with Toronto, with the maritimes. Instead of stark, bleak landscapes and stern puritanical personalities, we had barbers in Bombay, drunk cane cutters in Guyana speaking in dialect, a Rita Hayworth look alike in Africa. The great wars of the world, the great human struggles were no longer only those of Europe and America, but also the colonization of the third world by Europe and the subsequent independence struggles, the wars against poverty, oppression, nationalisms, fundamentalisms. The storehouse of stories included not only those told by the Greeks and the Old Testament, but also now those from the *Mahabharata* and the Puranas, the Arabian Nights and the Hadith, the Jatakas, and so on." (Presentation at a conference, unpublished)

Even at the level of style of writing, different laws of aesthetics appear to govern such writings:

> "I shan't call you reader. One who reads, hah! That's so undeclared. Blank as a daft blue form: "Resident of?" "In the Dominion of?" "Port of Embarkation/Disembarkation?" "Destitute-Festitute?" Blue muscle of power. Generic.
>
> Between you and me, there is no glint of a badge. Badges are razor sharp. Between you and me, the ink quivers. Beena exists declare (fetch the trumpet, fetch the *dholak: dha dhin dhinakd)* because of you and me. "A reader," you say? You correcting me? My Allah! You have joined the critic's English! May he forever be buried in the Sahara. *Readerji,* I command you, banish the critic from your eye, this instant, *fatafat!* Look at his beauty nose, wide as a camel's nostrils!
>
> My *yaar-Readerji,* sometimes with my own, I forget this definite and not so definite article stuff. Allah! You are turning gray because I call you my own! Readerji by bending, yes-Masta, yes-

> Masta, you follow the colonizer-critic to his bed!" ("Beena" in *Lion's Grand Daughter and Other Stories* by Yasmin Ladha)

It is difficult to find similar samples of stylistic experimentation in contemporary Canadian writings.

Let me conclude—finally—by observing that in the Seventies we pleaded for granting autonomy to genres and categories of writings lumped together under portmanteau categories like the Commonwealth Literature, Anglophone and Francophone Writings and created categories like Indian Writing in English, Canadian Literature, Australian Literature and African Literature. Later, the categories became more micro and we have Canadian Native Literature, Indian Women's Writing, Australian Aborigines Writing, Writings of Canadian South Asian Diaspora, African American Literature and even Holocaust Writing. However, during the last ten years or so, the concept of globalization has taken root—in letter and in spirit. Although some of us do not like some ramifications of the concept—particularly economic—we cannot wish it away. E-mail and mobile telephones, more than any other technology, have turned the world into a global village—truly and irreversibly. This has had its impact on writings and writers. Some of the labels we invented and used only a couple of decades ago are valid no more. Nor are the implications contained therein. Hyphenated identities like Afro-American Literature which later changed its character from compound to complex by dropping the hyphen and filling out the abbreviated 'Afro' to African too seem to have outlived their utility—too soon perhaps but such has been the staggering pace at which human life has moved during the last couple of decades. Let alone labels like Canadian South Asian writer, even a category like Canadian writer may prove to be inadequate. Perhaps we may need—sooner than later—to strip a writer bare—so to say—and call him a writer—simply. And if I may borrow a line from Lakshmi Gill to describe writers—all writers:

> "You will flow back into your beginnings."
>
> ("Pooja for Papa" in *Returning the Empties*)

Multiculturalism: The Immigrant's Dilemma

VIMAL DHAWAN
A.R.S.D. College, University of Delhi

From the 'Kamagata Maru' incident in 1914 when a boatload of Sikh immigrants were refused entry into Canada to the 'Multiculturalism Act' of 1988 which promotes multiculturalism as the official policy of the government, Canada has traversed a long distance on the path of assimilating ethnic diversity. The fact that Canada, at last, has acknowledged and reaffirmed the role played by ethnic minorities in enriching its cultural heritage augurs well for the minorities. However, the big question is—how has this policy of reconciliation percolated down and how has it been received at the socio-cultural levels. Has it made a dent in the politics of power, in the policy of exclusion or in racial discrimination? The paper will deal with this aspect by focussing on the literary voices of the geographically displaced and by highlighting the dilemma that immigrants face in the fast evolving 'mosaic' matrix of Canadian society.

Immigrant sensibility has traditionally revolved around nostalgia and lament. Caught between conflicting cultures, the immigrant writers often dwell upon the themes of dislocation, survival and loss of identity. The feeling of nostalgia is heightened if the writer happens to be a coloured immigrant in a predominantly white society. Writers of the Indian diaspora in Canada—Himani Bannerji, Bharati Mukherjee, Uma Parameswaran, M.G. Vassanji, Rohinton Mistry, Neil Bissoondath, Surjeet Kalsey, Lakshmi Gill—to name a few—often explore the crucial issues of racism, alienation and the attendant social tensions that crowd the world of an immigrant. However, the lived experience and its literary expression convey a diversity that cannot be easily categorized. The impact of the cultural shock varies "according to an intricate set of variables in the lives of both authors and chambers they create: the time and conditions of immigration, age, gender, class, religion, race." (Hutcheon, 6) These variables provide for thematic multiplicity and diversity. However, the most significant factor that oppresses the Indian immigrant writers' psyche in Canada appears to be racism which results in their marginalization and ghettoization. The hostility of the majority community, the insensitivity of their behaviour, the bitter stings of racism become the focus of their writing. The writers, by voicing the concerns of their society, to some extent fulfil the role that Achebe assigned to himself of exhorting the writers to act as teachers by taking up the task of re-education and regeneration of their people.

In "On a Cold Day," Himani Bannerji epitomizes an immigrant's rootlessness and facelessness. In order to exist in her new dispensation in Canada, Devika Bardhan from Calcutta changes her name to Debbie Barton. She has to develop the right attitude and right motivation, still she feels ignored and unnoticed. She is humble and deferential amongst the whites, at times wanting to be invisible. The whites lose their individuality and appear to her as one mass of a cold ice colour. "This feeling continued with her as she sat in the train making herself as small as possible. Two white people sat on either side of her, and they kept expanding, squeezing her out of the very little space that she took." (*Her Mother's Ashes*, 33) The symbolic meaning of the expansion and the squeezing can hardly be missed. At the time of leaving the train, she inadvertently banged into a white man, and even though she apologised, he shot back "fucking Pakis." Her total alienation is very poignantly projected when she comes across the dead body of an unknown Indian woman who has committed suicide. Debbie identifies with her so completely that she informs Abdul Jalal that the dead woman's name was Devika Bardhan and she was from Calcutta. Symbolically, Devika has died, but Debbie lives on. Another story by Bannerji "The Other Family" focuses on the fear of assimilation at the cost of one's identity exemplifying what Mordecai Richler has termed as "the familiar and agonizing process of alienation between immigrant parents and Canadian born children." (Intro, *Other Solitudes*, 7) The 'Other' in the title is a pointer to the otherization of the immigrant. A non-white schoolgirl asked to paint the picture of her family drew it from a book wherein she made her family white-skinned, herself freckled and her mother blonde. The mother panics and demands: "Where are you in this picture. . . . Where are we? Is this the family you would like to have? Don't you want us anymore? You want to be a *mem-sahib*, a white girl?" (143) The child's conception of her family differs from that of her mother. The child, a second-generation product, is culturally a Canadian too. The palpable tension is a by-product of the amalgamation of identity at one level and guarding of ethnicity on the other.

The women poets, by and large, are writing a literature of protest. The sense of languishing in Canada, the feeling of being trapped in an alien environment is evoked with considerable force by them through the use of the prison metaphor. In Himani Bannerji, feministic sensibilities seem to coalesce with her immigrant consciousness. In her prose poem 'Doing Time' she expresses frustration and bitter anger at the absence of personal freedom which alone would lead to a life of fulfilment: "If we who are not white, and also women, have not yet seen that here we live in a prison, that we are doing time, then we are fools. . . . The prison, it might be objected, is a metaphor, a myth that I, and others like myself, have constructed to mythicize our petty problems, to glorify, romanticize our trivial lives. . . . Instead I am saying that for us the much touted word "freedom" is the dishing out of a myth or a metaphor, covering up the prison in which we live, where, and I insist, we are doing time." (*Canadian Voices*, 116)

Surjeet Kalsey in "Migratory Birds" describes the immigrants' inability to extricate themselves from a web-like situation:

We
the migratory birds
are here this season
thinking

we'll fly back to our home
for sure
No one knows
Which invisible cage imprisons us?
And the flight begins to die slowly
in our wings. (*Canadian Voices*, 79)

Uma Parameswaran in her poem "Tara's Mother-in-Law" portrays an old woman who finds it difficult to exorcise the ghost of the past. The poem not only expresses the helplessness of the woman but also exposes the isolationist Western culture, the artificiality of Canadian life. The prison syndrome is used indirectly. The opening lines of the poem are:

What kind of place you've brought me to, Son?
Where the windows are always closed
And the front door it is always locked?

The nostalgia, the longing in the closing lines is pathetic:

Open the windows, son.
I am too used to the sounds
of living things;
of birds in the morning
of rain and wind at night. . . .
Open the windows, son,
And let me go back
to sun and air
and sweat and even flies and all
But not this, not this. (*The Geography of Voice*, 67-68)

In Lakshmi Gill's perception, Canada seems worse than a prison; it is a hell. In her poem "Letter to a Prospective Immigrant" she sends a warning to her countrymen not to expect warmth and comfort if they intend to come to Canada:

And what about that tired myth: Canada the Cold?
Not a myth, I assure you. Don't come naked. . . .
Joy? There is no joy. Just a long, dull ache
icehot (not even pain) of want. . . .
If you can bring blessings, come then
(don't expect blessings in return); hell does not give
but takes. (*The Geography of Voice*, 45-46)

The helplessness, the absence of joy, the loss of freedom inevitably lead to a sense of continuing apprehension and a feeling of terror. Himani Bannerji, in another prose poem 'Terror,' juxtaposes the normal city experience of Toronto with the underlying sinister implications which she alone is able to visualize:

> I think of my daughter. I grow afraid. I see designs against her deep-set into the concrete structures or embossed into their Education Act. The blue of the sky, the gold of the sun, become an Aryan-eyed blonde and her spiked heels into my bowels. Fear lurks in the trees and gives the leaves their sharp precision. (Qtd. Shahani, *Intersexions*, 184)

Structures representing establishment become symbols of exploitation for Bannerji and the world around her presents a spectacle of fear. Bannerji's poem "Paki Go Home" paints a gory picture of the plight of the immigrants who are habitual victims of racist abuse:

> And a grenade explodes
> in the sunless afternoon
> and words run down
> like frothy white spit
> down her bent head
> down the serene parting
> of her dark hair
> as she stands too visible
> from house to bus stop to house
> raucous, hyena laughter,
> "Paki, Go Home." (*Canadian Voices*, 118)

Lakshmi Gill in "Third Street" shows how an immigrant family lives under the constant threat of racial attack. The threat exists in their subconscious but the terror is real and all pervasive.

Anguished expressions like marginalized, otherized, exiled, victimized and terrorized project the preoccupation of the Indo-Canadian women poets: Sorrow, anger, pain, frustration, suffocation and insecurity are the emotions that dominate their psyches. The complaints are loud and clear. One is, however, tempted to ask whether they inhabit a country to which the majority of them have gone by choice or are they observing a prison term in enemy-territory? There is no denying the fact that the immigrants do face complex problems and often undergo emotional traumas. But there ought to be a flip side of the coin too. If the situation is really so frightening, why then all the subterfuge used and legal loopholes exploited to get to Canada? The real culprit may not be racism, but a mutual ignorance, a mutual incomprehension that leads to mutual suspicion, exaggerated fear and ultimately hatred.

Mordecai Richler in his story "The Street" describes street fights in Montreal in which he used to participate. Looking back, he concludes that the real trouble was an absence of dialogue between them (Jews) and the French Canadians. Neil Bissoondath comments that true racism is based, more often than not, on willful ignorance, and an acceptance of—and comfort with—stereotype. He further adds that the struggle against stereotype, the basis of all racism, becomes a purely personal one. In his story "Dancing," he successfully subverts the stereotype as one comes across the rare spectacle of a white man at the receiving end of racial abuse. Sheila, an innocent immigrant from Trinidad arrives in Canada but feels uncomfortable even with her own nationals as she disagrees with their assessment that Canadians are cold and uncaring. Though the blacks feel that they are unwelcome in Canada, yet, they insist that they have a right to stay and they are capable of giving it back as well as they receive. At a dance party, the loud music brings in a protesting neighbour, a white, who receives an unexpectedly hot welcome. "This son-of-a-bitch say music is too loud. He complaining. He say he going to call the police." Taken aback, the man replies: "I just want it turned down. I don't want to call the police." (*Other Solitudes*, 312) At this, one guy blows his nose twice, rubs the cold between his fingers and then wipes his fingers clean on the white man's sweater. The man runs away, the gathering shouts abuses like "Blasted racialist honkey," "son-of-a-bitch" and gleefully celebrates its victory. Disillusioned and bewildered, all Sheila can do is to keep on dancing. Bissoondath is accused of showing a lack of compassion for his own community. However, distancing himself from his community provides him with a certain degree of objectivity. This inverse racism is not just a of objectivity. This inverse racism is not just a figment of the author's imagination. Bissoondath comments: "I'm fearful of people over reacting: screaming racism simply because the two people happen to be of different races or different colours." (315)

Another example of mutual ignorance can be found in Bharati Mukherjee's story "The Management of Grief," which deals with the aftermath of the 'Kanishka' plane crash. The Canadian social worker's earnest attempts to help the bereaved families come to a naught as both the parties are unable to appreciate each other's point of view; the chasm between the two cultures becomes the real stumbling block. The bereaved families refuse compensation claims as it would not bring their dear ones back. Further, it could also amount to signing their death warrants.

Rohinton Mistry in his story "Swimming Lessons" also portrays the superficiality of living together without actually knowing each other. It is such situations that lead to alienation and isolation. Affirming that racial hatred and prejudice are a result of a misguided fear, Mistry contends that one thing that can cast out fear is education, "Education is respect for humanity essentially a turning away from fear" (*Other Solitudes*, 261). Mistry proclaims that racism exists everywhere, not just in North America. Citing the example of India, he points out that "the tall, wheat-complexioned north-Indian Hindu feels superior to the short, dark-skinned south-Indian Hindu. And within the same religion, the hierarchy of castes and sub-castes leads to a maze of attitudes which is quite bewildering." (261) This opinion is reinforced by Bissoondath who puts the Canadian racial intolerance in context: "Racism is as Canadian as maple syrup," he writes, "but it is also as American as apple pie, as French as croissants, as Jamaican as ackee, as Indian as aloo, as Chinese as chowmein" (qtd. Hutcheon, Intro).

Racism, thus, is a universal phenomenon, not peculiar to Canada and not confined to one time and place. Canada's track record may not be very good in respect of racism, yet among the nations of the world, Canada is a pacifist country, which makes Rudy Wiebe state that in that sense he finds Canada to be a good nation to be a citizen of. Bissoondath feels that adjustment is essential in every society: "I don't think we should expect the greater society to adjust to our ways . . . immigrants have to make a certain adjustment, just as society has to make an adjustment too." (Hutcheon, 316)

Adjustment, adaptability and acceptance are the key terms which immigrant writers seem to have ignored. In this connection, I am reminded of Margaret Laurence who migrated to Somaliland and Ghana during the British Raj. Laurence comments that if at all there was a feeling of alienation among the English, it was of their own making. When Laurence was given a bowl of soup with a dozen detached ant-wings and several frantic beetles, she did not start lamenting her existence. Instead, stoically, she spooned the bugs out and began to eat. She had gone there of her own accord, so there are no unnecessary tantrums. She accepted life as it came, without being hypocritical and without indulging in propaganda which the British were really fond of. One of Laurence's intuitions about human outlook that "it was not a matter of intelligence but of viewing the whole life through different eyes" which can generate either compassion or antipathy, thus stands vindicated.

If clinging to one's cultural baggage proves detrimental in one's journey towards acceptability at a wider level, it is better to shed some of it. One has to give up some of one's distinctive cultural identity in order to gain acceptance. One need not give up one's parent culture, but it needs to be redefined in the context of the adopted culture. Asked how much such a loss rankles, Uma Parameswaran replied that in order to gain something, one has to lose something, but in this case, the loss is worth it. She displays a similar positive attitude in her story "How We Won the Olympic Gold," which deals with the famous incident of the Canadian sprinter Ben Johnson who won the Olympic Gold Medal but was disqualified for using drugs. The "we" in the title makes a vehement assertion that Parameswaran is a Canadian. McGifford comments: "This 'we' is her insistence that she and her writing are Canadian, that she—and here I take liberties with

Margaret Atwood—has planted herself 'in this country/like a flag'" (Intro, xvii)

I would like to conclude by quoting Bharati Mukherjee's statement that totally reorients our perspective about the immigrants. She asserts that she "likes to think of her characters as conquerors. They are all minor heroes because they have the guts to sail the oceans and make new lives. They are not failures even though they have disappointments. Adventure can dent one in many ways but the bruising is a trophy."

NOTES

Bannerji, Himani. "On a Cold Day," *Her Mother's Ashes and Other Stories by South Asian Women Writers in Canada and the United States*, ed. Nurjehan Aziz (Toronto: TSAR, 1994).

Bannerji, Himani. "The Other Family," *Other Solitudes: Canadian Multicultural Fictions* (Toronto: Oxford University Press, 1990).

Bissoondath, Neil. "Dancing," *Other Solitudes*.

McGifford, Diane, ed. *The Geography of Voice*, ed. Diane McGifford (Toronto: TSAR, 1992).

Mistry, Rohinton. *Other Solitudes*. Interview.

Parameswaran, Uma. "How We Won the Olympic Gold," *The Geography of Voice*.

Richler, Mordecai. "The Street," *Other Solitudes*.

Confluences and Divergences: Short Story Cycles by South Asian Canadian Writers

DEVIKA NARULA
D.C.A.C, University of Delhi

The ideal global paradigm of a politico-socio-cultural construct is that of the multicultural society where people of different ethnic origins live in an amicable integrated totality. In theory this is the vision that all nations proclaim and that Canada has even put into legislation. But what is the ground reality? Is it really that people have submerged their feelings of "difference" and converged into a confluence of harmony to form a single political identity? Or is it that the declarations of global homogeneity are merely a projection of oneness to conceal the self-centred diversity of vested interests of people? The truth of the matter is that fear of the loss of individual identity, consequent upon a homogenization of different nationalities, is creating a greater awareness of the tradition, culture and history which define the roots of an individual. Hence the "confluences" of different nationalities have, in reality, made their mutual "divergences" more aggressive, and different ethnic groups are constantly challenging the idea of a uniform political identity.

Migration has become a global phenomenon that has induced a consciousness of borders and nationalities in the psyche of the migrant. This cultural reality is reflected in the use of the 'hyphenated' terminology that has become prevalent in referring to minority groups, for example, the Chinese-Canadians, the Ukrainian-Canadians, the Italian-Canadians, the South Asian Canadians and so on. The consciousness of their 'hyphenated' personality is reflected in their literature where they go back to their homeland to project their 'histories' and their socio-cultural ambience as a lived experience. In his essay "The Politics of Recognition," Charles Taylor states: "Identity is partly shaped by recognition or its absence, often by the *mis*recognition of others, and so a person or group of people can suffer real damage, real distortion, if the people or society around them mirror back to them a confining or demeaning or contemptible picture of themselves."[1]

The minorities have suffered '*mis*recognition' at one time or the other but in the changed political scenario of the present, they, too, are demanding 'recognition' and equal status. Their objective in 'voicing' their 'histories' is to present a realistic self-narrated version of their 'history' to counter the distorted one projected by others. To use Charles Taylor's words once again: "Democracy has ushered in a politics of equal recognition, which has taken various forms over the years, and has now returned in the form of demands for the equal status of cultures and of genders." (27)

Hence, in a multicultural society 'recognition' becomes an important factor for all ethnic groups desirous of obtaining an equal status. This may be the reason that in the last decade there has been a sudden spurt of interest in diasporic writings, and their objective of projecting the recent history of their race. They present a chronicled account of the history of their community through a narration of their personal histories which recount the life that they lived in their homeland or in the land from where they migrated. These narratives present the cultural divergences of different diasporas but they also contribute to a better understanding of the 'other.'

The present article considers some of the short stories by South Asian Canadian writers to explore the various nuances of immigrant literature and the feeling of 'otherness' that they experience. The short story cycle becomes particularly suited to the multiplicity of experience and perspective of a postmodern and postcolonial expose of an immigrant group that retains its distinct identity as a diaspora. It lends itself to an exploration of the particular/unique socio-cultural identity experienced individually as well as by a common group of people by depicting, through short narratives, the different aspects and nuances of the interaction of individuals. The short story cycle is an interesting form that is used by some of the diasporic writers to create and preserve a world that is slowly slipping away with the sands of time and change. Linda Hutcheon in her book *A Poetics of Postmodernism: History, Theory, Fiction* states that the "borders between literary genres have become fluid: who can tell any more what the limits are between the novel and the short story collection."[2] The short story collection, in its totality, becomes comparable to a novel because it depicts a repertoire of characters interacting with each other, in an imaginative/real locale over a certain period of time, and incorporates the progressive change in their attitudes. The short story collection also has the added advantage of the polyphony of voices in the different stories, and each story is independent and complete in itself and yet thematically and structurally related to the others. This genre is, in effect, a postmodern inquiry into the nature of subjectivity and, as Linda Hutcheon states, it poses a "frequent challenge to traditional notions of perspective." (11) Charles Russell, also, presents the view that with postmodernism we start to encounter and are challenged by "an art of shifting perspective, of double self-consciousness, of local and extended meaning."[3] These statements contest the existence of a unifying, thematic, universal concept of literature with its hegemonic impulse, and lead to a de-centring of perspective, so that the marginal and the 'ex-centric' take on a new positive significance, which is very appropriately expressed through the short story.

The stories in Rohinton Mistry's *Tales from Firozsha Baag*[4] revolve around three thematic nodules: first, the stories are concerned with the creation and preservation of a particular group of ethnically related people; second, they explore the intra-community dealings and reflect on the inter-racial relations; third, the scope of the stories goes beyond the geographical boundaries to depict the process of immigration and adaptation to another socio-cultural environment that any movement of a socio-cultural group from one geographical space to another would entail. Thus, the shifting borders of ethnicity in their location/dislocation discover their formal expression in the short stories that make up the cycle. The narrator in Rohinton Mistry's short story "The Ghost of Firozsha Baag" is a Konkani ayah, Jacqueline, who is employed by a Parsi family. She gives an outsider's view of the Parsis with their eccentricities and idiosyncracies: converting English words into Parsi-Gujrati, calling Jacqueline 'Jaykaylee,' their favourite dishes, superstitions, and their supercilious elitist behaviour. She explains that she has got used to living close to the floor because all the work she does is done at that level and she even sleeps on the floor. In adapting to their ways, Jacqueline has even forgotten her native Konkani and yet when unwittingly she frightens her mistress, who mistakes her for a ghost, she revels in secret at having outwitted her. The story reveals the inflexibility that is typical of the Parsi community. It also shows the submergence of the migrant Jacqueline's identity to assimilate into the culture of her masters, who, however, do not accept her and maintain the distinction of 'separateness.' "Swimming Lessons" is another story by Rohinton Mistry that reveals the ambivalence in the situation of the migrant. It depicts the experience of migration and dislocation through individual memory and individual perspective where the world described belongs to the past and yet it is a past that has determined and formed the present. The migrant is situated in a complex space between two worlds and two cultures, one is his ethnic culture and the other, the culture of his adopted land. The short story very succinctly brings out the dilemma that the protagonist confronts as he endeavours to adapt to his Canadian milieu.

The short stories written by M.G. Vassanji in the collection *Uhuru Street*[5] reveal another aspect of immigrant literature. The writings present a postcolonial discourse since the stories are situated in East Africa and describe the life and times of a colonized people. They deal with the experiences of the Asians in East Africa under the British rule and then, post-Independence, under the Africans. They depict the change in the socio-cultural construct of the Asians caused by the change in the political ideology. The hatred that the Africans nursed silently towards the Asians as well as the potential threat that they posed to the

Asians is evident in stories like "What Good Times We Had" and "Ebrahim and the Businessmen." The Asians are hated for being the middlemen, who were neither the colonizers nor the colonized in Africa, but only traders who benefited from the 'disadvantaged' Africans, employed them as servants and grew rich at their expense. The quarters of the Africans were hutments in the hinterland whereas the Asians built house after house as they flourished. Even in location, they occupied the middle space between the backward area of the Africans and the best locations of the Whites. After independence, the Africans took away most of their property in the name of socialism, as is shown in "Ebrahim and the Businessmen," even driving some to the point of suicide. But the worst is the revenge of the African bank clerk in "What Good Times We Had" who rapes and murders the rich thirty-five year old Asian woman who had, in her own life-time, employed and supervised over so many Africans. This dark face of Africa is also reflected in the fact that African quarters were out of bounds for the Asian boys and girls mainly because of their fear of the black magic associated with them and also the 'unknown' factor of their behaviour in different situations. The concept of Africa as a place to explore, inhabit and colonize is one aspect of colonization but the other aspect is the migrant's relationship with the alien land that he has set out to possess: does he accept his relationship with the land or does he merely use it and discard it? The Indian community calls itself African as far as political ideology is concerned but when it comes to the socio-cultural norms it considers itself completely Indian and above the Africans. The Asian community does not desire to mingle with the African community in a socio-cultural space: they cannot think of inter-marriage between the two communities. The short story, "Breaking Loose," however, is about a young Asian girl who falls in love with an African Professor and marries him, breaking away from the tradition-bound views of her society. She has the courage to cross the unnamed cultural boundaries that exist between the Asians and the Africans, and takes the bold step in spite of her mother's misgivings. The African connection is something that the Asians are not able to ignore because it is intricately tied up with its influence on their personality as migrants to East Africa.

This complex situation of the postcolonial perception of the diasporic writer may be symbolically represented by the two-way vision of the South Asian Canadian Diaspora whose literature explores the past but is actually a metaphor for the present experience. The diasporic writers may be writing about their homelands but the problematics of human constructs that they navigate in their postcolonial discourses are very much those of their present situation as migrants. In the stories that have been considered, the gender context of the location of the immigrant becomes a problematic of the 'double-bind' situation. Jaykaylee suffers a loss of her individual identity in her attempt to earn her living—she has been misnamed and she has even forgotten her Konkani language. The Asian woman who is murdered has to suffer the indignity of rape which is the easiest revenge that a male can claim to belittle an individual, a community and a race. On the other hand is the young Asian girl who takes the bold step of marrying an African Professor. Clearly the two stories reveal the negative and positive aspects of the same situation: in one the young woman had felt insulted when she received a proposal of marriage from an African Chief and remained a spinster, only to suffer the worst brutality but in the other instance the young girl had willingly married the African and hence embraced the land not only in how she could benefit from it but also in how she could also respond with affection for it. The kind of control that Africa, in its dark secret aspect, exerts on its inhabitants is almost as if the land avenges itself for being denied recognition and acceptance. This also creates the ambivalence in the 'positionality' of the insider/outsider situation which is as much true of the migrant in the present as it was in the past. Wherever he goes, the migrant carries his cultural baggage with him in the hope of establishing his roots in the new environment and yet he remains an outsider in the new milieu, either because he is not accepted by 'them' or he is not willing to accept 'them.'

The diasporic writers from erstwhile colonies are also conscious that their own colonial past has configured and variously distorted the view of 'home' and 'away' that people generally have, and that it has perhaps been further distorted by their neo-colonial present of being a minority group, so that they take pains to construct a viable representation of the 'self' as a located 'self.' What is at stake here is more than just local colour—it is an ambience that actually gives authenticity to their identity as he explores the intra-racial communication and associations between different races. M.G. Vassanji negotiates the imperceptibly changing scene with the withdrawal of the British and the feeling of oneness among the Asian and African students, along with the restraint that prevents Asians from assimilating into the African socio-cultural space by allowing inter-racial marriages, the revengefulness of the Africans and the vengeful power that they suddenly unleash on the Asians as they nationalize properties and deprive the Asians of the fruits of their hardships of over a century. There existed a binary situation between the White colonizer and the colonized Black and hence with the end of colonialism, in that particular situation of East Africa, the Asians occupying the middle space were abandoned by the colonizers to the mercy of the earlier colonized natives. The history of the Asians in East Africa, thus, involves not only the shifting boundaries of location and political ideology but also the socio-cultural and psychological changes that occur in the identity of an individual, as he is swept along the tide of confluences and divergences of cultures.

Francesco Lorrigio comments on the diaspora writers and states that they "often also act as the memory of the group: they are scribes who give voice to those who have lived or live in silence. By their mediation, because they managed to master a language, an experience otherwise lost, left unsaid, is communicated."[6] This statement is as true of diasporic women writers as it is of others. They, too, are 'silent' voices and have come to a consciousness of their 'disadvantaged position' by virtue of their gradual realization of their 'equal' status and the need for creating an awareness in other women through a narration of their own 'personal histories.' The context of themes and places become only means by which gender history, too, is inscribed into diasporic literature for the cognizance of others. The collective impression created by the anthology of short stories by South Asian women writers, *Her Mother's Ashes*,[7] is that of the gender problematic in the South Asian Diaspora. They project the feminine perspective and give an insight into the double marginalisation that the South Asian woman suffers—first, because of her race and immigrant status, and the second, because of her gender and the dependent secondary role defined by the patriarchal society to which she belongs. The stories also reveal that in spite of assimilating the essence of the host culture, they do not forsake the essence of their homeland-culture. For the women writers the short story becomes a metaphor to convey the complexity of their ethnic lives and the articulation of their subjectivity; sometimes it may merely be a statement of their suddenly dawned awareness of their own individual identity, but it mobilizes them into an assertion of the self, through action or through a conscious creativity. They create a holistic picture of the South Asian diaspora and the status of women within the diaspora.

"Lekythos," a story by Lakshmi Gill, has a situation where the husband does not co-operate with the wife's desire to write a novel so every day she completes all her duties as a wife before leaving for her friend's office to type her novel. She has to ignore the silent demands of her children and her husband because she realizes that she has a duty to her own self also. The effort is very fruitful and self-satisfying: through her experience of coming away from home to write, she has learnt to be more assertive, she has gained confidence and has seen the true chauvinistic character of her husband. She has realized the gender 'disadvantage' that she has to suffer in the patriarchal set-up but she has also been able to assert herself in her own way by writing the novel which become a marker of her identity. Similarly, in Lakshmi Gill's other short story "Altered Dreams," the protagonist Magdalena completes her doctorate degree not only under great stress to herself but also to her father. He is unable to last through the daily strain of commuting and baby-sitting, and finally collapses and dies in his effort to help his daughter obtain the degree. The story foregrounds the 'double-bind' situation of the woman who is not only expected to stay abreast of others' achievements to do well in her professional life but who must also perform all her duties at home as wife and mother.

Another interesting short story is "On a Cold Day" by Himani Bannerji. The story depicts the desperate need of Devika Bardhan to be assimilated into the Canadian society and its rejection of her because of her being the 'visible' other. Devika Bardhan has changed her name to Debbie Barton, she has changed her mode of dressing to the Western and has tried to pick up the right accent. But she is still not 'recognised,' to use Charles Taylor's phrase, and this leads to her feeling of being a non-entity. The metaphorical death that she experiences, over and over again in encounters with the WASP community, because of her 'otherness' is converted into a literal death transferred to the figure of the dead Asima. Moreover, the description of the "cold whiteness" of the day clearly projects how unsuited she is to her transplanted milieu, coming as she does from a warm climate. In this case, Devika Bardhan is not able to overcome the divergences of social and geographical environment to facilitate her confluence into the White Canadian society.

In their short stories women writers have also used parody and irony to implicate and yet to critique and challenge the male white tradition from within, exposing the double-standards that men employ vis-à-vis women. Arun Prabha Mukherjee's "A New Reading of 'The Wasteland'" reveals the hypocrisy in foreign-returned academics behind the modern attitude of free intermingling of the sexes. The professor encourages the young girl from the small town to shed her inhibitions because of the model of the West that he holds up to her, and calls her a prude when she refuses to sleep with him, but as soon as his wife returns he becomes absolutely sheepish and does not even have the courage to look her in the eye. The story reveals the duplicity that men employ of virtuous fidelity within the home and the moral laxity outside it. In another short story "American Date" by Nazneen Sheikh, the young female protagonist is sexually aroused at the prospect of going on a date with the handsome macho football captain who is also the most sought after boy in the school, only to discover that he is gay and has brought her out to deceive others about his true sexual preferences.

The Canadian multicultural society is a postmodernist society where different ethnic groups and different ideological social groups are constantly in a shifting situation; nothing is rigid. The stories reveal that attitudes of hostility, alienation, racism and manipulation are not determined by location or period (of time) but rather they are integral parts of the human psyche, whether coloured or white. Farida Karodia's story "Friends" is one such example where the Japanese Hiroko is ready to do anything, "even die," just to be considered a real Canadian and not just a hyphenated personality. She thinks the easiest way of becoming Canadian is to marry a Canadian man. To her own consternation she discovers the misconception of her ideas but by then it is too late and she falls to her death in the gorge. Women writers also develop the postmodern concept of the importance of the peripheral and the ex-centric, as a way out of the power problematic of centres and of male/female oppositions. In "The Icicle" Uma Parameswaran shows the other aspect of the man-woman relationship where the woman exploits the male and benefits from him only to strengthen her position before she discards him. Ranjit is too myopic to realize the need to change from the traditional sexist concept of the man-woman relationship engendered by a patriarchal society, when their cultural and working situation changes; but Deepa finds the whole effort of living out the traditional role of the Indian wife too taxing and, without being deterred by emotional sensitiveness, decides in a very cold calculating manner to just gradually draw away from him by putting distance between them and also to wean the child Anjali away from him though she is the centre of Ranjit's world. She does not see the love and pride that Ranjit takes in his family and the effort he puts in to keep the bond intact, but she only has her own constricted vision of things. She is depicted as a cold calculating woman who has totally overcome the traditional values, losing out even on the positive value of familial love, but nevertheless, she is also projected as a charming personality. Deepa privileges the personality of the new-age woman who is intent on the fulfillment of her own career-ambitions, ruthlessly employing her feminine charm for her advancement.

The stories thus reveal the changing attitude of women as they are transplanted into a different culture with different demands. The story "The Cat Who Cried" by Shauna Singh Baldwin is another example of the psychological oppression that the traditional role of a submissive wife can exert on the psyche of an educated independent woman and how sometimes the only option left is to assert one's independence, even at the risk of sacrificing marital harmony. Here the female protagonist tries to adjust to her mother-in-law's domineering interference but when she sees that her husband does not take a stand against his mother's unfair demands, then finally she is forced to take a stand herself even at the cost of marital harmony. The stories reveal the changing world of the South Asian woman in Canada as she becomes more and more aware of the need to assert her own individuality and the need to retain her own identity.

The socio-cultural vulnerability of the South Asian woman stems from her traditional role in the patriarchal society with its male domination and traditional ethos. The woman is expected to be an active economic partner thereby assuming a semblance of independence in the outside world, but within the home she is still expected to be a self-effacing silent non-entity. This creates a psychological confusion in her mind as to her real identity. The short stories depict an awareness of the new feminine psyche that no longer accepts the 'disadvantaged' role silently but finds the courage to resist patriarchal attitudes and 'privilege' herself. Bharati Mukherjee defines the South Asian woman very succinctly in an interview to Gillian Mackmay for the *Globe and Mail*, "Most Indian women do not give up easily: what foreigners perceive as forbearance is really a secretive love of revengeful survival." The South Asian woman has not only been taken out of her familiar homeland but has also been taken out of her familiar social role and milieu, with the double expectations of her adjusting to the new country and the new role of breadwinner while retaining the same mindset of the meek submissive self of her traditional role back home. This is the "double-bind" situation that she finds herself in, bound to patriarchal patterns of the homeland and maladjustment to the demands of the new adopted homeland and the stories show her effort to break out of such a situation.

Janice Kulyk Keefer states that the writing of immigrant experience disseminates understanding of the 'otherness' of the 'other' and acts as a bridge that crosses the chasm between cultural differences. She says: "It's a bridge . . . in which mobility vies with stability, a bridge over which people are constantly passing, jostling one another and stopping to exchange opinions or interpretations of the view. This kind of bridge points as much to the intractable chasm it was built to span as to the fact that a means of crossing that chasm now exists."[8]

The very fact that different diasporas are now projecting themselves through their literature, i.e., 'jostling one another,' reveals the gradual familiarity that is being developed with each other's 'differences.' The 'divergences' exist across the 'confluence' of different races and transnational borders. The idea of a singular uniform identity is challenged not only in the socio-political context but also in the gender context. 'Differences' are being 'privileged,' and the awareness of one's own identity and 'positionality' in social formations is gradually becoming more obsessive. The global cosmopolitan world of the present can be compared to a jigsaw puzzle in which, if each piece finds its location and space, there is perfect order, otherwise there is chaos.

NOTES

1. Charles Taylor, *Multiculturalism and "The Politics of Recognition"* p. 25.
2. Linda Hutcheon , *A Poetics of Postmodernism*, p. 9.
3. Charles Russell qtd. Linda Hutcheon, p. 11.
4. Rohinton Mistry, *Tales from Firozsha Baag* (New Delhi: Penguin, 1998).
5. M.G. Vassanji, *Uhuru Street* (Toronto: McClelland and Stewart, 1992).

6. Francesco Lorrigio, "History, Literary History, and Ethnic Literature" in Joseph Pivato, ed., *Literatures of Lesser Diffusion* (Alberta: Research Institute for Comparative Literature, 1990), p. 29.
7. Nurjehan Aziz, ed., *Her Mother's Ashes and Other Stories by South Asian Women in Canada and the United States*, 2 vols. (Toronto: TSAR, 1994 and 1998).
8. Janice Keefer Kulyk, "'The Sacredness of Bridges': Writing Immigrant Experience," *Literary Pluralities*, Christl Verduyn (Toronto: Broadview press/Journal of Canadian Studies, 1998), p. 101.

The Dilemma of Being an Immigrant: A Study of Bharati Mukherjee's *Leave it to Me*

G. DOMINIC SAVIO
The American College, Madurai

The statement of Uma Parameswaran, "Home is where your feet are" posits the theory that all immigrants get themselves acclimatized to the new land, uncritically accepting its protruding edges and glaring margins. But the picture that emerges while reading the immigrant literature is often different and disappointing. Pain, failure and nostalgia govern the life of the immigrants. Only a few of them show their mettle by integrating themselves with the new land, whereas many others fall a prey to frustration, despair and loneliness.

Though the wheat-granary of the world, Canada welcomes the immigrants by assessing them on standards that do not discriminate on the basis of race, national/ethnic origin, religion or sex, there is still discrimination. The "Keep Canada White" cry is loud enough. Economic exploitation and deprivation of the migrant labour force grows in leaps and bounds. Thus, the immigrants do not enjoy a paradise-like existence, for they are exiles, incapable of locating their real home. They further suffer a self-imposed segregation that hinders their acceptance by the native people. These immigrants simultaneously cherish a nostalgic attitude towards their home culture, thus glorifying the latter. Owing to this kind of conflict, the immigrants' cultural assimilation or dislocation is never total. They are dislocated and, at the same time, assimilated. Where are they?—in the new soil? Or, in their native land? Which is their real home?—The new land of which they have many dreams? Or, the one they have left behind?

Bharati Mukherjee's *Leave it to Me* subsists on the life of a young woman, Debby DiMartino, abandoned at birth in India and adopted by an Italian-American family in the Hudson Valley. The protagonist leaves the home of her foster-parents in search of her origin and identity. The author brings into focus how exiles, émigrés and outsiders tirelessly reinvent themselves, shedding their old life and lovers, and thus undergo a process of metamorphosis. Mukherjee views America as a country in which freedom has been translated into rootlessness and possibility into dislocation.

The present paper analyses the dilemma of the migrant, tracing his quest for inheritance. The study investigates whether the immigrant agrees with the paradigm "Home is where your feet are, and may your heart be there too," or not. (Jain)

The first level of investigation lies in unfolding the basic dilemma of the immigrant. DiMartino, the protagonist, suffers from an intense psychological problem of isolation and alienation. She is adopted and brought up by Italian-American parents, DiMartinos in an atmosphere of affluence and abundance. But she remains deeply distressed. The novelist makes use of the psychology of Freud in portraying the heroine as one who is longing for, knowing who she really is at bottom. Debby DiMartino is the Italian name she received from her adopted Italian parents. She feels that her "conscious" life in the terminology of Freud reveals only the superficial side of her peripheral existence. Her life in the cradle of adopted Italian parents is only a peripheral existence and her fundamental existence and the fundamental ground of her being lie elsewhere. She knows that she is a peculiar conglomeration of many odd realities: Indian father, American mother and Italian foster parents. She herself confesses in the language of T.S. Eliot that she is living, partly living and not fully living. When she discovers her origins of parentage, she cryptically captures her crisis in the lines, "Debby DiMartino is a lie . . . it's just that Debby DiMartino has no weight, no substance." (10)

To move out of the superficial self to the core self constitutes her struggle. Her life is an attempt at a long trial for knowing the mystery surrounding her own unknown parentage. The novelist calls her two-tire life as the upside and downside of her existence, what Freud would call 'conscious' and the 'subconscious' levels of existence.

The second level of enquiry for the heroine DiMartino is to know the history of what has pushed her to this crisis of identity. She is an immigrant born to an American mother and Asian father and exposed to Italian foster parents. In terms of her father, she makes a westward journey and in term of her mother, she makes an eastward journey. But her residence and upbringing are located in the west. Though born to an American mother, she feels that her American background is not her real side. The state of DiMartino being a cultural vagabond is worse than the state of being an immigrant. Her Indian father has avenged her American mother by making her an orphan through his illicit relationship with her American mother. It is the duty of the daughter to take vengeance on the Indian father who has made her life a big cultural mess. It is in this process of taking revenge on her Indian father, she makes the search for her American mother. The novelist brings in Indian mythology to throw more light on this cultural crisis.

The Indian mythology deals with the dual aspects of God. God is both male and female; but there are specific references to a male god and female goddess. The male god, according to the novelist, is Apollonian, namely, reason-oriented and the female god is Dionysian, namely, imagination-oriented. The female god is under the control of the male god. Similarly, in philosophy, imagination is under the control of reason. But the novelist being a woman is not satisfied with this kind of settlement of the issue found in Indian mythology. The first settlement, namely reason-conquering imagination is a kind of Aristotelian way of Apollonian settlement. What the novelist looks for is the Dionysian way of disposal of the issue in the conflict between reason and imagination. The novelist prefers Freudian-settlement of the issue: the subconscious (imagination and passion) prevails over the conscious (reason and mind). Roughly, it means passion is like a motor-car operating on the roadside of reason. The formula, when applied to the novel, runs like this: Debby DiMartino, an Indian born American is going to ride her motor-car roughly on the body of an Indian father whose cunning combined with treachery has destroyed the roots of her mother. DiMartino, according to the novelist's prologue becomes Mahisha-Asura-Mardini. Devi Mardini becomes the killer of the buffalo like Demon Mahisha. Here the analogy is that DiMatino will find out her Indian father and kill him by assuming the figure of Devi Durga. Problems coming from the subconscious cannot be solved by the criteria of the conscious. DiMatino had to assume the figure of Devi Durga (subconscious-Passion) in order to avenge the male Indian father (conscious-Reason)

There is an old saying that it is reason which promotes progress in life. But to the novelist, it is passion which promotes progress in life. Cultural vagabondage and cultural immigration come from passion impelling a person to choose a path and a home in accordance with his prompting. There are significant lines in the novel throwing light on this issue. DiMartino utters these lines in a mood of psychological anguish:

> and so I made up my mind to find out if I was someone special or just answer misfit I didn't write another poem but I began to understand about mugged identities. There was something to nature over nurture, and to the tyranny of genes. (16)

The last line 'nature over nurture' indicates the novelist's order of priority, namely the predominance of passion (nature) over reason (nurture). Her real residence is in her inner being. The outward being is only shallow with no weight and substance, in the language of the novelist herself. The dilemma of immigration is viewed by Bharati Mukherjee in Freudian terms. Without passion there is no movement in life. This is the inference which the novelist for a typical immigrant draws from Freud. It is only passion which drives one to be an immigrant. Reason settles the issue once for all whereas passion promotes life and puts it in progress and conflict. A crisis teaches a person more solidly than affluence and leisurely life.

The novel unfolds itself on five levels and at every level the cultural state of immigration is shown. For the novelist, immigration turns into a worse form of cultural vagabondage. The first stage of her life is seen in Catholic orphanage run by Gray Sisters. For DiMartino there is no birth certificate, no mother's name, no father's name—this seems to be the report of Catholic orphanage on her nativity and identity. The second level in her life is the training she receives from Frankie Fong who is a Hong Kong salad of racial genes. She loves him but Chime does not claim her being. That her psychological leanings are not towards China are brought out in the following lines:

> Frankie made an Asian childhood sound great fun, something I wanted to claim, something I'd been robbed of. (26)
> The charm of Frankie Fong started out as the charm of foreignness, of a continent I couldn't claim but which threatened to claim me. (36)

There are two cultural passages Euro-American and Eastern-Asian. The protagonist DiMartino is tossed between these cultural passages. Her difficulty of getting anchored in one or the other is the result of the cultural complexity hidden in her being. Perhaps cultural immigration can be taken as a synonym for cultural complexity. The heroine loves a Chinese but is incapable of loving China. It is true that cultural landscapes have particular psychological characteristics which touch deeply the chord strings of one's own inner being.

It is this truth which the passages quoted above try to establish. She is a typical cultural immigrant at the Catholic orphanage of Gray nuns and Fong Home products of Frankie Long. What the protagonist wanted is the passage of her knowledge of "shadowy parentage." (26)

The third level of enquiry into her parentage brings her subsequently to mind, fourth and fifth levels, resulting in her contact with Gabriel, Ham, Larry, Fred Pointer (a professional detective) and at last her Bio-mum (Jess—American woman—Hippie) and Bio-Dad (Romeo Hawk—Indian Guru and serial killer). Romeo Hawk was an Indian who was a Guru and a serial killer who ran a harem which attracted the American Hippies. Jess, her bio-mum was a Hippie who became a victim of his sexual treachery. The American Hippie tired of American life after the Vietnam War came to India for the purpose of mental solace. Commenting on her dream of India, Brandmark says, "Like so many young Americans in the 1960s and 70s Jess thought of India as a spiritual and sexual Never-Never-Land in escape from the moral confusion of her own country." (22)

DiMartino's mother Jess moves out of America under the garb of a Hippie to India. As an American, her cultural choice is with India. Jess is an immigrant in the sense that she expresses her desire to move out of America towards India for spiritual consolation. But DiMartino is an Italian by upbringing, Indian by fatherhood and American by motherhood. She is unable to absorb her being either into Italian or American parentage. Her Italian foster parentage is superficial and her American parentage is real but is unacceptable and her Indian parentage is acceptable because it is her real state of being. The heroine DiMartino experiences an intense agony of the dilemma of being an immigrant. She is tossed to and fro in the cultural waves of the sea without anything to hold onto. Her search for parentage makes her all the more pitiable because at every step she shows that she is a confirmed cultural immigrant from a condemned group.

The ultimate hope and desire of a human being is to search for everlasting and enduring happiness. If this view is taken as the yardstick for measuring life, then topography, geography, continents and landscapes have their role in determining the mental state of the human being. Why should Jess, an American woman Hippie, turn to India for solace? Her outward belonging to America has nothing to do with her longing to see India. It is in this context that the saying of Uma Parameswaran, "Home is where your feet are" gains significance. One cannot sustain the statement that one's own home is found in the mind. It may be true that it is the mind; but the mind gets attuned to some landscapes irrespective of one's own cultural origin. Two parentages are cited to prove the truth of the statement that the well being of mind is loosely bound with peculiar cultural landscapes. One would not have been born to a particular culture. But the strange irony is that one is at home with a foreign culture, on the other hand one would have been born to a particular culture but he is not at home with it. This is the paradox of life. In the light of these observations one is forced to recall the following lines, "when you inherit nothing you are entitled to everything" (67) and "Home is a place where your feet are." (Parameswaran 37)

One is tempted to accept these norms as something which lessens the intensity of the dilemma of being an immigrant. From a reading of the novel one comes to understand that the immigrants' dilemma is irresolvable as minds are varied in nature and function according to different wavelengths.

Bharati Mukherjee in her *Leave it to Me* captures the critical dilemma of an immigrant and offers a fluid solution which the title of the novel suggests. The dilemma of the immigrant arises out of many factors and the solution lies in this: leave me to myself and the crisis will resolve itself. The novel *Leave it to Me* meets the challenge of cultural diversity. One owns nothing and simultaneously one owns everything. This message is the novelist's answer to the challenge of cultural diversity. Expatriatism, immigration and diaspora are mutually exchangeable terms. Cultural origins and psychological origins have no resemblance and are disconnected. The immigrant's dilemma is born of the conflict between cultural origins and psychological origins. Disowning and disinheriting are acts of controversy but they are to be viewed in a sympathetic perspective. Disowning and disinheriting are mostly psychological problems. For men of such frames of mind, cultural problems are secondary and psychological problems are primary. It is in this emphasis that the whole dispute lies. One knows after reading the novel that the heroine DiMartino chooses what she prefers. Though Italian and American in background and upbringing she prefers to identify herself with Devi Durga of Asian mythology. Her choice is her own and it need not be the choice of somebody else. One cannot be very false at bottom to one's own self. It is the truth of being that drives an individual to make a choice. No crisis can go without a solution. One gathers this lesson from Hegelian philosophy. For the crisis engenders a counter-crisis and it forges a solution in its own way. The crisis of DiMartino is to know who her real parents are. The knowledge of her real parentage brings sorrow. Nevertheless that knowledge is very important to her in subconsciously facing herself. Her outward parentage is American-Italian but her real parentage is Indian-American. Instead of turning to America, she turns to India like her mother. Cultural vagabondage is the inevitable fate of an immigrant; this truth is well illustrated in the novel *Leave it to Me* from the life of the heroine, DiMartino. Cultural foundations are never fixed; they are found floating and the immigrant's dilemma pushes the person and throws him out of cultural fundamentalism because "When you inherit nothing, you are entitled to everything." (67)

Bibliography

Brandmark, Wendy. "Looking for Devi Dee." Rev. of *Leave it to Me*. *The Times Literary Supplement*, 4920, 18 July 1977, 22.

Jain, Jasbir, ed. *Writers of Indian Diaspora*. New Delhi: Rawat, 1998.

Mukherjee, Bharati. *Leave it to Me*. London: Random House, 1998.

O'Flaherty, Wendy Doniger, trans. *Hindu Myths*. Harmondsworth: Penguin, 1999.

Cross-Cultural Transactions and Evolution of Family in Bharati Mukherjee's *Jasmine*

VIJAY K. SHARMA
R.L.A. (Eve.) College, University of Delhi

Cross-cultural transaction is "an interactive, dialogic, two-way process rather than a simple active-passive one." It is "a process involving complex negotiation and exchange." In the postmodern climate, the notion of America as a melting pot for different cultures and the need for assimilation into what was thought to be the American culture is passe. Today the American attitude towards ethnicity and foreignness has changed. Ethnic difference is no more a matter of embarrassment. It is a matter of pride, instead. The metaphor of the melting pot has been replaced with that of a mosaic—an image used by Joan Morrison and Charlotte Fox Zabusky in their book *American Mosaic* (1980). Another image—that of a quilt—has been used by Wesley Brown and Amy Ling in their collection of short stories *Imagining America* (1991). Yet another image of a salad bowl has been used in this context. The emphasis in the last three metaphors marks a shift from the paradigm of assimilation to the acceptance of what used to be perceived as alien, and ethnic as part of the larger whole.

In any case, Bharati Mukherjee has the maximalist agenda as proclaimed by her in the *New York Times Book Review* (August 28, 1988) as against what she calls the "blind spot in American writing," that is, the minimalism which "disguises a dangerous social agenda. Minimalism is nativist, it speaks in whispers to the initiated. . . . I can feel its chill as though it were designed to keep out anyone with too much story to tell." Mukherjee recalls V.S. Naipaul's complaint that two of America's most celebrated authors, the two Johns, Cheever and Updike did not speak to him. Despite Naipaul's penchant for provocation, she finds that he was right. Writing in the late eighties, she felt that while "American fiction was sunk in a decade of minimalism, an epic was washing up on its shores." She goes on to imagine a poster over the United States Court House: "WELCOME MAXIMALISTS HELLO EXPANSIONISTS." Her Movement from Canada to the United States, she says, in the "Introduction" to the collection of her short stories called *Darkness* (1985) "is a movement away from aloofness of expatriation to the exuberance of immigration." (3)

Having argued for a new model of American literary scene, which is inclusive of the immigrant writings, Mukherjee, in her aforesaid article in *New York Times Book Review,* talks about what she calls "some forgivable fraud involved in the maintenance of expatriation." She feels that in "literary terms, being an immigrant is very declasse. There is a low-grade ashcan realism implied in the very material. . . . The exiles . . . come wrapped in a cloak of mystery and world-weariness. By refusing to play the game of immigration, they certify to the world, and especially to their hosts, the purity of their pain and moral superiority to the world around them. In some obscure way, they earn the right to be permanent scolds, soaking up comfort and privilege and nursing real grievances until privilege and grievance become habits of mind."

In *Jasmine* (1990), Mukherjee celebrates the freedom of anonymous in the U.S. and the American reverence for the autonomy of the individual. The energetic protagonist of the novel, who was born as Jyoti, metamorphoses herself into personae like Jasmine, Jase, or Jane, according to the requirement of the situation. By the time she starts her first person narrative, she has become a confident accomplished woman who is not only an adept "caregiver" to American households, "wife" to so many men, but also speaks with authority about diverse subjects such as farming, films, politics, science, medicine, accents of various Englishes spoken around her, Indian philosophy, Indian literature and social issues such as poverty. Her confidence level is very high throughout the novel, despite some real dark patches in her life. She finds herself being praised for her "great face" by an American woman professor. She is a source of love and inspiration for her "husband"-lovers—Prakash, Taylor and Bud. "You were glamour, something unattainable," says Bud (199) Her rival Karin needs her help: "Help me not to hate you Jasmine," says Karin (203) She perceives herself as the woman with "stark-white bobbed hair and a sad, heavy, wrinkled face. It's the face of poet or a philosopher, the face of a woman who has come to terms with all the Sukkhis and Half-Faces out there and is no longer afraid." (208) And finally unlike her adopted son Du, who chooses to remain hyphenated, she says, "My transformation has been genetic." (222) It is important to note that unlike an expatriate, Jasmine claims to have changed her very chemistry.

Jasmine's journey of self-actualization leads her not just to a comfortable life and fluid identities but to forging new alliances to form what she, as an Indian, is obsessed with—that is, family. One recalls Clark Blaise's documentation of his year-long stay in Calcutta in 1973-74 with his wife Bharati Mukherjee. His observations about Calcutta and Indian mores are typical of a westerner's viewpoint. He writes, "Family, family, family. In India all is finally family. If we in the West suffer the nausea of disconnectedness, alienation, anomy, the Indian suffers the oppression of kinship" (1977). One may not completely agree with Blaise's point of oppression of kinship; he, however, aptly marks the centrality of family in the Indian context. This is more than true in Jasmine's case. Despite her adaptations and accomplishments, she is out to forge familial alliances at various levels with different people. And one notices that these familial concerns and efforts almost subvert the very institution of family she is out to create. In other words, she creates new and rather unusual familial ties.

Before coming to America, Jyoti falls in love with the voice of Prakash who spoke of love and brotherhood in vicious atmosphere of Sikh separatism in Punjab. "I fell in love with that voice. It was low, grave, unfooled. I was prepared to marry the man who belonged to that voice" (66), she says. "Only a very tall and a very strong man could have a voice like that" (67), she adds. It is interesting that she is prepared to marry Prakash without any knowledge of what he looks like. She writes, "Love rushes through thick mud walls. Love before first sight: that's our Hasnapuri way." (67) Her only concern is whether Prakash spoke English or not. "I couldn't marry a man who didn't speak English. To want English is to want more than you had been given at birth, it was to want the world." (68) Assured by her brothers of Prakash's what they call "first class English" (68), she learns that he has plans to move to America. Jyoti has already set her heart on marrying Prakash without even knowing his last name. "An impression was all I had: dignity, kindness, intelligence. Maybe even humor" (73), she says. It is important that these are some of the qualities she appreciates in all her later "husbands" also. She chooses to marry unconventionally: "Ours was a no-dowry, no-guests Registry Office wedding." (75) Her village-friend Vimla observes rather pontifically "that once you let one tradition go, all the other traditions crumble." (75) And this proves right too in Jyoti's case. She prides in the fact that her husband Prakash Vijh was "a modern man, a city man. He did trash some traditions right from the beginning." (76) His friends were like him: disrupters and rebuilders, idealists." (77) She likens him with Professor Higgins as he "wanted to break down the Jyoti I'd been in Hasnapur and make me new kind of city woman. To break off the past he gave me a new name: Jasmine" because she was, as he called her, "small and sweet and heady, my Jasmine." (77)

Another important need Jasmine feels throughout her life is to get pregnant and mother a child. But then, "Prakash yelled every time I told him I wanted to get pregnant," she says, because he felt that they should wait for more prosperous times, which were never to be. Prakash falls prey to the bullets of a terrorist and thus Jasmine fulfils one of the two prophecies of the village astrologer—that of widowhood. The other one, that of exile, is what the rest of her story is.

But Jasmine is a fighter, survivor and achiever. She recalls that if "we could just get away from India, then all fates would be concealed. We'd start with new fates, new stars. We could say or be anything we wanted. We'd be on the other side of the earth, out of God's sight." (85) Jasmine sets out for America to fulfil her husband's mission in a rather strange and unique way—to commit *sati* in the university where Prakash was to become a student! Sounds rather regressive, especially from a person like Jasmine. Braving illegal migration, hunger, cold and even rape at the hands of an ugly monster appropriately called Half-Face (whom she murders eventually in the role of goddess Kali), Jasmine sounds philosophical, typically in the Hindu way when she realizes: "My body was merely the shell, soon to be discarded. Then I could be reborn, debt and sins all paid for." (121)

Her next incarnation takes place in Wylie and Taylor Hayes's household in New York where she works as a "caregiver," a position of respect, where her job is to look after their young daughter, Duff. Significantly Jasmine feels comfortable there because, she says, "Wylie made me feel her younger sister. I was family, and I was professional.." (175) By family, she means here a sense of belonging to the household. She has now acquired a new name. Jasmine has been shortened to Jase by Taylor in a typically American fashion and she becomes Duff's "day mummy." Gradually the scene changes. Wylie goes to Europe with her lover-friend Stuart to Europe while back at home Taylor falls for Jase. She admits, "On those nights, we—Duff, Taylor and I—became a small, sufficient family and I told myself guilty, that everything might really work out all right. I prayed that Wylie and Stuart would take all the time they needed in Europe, because I, the caregiver, was eager to lavish care in my new, perfect family." (183) One cannot help noticing the use of the term "family" here twice, this time in a more specific way than merely in the sense of belonging. Jase has replaced Wylie in the "family."

Taylor accepts her as she was. "Taylor didn't want to change me. He didn't want to scour and sanitize the foreignness," she says (185). But unlike the expatriates, Jase chooses to change—by choice, to be able to be one of them. She says, "I changed because I wanted to. To bunker oneself inside nostalgia, to sheath the heart in a bulletproof vest, was to be a coward. On Claremont Avenue in the Hayses' big, clean, brightly lit apartment, I bloomed from a diffident alien with forged documents into adventurous Jase." (185-86) Jase feels that she could have founded a family even with the vain and solicitous Stuart, Wylie's lover, but she was in her own words, "heads over heels" in love with Taylor (186), "who had been unfailingly kind, never condescending, always proud of my achievements." (187) Besides, she finds Taylor inspiring too. He tells her: "Weak gravity is what keeps your dreams inside your head so that they don't go flying out." (178) But in Jase's head "bat-winged nightmares flapped frantically; I didn't want them flying out of my skull," she says (182). Her realization that "America may be fluid and built on flimsy lines of weak gravity, but I was dense object, I had landed and was getting rooted." (179) proves wrong when she finds her husband Prakash's murderer recognizing her. Jase decides to leave New York for Iowa where she will be Jane to her new "husband" Bud Ripplemeyer.

"Iowa was a state where miracles still happened," (197) says Jane. Bud, a big, hearty, divorcee of fifty-three was older to Jane by thirty years, a fact she couldn't consider at all between them. She sums up her Iowa experience as follows: "Bud wants me to marry him 'officially,' he says before the baby comes. People assume we're married. He's a small-town banker, he's not allowed to do impulsive things. I am less than half his age and very foreign. We're the kind who marry. Going for me is this: he wasn't in a wheelchair when we met. I didn't leave him after it happened." (7) And, "Bud was wounded in the war between my fate and my will. I think sometimes I saved his life by not marrying him. I feel so potent, a goddess." (12)

Bud and his Asian wife have an adopted son Du—Du Ripplemeyer who was born Du Thien, a hard-to-place Vietnamese orphan. "He barely spoke English when he arrived; now he is fluent, but with a permanent accent. 'Like Kissinger,' he says." Du is a precocious child. Like Prakash, he has a surgeon's touch. Jase feels that he "is the son Prakash and I might have had." (155) But Du does not feel belonged to this family; he remains what Jase calls "hyphenated." He is indebted to Jase for giving him a new life, but leaves Iowa for LA to his community people. Jase observes, "Blood is thick, I think. Du, my adopted son is a mystery, but the prospect of losing him is like a miscarriage." (221)

Jase's Ripplemeyer attempt at family-formation is laudable but abortive. How can she fight the forecast of an old fakir sitting under a banyan tree in her village? And then now the divorced Taylor Hayes and his daughter Duff are on their way to reclaim Jase to form what he calls an "unorthodox family." Karin is back to Bud, thanks to Jane; and now, she says, "I cry into Taylor's shoulders, cry through all the lives I've given birth to, cry for all my dead." (241) Jasmine has lived many lives; in each incarnation she is a new woman. "I have had a husband for each of the women I've been. Prakash for Jasmine, Taylor for Jase, Bud for Jane. Half-Face for Kali." (197) One is naturally surprised if a rapist is called a "husband," especially the one who is murdered by her in anger soon after the rape. What is the meaning of the term "husband" for Jasmine? One assumes that marriage is central to family both in the Christian and the non-Christian societies. In the case of Jasmine, who has been a rebel of a sort from her childhood, social ceremony may have little relevance for her. In any case, the social or legal processes of getting married have no meaning for Jasmine, as she never married anyone of her so-called "husbands" except Prakash. But here she equates even rape with marriage! In her feminist zeal, she seems to subvert even the very fundamental feminist position for sexual freedom.

What concept of a "family" is Jasmine advocating? The unorthodox one obviously, even by the very strict feminist standards. On the one hand, Jasmine is a practitioner of feminist credo according to which the social and legal aspects of ritual of marriage are not central to one's existence; on the other, she seems to seek personal and social acceptance of such relationships as familial. As an Indian, she finds family to be an indispensable social institution. She creates unorthodox varieties of family that are possible only in the liberal climate of America.

On the basis of the above reading of *Jasmine*, I would like to suggest that South Asian American literature like the literature of the other marginal, ethnic, racial or cultural groups in America, contributes to as well as complicates the traditions and mythologies of American literature. These literatures re-form the contemporary literary scenario and reflect the changing patterns of life and society in America. To read these works as "merely ethnic" and as "ethnic documentaries" would keep them somehow apart from our serious readings and discussions of twentieth century American literature. Besides, while there remain a number of problems in cross-cultural transactions, creative writers and community workers cannot continue to sit on the margins, content to serve their little "ethnic" communities. They feel the need to understand the history of America, its founding ideals, and the "common vision" and contribute to them positively. May I conclude my paper with Jasmine's optimistic remarks about her future, at the end of the novel: "Time will tell if I am a tornado, rubble-maker, arising from nowhere, and disappearing into a cloud. I am out the door and in the potholed and rutted driveway, scrambling ahead of Taylor, greedy with wants and reckless from hope (241).

Works Cited

Blaise, Clark and Bharati Mukherjee. *Days and Nights in Calcutta.* New York: Doubleday, 1977.

Brown, Wesley and Amy Ling, ed. *Imagining America Short Stories: An Anthology of American Fiction.* 1991. New Delhi: UBSPD, 1995.

Morrison, Joan and Charlotte Fox Zabusky, ed. *American Mosaic: The Immigrant Experience in the Words of Those Who Lived It.* 1980. New York: New American Library, 1982.

Mukherjee, Bharati. *Jasmine.* 1989. New Delhi: Penguin, 1990.

Mukherjee, Bharati. *Darkness.* 1985. New Delhi: Penguin, 1990.

Mukherjee, Bharati. *New York Times Book Review.* August 28, 1988.

A Psycho-Analytical Study of the Protagonist in Bharati Mukherjee's *Wife*

MONIKA GUPTA
H.N.B.Garhwal University, Srinagar-Garhwal

Indian literature written by resident Indian and by writers of Indian origin, has received international recognition. Bharati Mukherjee is one of the leading fiction writers of South Asian Diaspora. She has written novels *The Tiger's Daughter, Wife, Jasmine, The Holder of the World, Leave it to Me* and short stories like *Darkness* and *The Middleman and Other Stories*. The major themes reflected in her works are issues related to women; their self-actualization, psychological transformation, problem of identity, issues of gender and culture and most importantly problems and challenges faced by the Indian communities especially by women in foreign countries. Bharati Mukherjee's works from *The Tiger's Daughter* (1972) to *Desirable Daughters* (2002) reflects her expatriate, immigrant and diasporic identities. She herself accepts that her works are about "psychological transformation, especially among women immigrants from Asia" (*Iowa Review*, 15). Her own experiences in Canada and America as an immigrant reflect her works. Although Bharati Mukherjee is now an American citizen but India and its culture is the central figure in her novels. Her second novel *Wife* (1975), presents protagonist's alienated life in immigration resulting in neurotic behaviour and her journey from marriage to murder. The present paper attempts to focus the psychological strains and causes of abnormal behaviour of Dimple Basu, who tries to relate her Indian traditional values with modern American culture. *Wife* is the novel, which she has started in Calcutta but her experiences in Canada overshadow the story. one can easily find influence of Canadian identity on her imagination.

As a young girl Dimple Basu is looking for a smart handsome husband who can provide her everything in life. The desire of Dimple is clearly indicated in the very first page of the novel:

> Dimple wanted a different life—an apartment in Chowringhee, her hair done by Chinese girls, trips to New Market for nylon saris—so she placed her faith in neurosurgeons and architects. (3)

Her marriage was settled with Amit Basu, a consultant engineer. After marriage, Dimple tried to please every member in traditional Calcutta-based Bengali joint family. When her husband and mother-in-law changed her name, she also accepted her new identity. When she heard the news that her husband was planning to go to America, she felt that this decision of her husband could provide freedom and liberty. Both husband and wife are excited to fly but their reason for going to America is totally different. The major cause of going to America for Dimple was to be liberated from all customs and traditions. She started dreaming about her stay abroad without knowing the practical problems she was going to face there. In order to fulfill her dream, she aborts her child which can be an obstacle in her happy life. She did not want to serve her old mother-in-law. Regarding fantasy it has been said, "man can continue to enjoy a freedom from the grip of the external world, one which he has long relinquished in actuality" (Freud, 381). Dimple understands that marriage and family are very central to Indian life and to fulfill her dreams she has to continue her confirmative role. Moreover she retreats into "an entropic state of inertia, exhaustion and endless indecisiveness" (Liew-Goek Leng, 487).

During her pregnancy, Dimple's act of killing a mouse clearly reflects her mental disorder. Mukherjee writes, "and in outburst of hatred, her body shuddering, her wrist taut with fury, she smashed the top of a small gray head." (35) In one way she was killing a part of herself because the dead mouse looked as pregnant as herself. On the other hand, it is a symbolic suicide of her self because with the end of the mice, her intense feeling has disappeared. This is a kind of catharsis for Dimple and, by giving vent to her feelings, she finds great relief from her internal tension that dogs her day and night. Dimple, unlike other normal women, discards the greatest gift of motherhood:

> She began to think of the baby as unfinished business. It cluttered up the preparation for going abroad. She did not want to carry any relics from her old life (42)

During her pregnancy, her abnormal thoughts and act of self-abortion once again remind readers about her frustration and dilemma:

> She had skipped rope until her legs grew numb and her stomach burned; then she poured water from the heavy bucket over her head, shoulders, over the tight little curve of her stomach. She had poured until the last of the blood washed off her legs; then she had collapsed. (42)

We cannot ignore that her action "is a sacrament of liberation from the traditional roles and constraint of womanhood" (Sharma, 15). Thus, her present state of consciousness is regarded as necessitated by our previous states and the externality of her perception is warped.

When she reaches America she becomes fascinated by every thing; the language, culture, society, even the Apartment in which they are living. But in few days, the cloud of uncertainty and confusion rules her. Mukherjee writes:

> She was caught in the crossfire of an American communalism she couldn't understand. She felt she'd come very close to getting killed on her third morning in America. (60)

All her dreams are shattered and she is unable to analyze her own existence. This is the stage of her psychological transformation and her personality turns into disequilibrium. Dimple faces cultural encounter between India and America. Now she begins to compare Calcutta and America. Her immature mind is not able to decide which culture she has to choose. She is very conscious of American surroundings and pressures which she is facing in alien country. Linda Sandler is of opinion that Dimple suffers from "a subterranean streak of violence. She is uprooted from her family and her familiar world is projected into a social vacuum where the media become her surrogate community, her global village. New York intensifies her frustration and unhooks her further from reality; she kills easily, like a sleepwalker." (76)

When Amit is not able to find a job, Dimple becomes disappointed and thinks of different ways for suicide. Psychological studies have proved that the people with suicidal tendencies suffer from interpersonal crisis, failure and self-devaluation, inner conflict, loss of meaning and hope. Dimple's sense of self-esteem has been crushed beyond measure and she plunges headlong into the depths of despair. Suicide is a delirious mania in which "the individual is confused, widely excited and violent" (Colmam, 343). She tries to learn Western culture, thoughts, activities, dresses but fails. After Amit gets a job, she is left alone all the day and from here her dilemma starts. She becomes involved with Milt, and finally kills her husband with a knife. His relationship with Milt made her more violent and her guilt is shown by the novelist:

> She would kill Amit and hide his body in the freezer. The extravagance of the scheme delighted her, made her feel very American somehow almost like a character in a TV series. (195)

Dimple is a complex character, suffering from schizophrenia, a group of "psychotic disorders, characterized by gross distortion of reality; withdrawal from social interaction, and the disorganization and fragmentation of perception, thought and emotion" (Colman, 292). Life or constructive instinct are always opposed to death or destructive instinct and Dimple suffers from different types of stresses—frustrations, conflicts and pressures. In the first part of the novel, her early marriage, unwanted pregnancy and troubles in Amit's house are the reasons for her stresses. To analyze her character, we must not forget her life before marriage. She belongs to a middle-class family where to find a good and prosperous husband a girl must be beautiful. Before marriage also the novelist has clearly indicated her abnormal behaviour:

> In the moments immediately after a power cut, when the street noises were sharp and distinct, she heard the boy next door scream

> in pain because of water in his head. She visualized his head as a giant balloon battered by the monsoon rains. (7)

Her complexion, flat breast and middle-class background are the reasons for her inferiority complex. She was only twenty when she got married and was not able to complete her education. Her concept of marriage is totally different:

> Marriage would bring her freedom, cocktail parties on carpeted lawns, fund raising dinners for noble charities. Marriage would bring her love. (3)

Due to all these circumstances she tried to please her husband and in-laws and lived in uncomfortable atmosphere in Amit's house. Coming from middle class, she adores prosperity. Her middle class mentality shrouds her way of thinking and she tends to place self before everything. She goes through an emotional crisis during her pregnancy. Her desire and ambition force her to go to the extent of aborting the child. Readers may think that she was wrong in doing so, but for her, the first pregnancy was not welcome. During the pregnancy her mental condition became worse and she became violent.

To get rid of her role of traditional wife, she left India. After a frustrating life in Calcutta, Dimple escapes to U.S. without understanding that her essential problems remain. Once again she was not able to adjust herself in America. She has a strong desire to forget Indian culture and tradition but simultaneously feels inferior in the company of Indian immigrants. Cultural and racial difference and her failure in speaking fluent English cuts her off from other Indians. Even she was not able to make strong relationship with the society. So, she suffers from an identity crisis and loneliness seems to tear her individuality to pieces. She seems to have depression and suicidal tendencies cloud her thoughts. She fails to assert her individuality in the quest of her authentic self. Under these circumstances, when Amit rejects her proposal for a job, she has to sit at home without any constructive work. Her independence on Amit for economic and emotional support leads her towards isolation. She starts watching television especially American thrillers where sex and crime are projected in a glorious way:

> Everything she saw on TV was about love; even murder and death, the scary, ugly kind of death, random and poorly timed. . . . And she gave up trying to make friends with children. (73)

She now started suffering from hallucination, suicidal dreams and violent dreams. Her isolation has a destructive effect on her psyche. Her abnormal and aggressive behaviour became more pathetic when Amit did not notice changes in her behaviour and involved so much in his job that he did not pay proper attention to her emotional and mental needs. As Amit is busy in his daily schedule and work, Dimple does not share her secrets with Amit:

> She does not tell him about her immoderate daytime sleeping either. They were unspeakable failings. She thought of them as deformities—sinister, ugly, wicked. (115)

Dimple's boredom and careless attitude of Amit lead her to become so violent, that she kills her husband. The last chapter of the novel clearly presents her violent thoughts of suicide and idea of murdering her husband:

> Her own body seemed curiously alien to her, filled with hate, malice, an insane desire to hurt, yet weightless, almost airborne. She dug her chin deep into the depression, so deep that she squirmed in sleep. With viciousness she thought inappropriate to her wifely status. (117)

Jasbir Jain opines, "Dimple is an escapist and lost in her private world of fantasy." (8) Dimple is not able to distinguish between fantasy and reality, and learning to cope with disappointments and frustration of living resulting in such a furious act.

Before her marriage to Amit, Dimple had a dream of marrying a neurosurgeon. This is her picture of an ideal husband:

> She borrowed a forehead from an aspirin ad, the lips, eyes and chin from a body builder and shoulders ad and put the ideal man. (23)

In a very general view her attitude and choice for a husband is quite natural. So, obviously Amit was not her first choice rather she did not have any other option. In U.S.A. she gets disturbed when Amit cannot find a suitable job which can provide them a happy and prosperous life. Amit has proved himself a failure. At this stage she has negative feelings for Amit also. She realizes that Amit was not the person of whom she has always thought:

> She was bitter that marriage had betrayed her, had not provide all the glittery things she had imagined, had not brought her cocktails under canopied skies and three A.M. drives to dingy restaurants where they sold divine *Kababs* rolled in *roti*. (102)

Even later on, after getting a good job, Amit's careless nature had negative impact on her. On one hand Amit burdened her with household work and on the other hand he always ignored her. He is not able to give her a positive solution. Moreover, there is none with whom she can share her problems. Dimple is not satisfied with Amit and her life:

> He did not feed her reveries; he was unreal. She was furious, desperate; she felt sick. It was as if some force was impelling her towards disaster, some monster had overtaken her body, a creature with serpentine curls and heaving bosom that would erupt indiscreetly through one of Dimple's orifices, leaving her, Dimple Basu, splattered like bug on the living room wall and rug. The cataclysm embarrassed her. (156)

Through Dimple-Amit relationship, Bharati Mukherjee has tried to raise the problem of compassion which involves 'the feeling of sympathy with, and understanding of, another person's feelings.' If Amit was able to understand his wife's problems, the situation would have been different. Middle class Indian women are not only economically and socially dependent on their husbands but their emotional and psychological needs get satisfied in their husband's company. If Dimple was educated and had her own interests and hobbies, she would have not reacted in the way she did.

Dimple's increasing desires and inactive life bring her closer to Ina Mullick, who is a vulgar and selfish woman. Dimple learns a lot from Ina about new culture and modern life, but later on she wants to get rid of Ina. In fact Dimple's illegitimate relationship with Milt is the result of her friendship with Ina. Here we should not forget the immature age and incomplete education of Dimple. She easily gets fascinated by new objects and people without thinking of their reality and importance in her life. She is forever looking for something new without thinking of the consequences.

Commenting on the concluding part i.e. Dimple's violent act of killing her own husband Bharati Mukherjee explains:

> So instead of committing suicide, turning the society-mandated violence inward, she, in a misguided act, kills the enemy. So, of course, I am not approving of murder. It's meant to be a positive act, self-assertive. (*Iowa Review*, 200)

Bharati Mukherjee has beautifully portrayed her protagonist, Dimple Basu, who is in her identity crisis and self-individualization. She is not able to understand her potential and wishes. Studies say that there are four important wishes that arise in our mind: security, new experience, response and recognition. She wants all of them together without making any positive efforts. Her daydreaming and withdrawal form reality make her life a hell. As a woman, wife and immigrant she fails to establish significant role for herself. Dimple is unable to face the gross reality of life and cannot discern the way to deal with her psychological problems. This is responsible for the ruination of her 'inner self.' The amicable solution lies in facing the problems as they come. Dimple is caught in a web or fantastic world, which is created by her. It is clear that "a person's maladaptive behaviour might be caused not only by personal problems but also by abnormal conditions in the surrounding social environment" (Carson and Butcher: 91). Her incapability of facing and fighting with her psychological problems compels her to act in such a manner. Bharati Mukherjee portrays the extreme case of women and Dimple's "final act of violence is unconvincing on a realistic level, yet really is an attempt at trying out a mode other than realistic"(Meenakshi Mukherjee, 237).

WORKS CITED

Carson, Robert C. and James Butcher. *Abnormal Psychology and Modern Life*, ninth ed.,New York: Harper and Collins,1992.

Colman, J.C. *Abnormal Psychology and Modern Life*, Scott, Foresman, 1972.

Freud, Sigmund. *A General Introduction to Psychoanalysis*, New York: Washington Square Press, 1968.

Jain, Jasbir. "Foreignness of Spirit: The World of Bharati Mukherjee's Novels," *Journal of Indian Writing in English*, Vol.12, No. 2 (July 1985).

Jessie Glearson and Tom Grimes." An Interview with Bharati Mukherjee," *Iowa Review*, Vol. 20, No. 3 (Spring 1990).

Leng, Liew-Goek. "Bharati Mukherjee," *International Literature in English,* NewYork: Garland, 1991.

Mukherjee, Bharati. *Wife.* New Delhi: Penguin, 1975.

Mukherjee, Meenakshi. "The Theme of Displacement in Anita Desai and Kamala Markandaya," *World Literature in English* (April 1978).

Sandler, Linda. "Violence as a Device for Problem Solving," *Saturday Night,* October 1975.

Sharma, Maya Manju. "The inner World of Bharati Mukherjee: From Expatriate to Immigrant," Emmanuel Nelson, ed. *Bharati Mukherjee: Critical Perspectives*, New York and London: Garland, 1993.

Critiquing Patriarchy: The Literary Works of Suniti Namjoshi

SAVITA GOEL
Savitri Girls College, Ajmer

Suniti Namjoshi, an Indo-Canadian writer, believes that the inequality between the sexes is not the result of biological necessity but is produced by the cultural construction of gender differences. In her literary works, she tries to comprehend the social and psychic mechanisms that construct and perpetuate gender inequality. She asserts that women should claim for more space within the existing social structures, and try to dismantle the prevailing status quo. Suniti Namjoshi does not use conventional narrative in order to highlight the feminist concerns. She uses the fabulative mode which is extremely effective in focussing attention on the questionable workings of patriarchy. The present paper focuses on her novel *The Mothers of Mayadiip*[1] and her collection of short stories called *Feminist Fables*.[2]

The Mothers of Mayadiip is a feminist fantasy, where she explores the problems of women in a patriarchal structure through the construction of society where women are the dominant sex. Though Namjoshi critiques patriarchy through her tabulation, she also moderates feminist euphoria. As opposed to Simone de Beauvoir, she considers 'men' the 'second sex.' In the novel the term 'woman' is always positive, standing for the norm, man is the secondary term, what is other to the norm, and so man does not have a positive meaning in its own right, but is defined in relation to woman—as what woman is not. Here, 'man' functions as the 'other' which allows woman to construct a positive self-identity as feminine. And because what is other does not have identity in its own right, it often acts as an empty space to be ascribed whatever meaning the dominant group chooses. By seeing men as other to themselves, as not women, women can read into 'feminity' whatever qualities are needed to construct their sense of the feminine. So a mythicized man becōmes the imaginary location of female dreams, and masculinity is found to represent beauty, so the boys are called 'pretty' boys, which demeans them to the level of objects and denies any meaning or significance to them.

The novel is a fantasy where the patriarchal structures are dismantled and the society is matriarchal, where the interests of the males are sub-ordinated to female interests. The women have all the space for themselves and men or the pretty boys do not possess any identity and are like puppets whose strings are controlled by women. The boys are used for their semen because it is necessary for reproduction in the Mayan state and they are discarded after.being used. When the Blue Donkey questions as to how mothers conceive their children, Valerie explains that the mothers milk the pretty boys of semen before they dive into the sea and turn into foam. Boys are not the norm here, they fight among themselves and mothers of Maya let them. Eventually, there is nothing left to fight except the waves and they turn into foam. The Mayans think that except for the semen the lives of pretty boys are perfectly pointless. Valerie says that "the mothers of Maya don't regard them as their own children—just as necessities." (161) The pretty cannot rebel because they are unorganised and their rebellion is turned against themselves. They are the passive victims of female oppression. These boys reflect on the plight of women in a patriarchal society, where they are treated as objects. The attitude of the ruling sex towards the subordinate sex can be epitomized in what matriach says to her daughter, Asha, the Apostate: "My dear, whether or not they can be civilized was never in dispute. It is just that it was never considered particularly worthwhile (184).

However, there are hierarchies in this matriarchal society, too. All the daughters of Maya look to the Matriarch as an incarnation of Supreme Mother. She has made some rules for this society and defiance of the rules leads to punishment. Jayanvi, an Indian feminist is locked up because she has offended the Mayans for disliking children. She has sinned against motherhood—against the care of their identities, their religion and their family structure. In Mayadiip, there is no army, just the Therapists' Guild, who serve as the police. They deal chiefly with crimes of passion i.e. "maladjusted mothers, unsisterly sisters, rivalries and jealousies of diverse sorts, non-conformity with Mayan customs . . the problems of lovers." (127) The Matriarchi's eldest daughter, Asha was debarred from the succession and sent to exile for being a heretic. She said that the pretty boys deserved better. The social structure is extremely important and personal relationships are subordinate to that. When Asha is exiled, there is a conflict between the matriarch as a mother and as a ruler. In this conflict, matriarch as a ruler wins, and she upholds her ideology and declares her daughter a rebel.

The Mayans believe that a woman is not a complete individual until she becomes a mother. Motherhood makes her life purposive and she cannot reach an adult status unless she is a mother. Grade A mothers are the chosen few. They pass all the tests and go to become the Chief of Guilds and so on. Their main privilege is that they are expected to have daughters just right away. They usually bear their own daughters but not always. They are like males in a patriarchal structure and do not have to do the chores of looking after the needs of children. Grade B mothers are biological mothers and their position is better than Grade C mothers who have to work and look after the children borne by the other women. When they have worked long enough and can pay to have a daughter, they can apply for Grade A status. This means that social status depends on economic status. In this society, young girls are trained to be good mothers. Gagri the good, the matriarch's granddaughter is compelled to undergo some tests to find out her aptitude to be a future mother and her skill with babies. She wants to go out and play but is not permitted as the baby is more important than one's own desires. Shyamila tells a story about the child who wished to be a boy and who did not play will dolls but with pretty boys and as she grew up she refused to be a womanly woman. When she was fifteen years old, she discovered that though still a child, she belonged to no one. Shyamila concludes by saying, "If you see an elderly woman walking the streets who begs to be mother— why that's her. . . . A pitiful spectacle." (123) This story amply portrays that in this society there is no place for childish women and motherhood is essential to endow meaning to a woman's life. Jyanvi is very candidly told that if she desires to remain in Mayan society, she must have a function and possess some status.

However, even in this matriarchal society, the problem of equality exists. There are no men to exploit women but the hegemonic structure still prevails and a woman has to face discrimination on the basis of whether she is grade A, grade B or grade C mother i.e. whether she is the guardian, mother or caretaker of the child. Everyone is not equal in this society. Money is distributed according to a woman's rank which depends on birth and merit. To make money, an ordinary woman has to sell her skills and if she has any children, there are the bonuses that accrue from the children. In Mayadiip, the children are glorified too much and lives and longings of women do not matter. It is the duty of every Mayan to sacrifice herself for the welfare of the children. However, hypocrisy prevails here, also. Jyanvi wonders why the more powerful mothers hire other women to care for their children, and if being a mother is such a marvellous thing, then why do the mothers pass off the chores to other. In this society the more powerful the mother is, the more privileged the child is and to be allowed to care for Mayan daughter is a great privilege.

When the matriarch, the supreme authority, is deposed by a coup and Shyamila usurps the throne and she is sent to the forest, Asha invites her mother, her elder sister, and others to Ashagadh, the Fortress of hope. Here, there is a tree in the forest which they call the tree of life, underneath which they find boy babies. They are, in fact, the pretty boys rejected by the Mayans. Saraswati wonders why do they steal the pretty boys who are left under the tree by the Mayans, they are warlike and sterile and cannot even reproduce themselves. Now they want the help of Asha's pretty boys to regain the Matriarchate of Maya. In return Asha wants a change in the institutions of Maya and equal rights for boys. She says, "Boys should also be given a decent education and allowed to grow up into mothers like everyone else." (188) The pretty boys cannot become biological mothers, but they are certainly capable of grade A and grade C status, and this has been proved. The patterns and hierarchies of Mayadiip are maintained here. This reflects on the heirachies in the patriarchal structures of power.

The concept of father is unknown in Mayadiip. When Jyanvi says that in her own society, she applied for the status as a co-mother, but was rejected on the grounds that the father would be more useful. Malini Devi questioned with surprise: "what is father?" It was explained to her that in patriarchal societies, the pretty boys are trained alongside the daughters. They grow up to a larger size and attempt to rule and many of them take up the functions of co-mothers. Valerie explains that in a patriarchal society, the Ashans and the Mayans live together and very often the Ashans bully the Mayans and they want the Mayans to bear their children: "the Ashans enslaved the Mayans and divided them up among themselves. The more important the Ashan, the more Mayans he owned." (192) The Ashans possess all the power. "Every Ashan thought of himself as a kind of farmer, and of every Mayan as bit of land or a field which could be his property." (192) This focuses on the status of men and women in the patriarchal society where women are the victims of male oppression and are treated as objects rather than subjects. Valerie explains that an Ashan is a grade A mother, and a Mayan is always the grade B mother. Valerie is put into jail because she described a society in which there were male masters and female slaves and acquainted the young Ashans with the concepts of slavery, rape and war. Throughout the novel, Namjoshi critiques patriarchy and interrogates the marginalisation of women in patriarchal structures of power and inspires them to struggle for self-identity and autonomy.

In *Feminist Fables*, too, she discusses the plight of women in a partiarchal society. Here, she reworks ancient myths, legends, fairy tales from East and West and makes them a vehicle of new vision through exploration of the female condition. In these hilarious, witty and elegantly written fables, she has invented a mythology that is simultaneously thought-provoking and entertaining and deals with the aspects of women's lives that have been erased, ignored, demeaned and mystified. The stories explore with playful irony the concepts of decency, honour and status of women. While some fables employ mythical characters or animals (dragons, ducks, swans, lizards) bridging the animate and inanimate with human consciousness, other stories depict characters like the New Woman, the Incredible Women and the handsome young dyke.

Women are relegated to a subordinate status in family and society, have been passive victims of male-oppression and are denied a social identity. "The Anthropoi" portrays women as species resembling men, who transferred to them the burden of child-bearing and child-rearing and other laborious tasks which had no prestige or required no intellect. Bluebeard in "A Room of this Own" and Jack Cleverfellow in "The Tale of Two Brothers" hired a wife to perform the domestic chores. The "Heart" portrays a "Headless Woman" who cooked, cleaned, scoured, was kind, caring and gentle, served her family and other people with a willing heart and never once complained of feeling exhausted. These women have moulded themselves according to men and their lives are nothing but a calm recurrence of those peaceful home duties in which men feel that their true vocation lies. The "Green Slave Women" depicts how men transformed the wild and energetic women and gradually trained them for slavery. These women were so bestial, vicious and wild that no human male was able to resist them and they were a menace to the whole world. This fable deals with the encounter of the Green Slave Women with the Space Captain and "the final submission of the woman to the man with its ensuing benefits, in particular, a guaranteed supply of docile slaves—all this is history" (67) and since then, men have been exploiting women.

Women are particularly vulnerable to inequity and exploitation because they are too timid and submissive, lay greater emphasis on compromise rather than confrontation, adapt themselves according to men and follow them. In "Ostriches," Namjoshi says, "Ostriches in their wisdom travel in herds, lionesses in their pride follow the lord" (48) and even the female chimpanzee is duly subservient and the prized possession of the males who fought. This happens because women are economically dependent on men. In "Next Time Around," a woman slept for thousand years and when she woke up she discovered that the plight of woman has not ameliorated even after so many years, "our women looked after; and every single man has a house of his own and a reasonable income." (64) Namjoshi feels that women should become self-sufficient and cease to be parasites, then the system based on their dependence will shatter and between them and the world there will no longer be any need for a masculine mediator.

The writer contends that daughters are conditioned to be passive, extremely patient and docile and to "hold their tongues" (8) ("The Lesson") and these qualities are considered to be positive traits in them and negative traits in their brothers. In "Nymph," Daphne runs away, when God chases her and is transformed into a green laurel, "It obviously means that trees keep quiet." (4) In "The Doll," girls make a male doll out of sticks; a boy, on hearing that the name of the doll is "Brittle Boy," smashes it. The girls get very angry but possess a lot of patience; they pick up the sticks and start all over again. All these fables are highly symbolic.

In a patriarchy men are considered to be powerful, strong and rational, whereas female sex is regarded as frail, emotional and demure. In "Exegesis," the writer points out that the sun must be male and the earth must be woman. "Look at the gashed and fissured earth. Look at the fierce and light-giving sun." (57) Wisdom, knowledge and ability to excel are not considered to be womanly qualities. "The Gods" depicts the daughter as a precocious child, who could run faster than anyone in the village, excelled in music and studies and was blessed with great abilities. Men, in the society criticized her and said, "To be so damned good is not womanly." (37) "The Female Swan" shows that in the social hierarchy, women occupy the lower rungs. In this story a duckling aspired to be a swan. "A duck by definition, is inferior to swans." (19)

Namjoshi asserts that patriarchy defines the precincts of women and even a slight infringement on their part is sufficient to arouse the wrath of men. Women are relegated to a subordinate status in family and society and obedience and compliance with the wishes of men are expected from them. The wife in "The Fisherman's Wife or the Foolish Feminist" asks for a boon for greater power and freedom and is told, "What she seems to want is a simple divorce" (59) and she is cast out. That an ambitious girl who tries to fly very high is slain by the society is illustrated in "Dragon Slayers" where the girl is "crippled" and the beast is shot. The girl child in "Bird Woman" sprouted winds, the horrified neighbours advised the parents to have the wings cut. On the parents' refusal, they returned a few weeks later and said, "If you won't have them cut, at least have them clipped." (18) Men can never accept the superior position of women. In "The Little Prince," the public shouts, "We will not be ruled by a woman" (17) and compels the prince to be their ruler and in "Thorn Rose" the princess brother lopped off her head because "women cannot be kings." (10)

The writer points out that the birth of a son is greeted with joy, but the birth of a daughter causes distress ("Local History") and people always desire a male offspring. In "From the Panchtantra" a Brahmin prays to Lord Vishnu to grant him a son. Similarly in "The Dower" the King is disappointed when the first child is born, he had wanted a son instead of a daughter, maybe because he is worried about the daughter's dowry. This story also illustrates that the worth of a girl is directly proportional to the amount of dowry she brings. The first and the second princesses got married to the princes of the neighbouring kingdoms because wherever the first princess walked, flowers sprouted and when the second one walked, pearls would be found. However, the third daughter has nothing to offer, so in sheer desperation the King married her off to a poor Swineherd. In "Jewel" the toad who had a precious Jewel on her forehead is worried that when she gets married she will lose it as it will be given in dowry and her parents said that "Then it really won't matter whether or not you are precious." (55)

Namjoshi deplores the disappointments, deprivation and anguish faced by women who deeply aspire for more space within the existing social structures. In "Broadcast Live" the Incredible Woman visits her psychiatrist and says that since she is at heart a womanly woman, "all she wants is a normal life" (63) and in "From the Panchtantra," the Brahmin who becomes a woman in the next birth clamours for dignity and human status. The woman in "A Quiet Life" leading a fearful, pathetic life says, "I don't want to be a woman." (51) She desires to be transformed into a rabbit or a squirrel or a mythical animal and lead a quite life. Rupanzel in "Rescued" dreams of a castle with wide moat and four strong walls and a room of her own where she is perfectly safe.

Women can never be ruled by men if they are intrepid and develop a habit of freedom in themselves. In "Liberation" she transforms herself into a colourless bird and it feels like freedom. The writer discusses the resurgence of 'new woman.' The daughter in "Her Mother's Daughter" is a feminist and resolves to fight against male chauvinism and oppression. She wants to avenge the wrongs that her mother has suffered and tries to change things. She realizes that "in a good patriarchy the women are dependent, but they are not allowed to know it" (96) and wonders why women do not have their own identity and are known through their relationships with men. In "And then what Happened?" Cinderella simply walks away from home and asserts her sense of self like Ibsen's Nora. Liberty for her means the deconstruction of social structures, so that they do not retain the shape which men have given them and she is fully aware that the world belongs not only to men but also to women.

Some fables portray the powerful figures of the Giantess and the She-Monster towering over men and thwarting their attempts to comprehend them. In these stories there is a reversal of the conventional roles of men and women. The strong giantess in "Jack Three's Luck" makes men succumb to her wishes and perform domestic tasks. Jack of Beanstalk and his two younger brothers, seized by the giantess, were told that she would keep them as husbands, but they must cook and clean and make themselves useful to her and be generally pleasant. The two elder brothers refused and were killed but the younger agreed and did his best to be pleasant and useful, so the giantess loved .him and "they lived happily ever after." (98) The giantess in the story "The Giantess" is an extremely strong ruler of a small kingdom and is a mother figure for the men there, consoling them in their hours of distress and feeding them when they are hungry. The central figure in "Legend" is the Dreaded She-Monster, whose fumes are noxious to men.

Namjoshi's literary works help women live and dream as women. She tries to combat women's feelings of isolation and inadequacy. She feels that women should realize that their own existence is meaningful, that their view of things is valid and intelligent, that their suffering is imposed and unnecessary and have firm belief in their own potential and strength to remake their lives. *The Mothers of Mayadiip* and *Feminist Fables*, are about self-definition and self-affirmation. Here, the writer has experimented with the fable form and has employed an innovative narrative technique and style. The narrator like her characters belongs to no time, no place and the stories have a universal significance.

NOTES

1. Suniti Namjoshi, *The Blue Donkey Fables and The Mothers of Mayadiip* (New Delhi: Penguin, 1991).
2. Suniti Namjoshi, *Feminist Fables* (1981; Penguin, 1995).

Passion and Devastation beneath Ethnic and Polytropic Identities in Michael Ondaatje's *The English Patient*

RASHMI GAUR
Indian Institute of Technology, Roorkee

Born in Colombo, Sri Lanka in 1943, where his family owned a tea plantation, Ondaatje immigrated to England, at the age of nine, and then to Montreal, at the age of nineteen. He has written poetry, fiction, criticism as well as screen plays (Elliott 800). *The English Patient* is his best known novel, which won the Booker Prize in 1992, the very year of its publication, and also a number of other awards. The cinematographic version appeared in 1996, produced and directed by Anthony Minghella, with the cooperation of Ondaatje and received seven Oscars (Tötösy 2). The novel has been analysed from various angles: its colonial context, introduction of fragmented cultural identities, ethnic issues, subtextual richness, poetic weaving of the past and the present, and above all, its treatment of history have always attracted critics—towards the novel, as well as towards the film. The present paper discusses these themes briefly and tries to analyze how these are ultimately linked with the dominant theme of complex human passions and devastation of internal and external landscapes.

The colonial context is present in *The English Patient* not only as a force of political change but at a subtler level also, as a vehicle of gradual yet permanent socio-cultural shifts. This aspect is unobtrusively presented by the explorations arranged by the British Royal Geographical Society during the two Wars. The English patient recalls it: "Look at a map of the Libyan Desert and you will see names. Kemnal el Din in 1925, who, almost solitary, carried out the first great modern expedition. Bagnold

1930-32. Almasy-Madox 1931-37. Just north of the Tropic of Cancer." (137) Leaving their "civilized" societies these adventurers go to a desert and face its primitive challenges. These exploits echo the natural scientists' dream of mapping the unchartered desert and also the colonial argument for political expansion of power, as the desert was soon to become the strategic arbiter of military wins. The pure scientific attitude is represented by Madox who, unable to accept the cruel realities of the war, commits suicide in a Suffox home: "Someone's war was slashing apart his delicate tapestry of companions." (241) The scientific aspect of explorations is soon replaced by the camouflage of agents like Clifton whose motive is to exploit scientific knowledge for colonial expansion. "He was not just an innocent Englishman. . . . As far as the English were concerned, he was keeping an eye on your strange group in the Egyptian-Libyan desert." (252) Against these circumstances the Bedouins are also unable to retain the unperturbed innocence of their tradition and learn to save a burning pilot for trading his skills. Western forces used the Bedouins for their "military aims and often infiltrated them," forcing them to shun their friendly and hospitable ways (Paula 45).

The representation of fragmented cultural identity is as acute in suggestivity as the colonial context is in the novel. The characters in *The English Patient* do not have a well-defined cultural identity. The characteristics are over-lapping and mixed and a "plural notion of identity that belongs to different cultural spaces" has been presented (Corina 75). Juxtaposed against it is the awareness of race and ethnicity codified as an indicator of behavioural responses during the significant moments of national loss and gain. The war makes the ethnic divisions more conspicuous. The characters' response to the atomic bomb illuminates the extent to which ethnic identity conditions and generates reactions. Kip realizes it after the bomb, "You and then the Americans converted us. With your missionary rules. And Indian soldiers wasted their lives as heroes so they could be *pukkah*. You had wars like cricket. How did you fool us into this? Here—listen to what you people have done." (283) Ethnic and racial awareness b comes a way of focusing larger issues within a particular perspective. W.E.B. DuBois has rightly suggested that race "as a socio-cultural construct was the battleground for the delineation of a modern self within society" (*The Souls of Black Folk*, 1903, qtd. Elliott 413). The concept of racial inferiority was developed as a debilitating weapon to subvert the potential development of societies, and is central to the unraveling and decoding of the true history of the 20th century. DuBois further states, "The history of the world is the history, not of individuals, but of groups, not of nations, but of races, and he who ignores or seeks to override the race idea in human history ignores and overrides the central thought of all history" (ibid). The bomb startles Kip into a sudden awareness of the commonality of Asian aspirations and he aligns himself to the vision of his brother.

The colonial context, ethnic insecurity and alienation are vividly present in Kip's portrayal. Nonetheless, along with other major characters of the novel, his personality can also be termed as "polytropic." The word itself can be interpreted as "having 'many ways of being,' always turning in various directions and multiplying the ways of his nature" (Corina 75). The English patient has a "hybrid of identities." (3) He is an engima, a mystery, the despairing Christ of Hana. He compares himself to Kip, calling him an "international bastard." (176) He does not want to belong to anyone, to any nation, and uses the multiplicity of his identities to transmit different versions about himself. Similarly, Hana moves around in an alien territory trying to look within herself and find her true self. She also does not possess any fixed identity. She cannot relate herself to the ravages of war. Sick of Europe, she does not want to go to Canada either. War has changed this innocent youth into a disillusioned being. The patient identifies it. Hana goes into a withdrawn self-imposed exile in the villa and like a nomad keeps on searching for oases. She prefers to be "nomadic in the house—living like a vagrant." (13) Caravaggio too is a traveller with multiple and polytropic identities—the thief, the double agent, the drunk, the lover, and the uncle. He systematically reawakens the memories of a pleasant past in Hana—dance, music and the Marseillese. The polytropic identities are clear in Kip too, despite his ethnic background. Away from his country, he is constantly on movement, sweeping land in different countries to detect unexploded mines. He does not share nostalgic reconstruction of the past with other characters and seems to be rooted in the present. Like the burnt patient he too sees "reason in everything." (84)

The English Patient has the discernible presence of three books which illustrate and heighten the significance of the different contours of the novel. The most quoted book is Herodotus' *Histories*, which provides the framework for the desert explorations of Almasy and others. The English patient's copy of *Histories* also doubles as his diary in which he jots down notes and pastes photographs. It also occasions many memories and constantly acts as a reference point for him, "'This history of mine,' Herodotus says, 'has from the beginning sought out the supplementary to the main argument?' What you find in him are cul-de-sacs within the sweep of history—how people betray each other for the sake of nations, how people fall in love." (119) The connections between Herodotus and the novel are "more than just the sum of a number of references" as the structure and themes of the ancient treatise are echoed in the novel (Harrison 1). *The Charaterhouse of Parma* discusses Napoleon's invasion of Italy and is a parallel discourse on the occupation of the same territory by aggressors. Rudyard Kipling's *Kim* is an artistic counterpoint to the sapper's life. The intertextuality and historical references impart a sonorous depth to the non-linear presentation of the story. The weaving together of the past and the present creates a multilayered poetic richness of suggestivity which could not be realized through traditional methods. It is enhanced by Ondaatje's method of fictionalizing the historical figures and events. Without going into a debate on whether he was aware of the history of some of his characters or not, it can be safely stated that many of the characters in the novel possess real life parallels, and their real story is selectively translated into the fictional mode. The English patient Almasy himself is a sketch of the Hungarian aristocrat, cartographer, explorer and military officer of the same name (Tötösy). The details of the real life match with the fictional representation of the personality. The real Almasy had discovered the legendary oasis Zarzura in the Libyan desert and the prehistorical paintings in the caves of the Uweinat mountains—these facts have been retained in the fiction. However, this curious overlapping of history and fiction is not maintained as closely in the case of other characters—viz., Katharine, Kip and Caravaggio. Katharine is modelled on Lady Clayton, but the fictional representation is not truthful to the real individual (Tötösy 5). It is mentioned that Kip is a portrayal of Lt. General Inder Singh Gill, who died recently. Lt. General Gill had served in Italy during the second World War. Trained initially as a sapper, he was linked with the bomb disposal units. Not much evidence has been unearthed about this link, though strong parallels exist. Caravaggio is not modelled after any historical person, but his name points to the Italian Renaissance painter, Caravaggio, whose painting "David with the Head of Goliath" is referred to by the English patient as an illustration of his attitude towards Kip. It is assumed that "the face of David is a portrait of the youthful Caravaggio and the head of Goliath is a portrait of him as an older man, how he looked when he did the painting—I think—that Kip is my David." (116)

Ultimately, however, these themes seem peripheral in comparison to the depiction of the deepest and most turbulent passions of human life and the suggestive rendering of the devastation littered in the internal and external landscapes of the contemporary world. Ondaatje has depicted the intensity of human passion and love which has always intrigued mankind. The love he describes is laced with struggles, disillusions and suffering, and its treatment reminds us of Turgenev's stories, particularly "Asya." Set against turbulent times of war and a presentiment of an impending catastrophe, it throbs with an alarming rhythm. The destruction and devastation wrecked by warring nations is matched by the inner desolation and tragedies of the characters. The polytropic and ethnic identities of the characters are significant pointers to the development of their attitudes, but beneath these identities a story of desperate passion, longing and devastation unfolds before us leading us to the denouement that human beings should preserve, and not violate the sacred life and its emotions.

The English Patient is a story about trapped people—people who are trapped in their past casting its shadow on their present, and struggling to somehow possess a hold over life. Almasy is trapped in his past, reliving it constantly to escape the pain of the present. Hana too does not have the freedom of mind and is yet to overcome the loss of her lover, child and father in the war. She retreated from everybody around her except the child with whom she shares everything in her mind (82). She wanted to go home; unable to do so she opts for the next possible action—stepping outside the war and staying with a patient, "she hardly talked during the war. She needed an uncle, a member of the family. She needed the father of the child." (85) With determination she creates a barrier of silence around her, using her experiences as nurse, using even the hammock and the shoes of the dead (47) to live and underline the determination of not falling apart "at this." (48) She "would have nothing to link her, to lock her, to death." (50) What Ondaatje has presented before us is a picture of life pitted against death which is duplicated by the setting of the Tuscan villa. Mined and ruined, its surroundings are littered with death and devastation. In sharp contrast the villa itself is painted—each room with a different season, as if in celebration of life. Inside the villa, Hana is brought back to life once again by the English patient in whose presence she "could turn away from being an adult." (52), and Caravaggio,–who brings back her past to her. Hana's journey towards life completes with her passionate love for Kip. Their friendship starts with a functional note and soon develops into an intimacy: "As they grow intimate the space between them during the day grows longer" giving them a private energy (127). Though intimate, their passionate relationship is rather unsure and tentative. Kip does not allow himself "to be beholden to her, or her to him." (128) The psychological depth of his passion again reminds us of Turgenev's handling of similar themes. Kip realizes that "he could never turn and inquire of her what deepest motive caused this relationship. He held her with the same strength of love he felt for those three strange English people." (197) Kip, who remains a foreigner to others (105), is able to overcome his colonial background in his relationship with Hana, till the tragic occurrence of the Bomb. Their passion for each other is suffused with a lyrical note, as the love they have known remains with them forever.

The passionate and rather tragic love story of Hana and Kip is paralleled by that of the patient and Katharine. The patient had noted down on his copy of the *Histories*, "A love story is not about those who lose their heart but about those who find that sullen inhabitant who, when it is stumbled upon, means the body can fool no one, can fool nothing. It is a consuming of oneself and the past." (97) Katharine's reading of Candaules' story becomes the first errant step towards their mutual passion (233). Helplessly they are drawn towards each other, unable to decide whether it was betrayal of those around them, or the desire of another life (238). Madox gives a warning signal through a paragraph from *Anna Karenina* which is strengthened gradually and Katharine ultimately returns to her husband, "From this point on, she whispered, we will either find or lose our souls." (238) Their intense passion for each other draws them together once again in the final moments of Katharine's life. She is left in the "Cave of Swimmers" while Almasy goes to seek help, is captured and comes back after three years. The passages describing their ardent love throb with a passionate intensity which is relived constantly and repetitively by the English patient. His constant speech which fills every waking minute reconstructs his love and also enacts barriers—as Hana's silence has done for her—around him and his love. His pain, separation and suffering compel him to look within and find solace in vocalized memory.

The passionate concern for each other in these relationships is ultimately thwarted by war. Ondaatje has captured and presented the intensity and the rhythm of passion by presenting disjointed mental process in the non-realistic convention of the poetic novel. The failure of individual sensibility and passion in those times which justified all sorts of cruelties in the name of reason has been polemically presented by the author. The spirit of war broods over the novel and images of death and devastation permeate its world. The desolation is clearly present in the surroundings of the villa. Retreating German forces mine the houses (11) using every conceivable object—wooden boxes, pipes, vehicles. "Italy was worse than Africa—As Sappers entered cities they walked along avenues where corpses were strung from trees or the balconies of buildings—Some of the hanging corpses were mined and had to be blown up in midair." (275) We have images of death, diseases and senseless devastation: typhus epidemic breaking out, people bombed inside tunnels and ships freshly mined underwater. Madox kills himself in silent protest against war, Almasy is arrested and can't reach Katharine with help in time, Hana withdraws within herself, Caravaggio's thumbs are cut off and Kip lives by defying the bomb wire.

These images are intensified in the ultimate expression of devastation, i.e. the bombs dropped on two Japanese cities. The colonial context once again becomes dominant as Kip recollects that his brother had advised him not to turn his back on Europe, "The deal makers. The contract makers. The map drawers. Never trust Europeans, he said." (284) Caravaggio also feels that such a bomb can never have been dropped on a white nation (286) Once Kip leaves the villa, Girolamo he does not look back. The atmospheric devastation has swallowed up his passion. Yet the love is never forgotten, the passion remains and sustains life. The patient lives through the memories of Katharine and her love, and in the same manner Kip harbours Hana's love in the centrality of his existence. Ethnic and polytropic identities and the difference therein do neither mitigate the intensity of passion nor softpedal the introduction of devastation as an overpowering reality of their day.

Thus we find that the thematic rendering of *The English Patient* possesses a multiplicity. The core story develops and unfolds as a tale of intense passion and complex sensitivity, which burgeons amidst chaotic, meaninglessly acute and immediate devastation. Despite the overpowering oppression, Ondaatje has been successful in communicating the message that passionate love imparts meaning and purpose to life despite constraints, and is capable of creating some permanent, transcendental vision within the self amidst the haze of pathetic diablerie.

Works Cited

Corina Ana Anghel, "Polytropic Identities in Michael Ondaatje's *The English Patient*," *Journal of Indo-Canadian Studies*, Vol. 1, No. 2, July 2001, pp. 73-86.

Emory Elliott, *The Columbia History of the American Novel*, New York: Columbia University Press, 1991.

Michael Ondaatje, *The English Patient*, New York, Vintage International, 1992.

Paula Garcia—Ramirez, "The Colonial Context of Michael Ondaatje's *The English Patient*," *The Atlantic Literary Review*, Vol. 2, No. 1, pp. 42-49.

Steven Tötösy de Zepetnek, "Michael Ondaatje's *The English Patient*, "History and the Other," <http: //clcwebjournal.lib.purdue. edu/ clcweb99-4/ Tötösy 99-2html.

Thomas Harrison "Herodotus and *The English Patient*," http: // www.ie/~classics/98/Harrison98.html.

Heirloom of Expressions: A Study of Yasmin Ladha's *Women Dancing on Rooftops*

VIJAY SHESHADRI
University of Mysore

Today large-scale migration of peoples across countries has occurred due to political instability, Globalization, rabid technology marked by uncertainty, despair, contemporaneity and changed circumstances. One of the vital developments in the age of Globalization is the "fecundation" of several nations within the encapsulated single body also known as the Nation. These variegated nations are constituted on various criteria such as class, gender, caste, ethnicity, pigmentation, migration etc.

Multiculturalism or Polyculturalism is an attempt at framing a society where various cultures intermix and co-exist complementing each other thereby forming an active cosmopolitan society characterized by consensual pluralism. In other words, it is perhaps an administrative device for sorting out social contradictions and conflicts, espousing a desire for harmony of difference, echoing the biblical shibboleth, *love thy neighbour*.

Interestingly, Polyculturalism in Canada is an Anglo-Canadian culture where Biculture and Bilingual is the ethnic core tolerating and hegemonically arranging others round it. Thus, Multiculturalism or Polyculturalism focuses on the citizenship of the settlers—an ideological slogan. Multicultural policy of Canada in the words of M.F. Ramasay is to eschew this notion, "to be a Canadian is no longer to be white in colour, French or English in Language, Catholic or Protestant in religion but to encourage settlers to preserve their cultural heritage within the Canadian mosaic."[1] To be precise, Canada's Polycultural philosophy projects Canada as a *masala puri* with each ingredient contributing its own flavour for a better comestibility.

Canada is a nation of immigrants where 1/3 of all Canadians cite origins that are neither English nor French. Most of the immigration centres around Vancouver and Montreal. Today, the Chinese have displaced the Italians in immigration to Canada. Most of the movement of the peoples to Canada is from South and East Asia, Africa and the Caribbean displacing the Europeans, to a country once described by Voltaire as "a few acres of snow" or a land from where Santa originated.

Incidentally, the bilingual and multilingual situations in Canada and India provide a general atmosphere of inquisitiveness. Interestingly, Polyculturalism in a bilingual and multilingual context takes on a different meaning in both instances—an exact point of divergence rather than convergence. In a bilingual situation like Canada, it is the state that empowers two languages, the Anglophone and Francophone, hence two cultures, the English and the French as the canon. In this process, the dynamics effaces all other languages and their associated cultures. Such an event in fact necessitates a strong resistance for the flowering of Polyculturalism while in a multilingual situation like India, the state makes room for each language and hence cultures to flourish. One can see here an instance of the politics of dissonance as a necessary conflict in the face of the agenda of *lingua universitas*.

Multiculturalism or Polyculturalism within the fabric of the Canadian mosaic is a mind-boggling issue. Moreover, Globalization is a ubiquitous and cockroachean phenomenon. Polyculturalism is no exception to this as it is connected to changes in social condition. Since Canada has journeyed from industry-based society to a society of electronic automaton, it has ushered in "contest mobility"[2] (the best gets the best), intergeneration mobility, eschewing sponsored mobility. Such a situation in fact prompts a model of equitable participation.

Since individual's identity and personal worth is determined by ethnic, racial membership, the multicultural or Polycultural agenda of treating all moral views and cultures as equal regardless of difference appears as altruistic, collectivist utopian venture. Institutes like Ayn Rand view multiculturalism as racism in a politically correct guise. Does it mean to say that Multiculturalism or Polyculturalism means all kinds of life styles and ideologies? No enemy but for the one who does not invite people with open arms? Is Canada then a nation of more public space than a private preserve for some.

Since the Kamagatamaru incident in 1914, which in a way was responsible for the implementation of multiculturalism Act on 21st July 1988, Canada no doubt has journeyed on the path of acculturation. This act was brought in view of the fact that in a bilingual situation Polyculturalism would really help one in effacing polycultural jealousies.[3] Unfortunately today, out of fifty-three aboriginal languages only three in Canada are said to have survived.[4] How would one account for this or react to such a disturbing statistical information. Perhaps the "idea of Multiculturalism in Canada can no longer be seen merely as an ideological tool of British hegemony or the wider corporate elite. It is actually characterized by the dominance of government rather than any grassroots or social articulation of its definitions and reality."[5] Or is Canada's multicultural policy a "spin doctor"[6] as Lorne Foster avers in her book *Turnstile Immigration*. One need to sit with one's fingers crossed or be an optimist by nature since ethnic and racial tensions especially in today's contexts are often fuelled by a climate of imbalance in economic uncertainty. Is Individualism then the only cure to racism? Or is Multiculturalism of Canada a "revolutionary nostalgia" (Walter Benjamin's term).

II

Most of today's global population is at least bilingual. Fortunately few are writers! Being a translinguist, Canada to Yasmin Ladha is a suitable country for its social paradigm is a "mosaic" providing a fertile ground for what Eva Hoffman opines "Nothing fully exists until it is aritculated."[7]

Women Dancing on Rooftops: Bring Your Belly Close by Yasmin Ladha, a Muslim from Calgary, Alberta, is a remarkable work criss-crossing boundaries, genres and cultures. Reading the book is like an esoteric excursion into diverse lands and its peoples—from the prairies of Canada to the gullies of Delhi, Bangalore, Kashmir, Cochin and through nostalgia to small town Africa.

Through the consciousness of an immigrant and a woman, the book juxtaposes the social, political, economic and historical issues/problems confronted by women in a first world and "non-first" world civil polity. For instance, "Lakshmi," the first story of the collection, through wit and irony, very succinctly captures the role enacted by a woman and the double standards operating in a sexist society: "her first steps in her married home are the Goddess's, forever a giver. She demands nothing in return."[8] Again, stories like "Two Friends," "Rooftop Women," "The Dancer," "When I Love a Man I Deify Him," "There are Mistresses even in the Internet Age," "Hair" and "Hey Woman," further explore such a dimension in its myriad manifestations. For instance, in the story "Hair," women's notion of beauty permeates through cosmetics especially through Ayurveda to be natural which in fact is a response to demands of a male desire of the beautiful since time immemorial: "Ancient Ayurvedic pastes and powders of *vaidans* and healers has gone Body Shop, filling maa-earth in translucent reusables. The whiz idea of au naturale on skin in healing maa-earth. . . . But even in Aryan-ancient of four thousand years ago, Ayurveda had a happy name—the green medicine shop." (145)

Similarly, the story "There are Mistresses Even in the Internet Age" exhibits how the institution of marriage as well as prostitution which again are androcentric prerogatives ushers in domination and subordination among women: "The wife's breezy touch is an awesome declaration—who belongs to whom this breezy touch legalistic. Testaments are made between parties who touch, declare this; affidavits of blatant belonging." (137)

The erasure of the doubly othered woman, the Mistress, sails into anonymity: "Intuitively, the mistress slides into her drafty, ghost step. She understands renunciation more fiercely than a nun on a hilltop monastery, nor is the mistress a dazed, fresh widow who is told to yank of all desire now. The mistress is neither of the women. She is both. She is nothing." (140)

The diasporic consciousness/cognition of an individual through a binary structure that of man/woman gets indented remarkably in "Luggage of Bride, of a Mujahideen." The story highlights the fact that (im)migration is not a completely finished process of body, mind, and soul: "When you flee, you never flee whole. Parts of you are severed, flung aside: heirlooms, toys and graves." (82) The dress of Sushma the Bride, who flees from Anantnag to New Delhi in a pheran, the baggy out-coat dress of Kashmir losing all her family gold (symbol of her marriage) metonymically posits the fact that women are potential victims during peace as well as war but "who are most unselfish in war, most insignificant in war." (84) Juxtaposed with the Bride is a Mujahideen whose luggage symbolizes power and possession: "A Mujahideen's luggage; AK-47, Koran, wireless set, coffin, rosepetals. His song: One day we will yank back our freedom from Hindustan." (94)

Kashmir, that violence-ridden state, is the making of the policy makers and their politicking: "Article 370 must go. India is a weak father. . . . Tell me, if Mohammed Bashir can buy property in Delhi, why can't Ramprasad of Delhi buy property in Kashmir? It is this Article 370 causing so much havoc of separatism. You get me sister?" (97)

Interestingly, Religion, that soul force of humanity comes under severe scrutiny with an ironic touch in Yasmin's hands. For instance in the story "Circling my Allah," a woman is pushed into a male hand when Allah turns chauvinistic, a typical instance of biological determinism marked by contradictions: "Rabbits breed and barrage and mirrors are multiplied on women by the mullah-mujahideen clan. In Arabic, a woman is *fitna*, one name for chaos and beauty. In Urdu, she is *rundi*, one name for whore and widow. Only Mother is pure and heaven is at a Mother's feet." (107-8)

Such lopsided double standard is brushed aside nonchalantly by Yasmin using the *talaq* version in a dystopian fashion:

> Then I a Muslim woman, want to denounce Islam thrice,
> I denounce you once
> I denounce you twice
> I denounce you thrice (108)

Juxtaposed with Islamic fundamentalism is the Hindu fanaticism which is ironically laughed at in the story "Slaughter of Babri Masjid" by an admixture of levity and seriousness:

> Lord Vishnu, mender and Diplomatic of all gods. Where the hell are you?
>
> Only this time, don't pop up in your 7th incarnation of Rama the noble.
>
> Ayodhya will scorch you! The mad head has risen. Extreme Hindus claim that Ayodhya mosque was built over your temple. Now in the name of virtuous Rama, they are going to exterminate it. (23)

The story comes to a close with a disturbing response that is indifferent and appears out of context, that of an immigrant who declares: "I crave nothing more than Smucker's Jam." An instance of an insider becoming an outsider, culture over nature!

Divided into six sections, the book through its fabulous experimentation of language like, "gully women tamper on way to temple/most beautiful look down, part of gully poetics" (22); "Her British speech teacher insisted that she speak from the pelvis" (25); "The slender flute is lord Krishna's mistress. But Krishna is Radha's. Her devotion to his is torrential. . . . Yet it is the bamboo mistress who shares the intimacy of his breath" (43); "Immigrant dream persistent as polyester pants" (46); "A refugee's luggage is nourishment" (84); "Hatyaar means 'friend of hand'" (94); "one who is raped has been well chewed" (99); "(male pleasure/an unfettered burp/a good scratch on the crotch. At the Janpath phone booths a lot of scratching) (114); "Bhring Raj oil becomes Bio Bhring Raj in an environmental age" (145); "Upper class Indians give their children Avante Garde names like Pinkie, Dimple, Puppy" (155) "Ganesh with panache" (170) etc., to mention a few, churns up an immigrant sensibility providing what Fred Wah aptly avers: "This 'Rooftop' writing is brilliant for its panorama of sensation and intelligence. The view from here is stunning and we are privileged to share it." (From the blurb)

Through its eye-catching appellation of chapters, *Women Dancing on Rooftop* makes a fascinating read, exhibiting a confluence of variegated genres, voices, images and experiences, permeated through an immigrant psyche. Taking recourse to genres such as Autobiography, Travel literature, Prose, Poetry, Epistolary features, the book leaves a mark on the reader by its experimentation of language. The *readerji* ends up experiencing globetrotting and is inveigled to view the world as "*vasudhaiva-kutumbakam.*"

The mode of writing in *Women Dancing on Rooftops* is a successful translingual enterprise exhibiting hybridity. Creation of a new voice invariably means the invention of a novel self. Adopting a language in Yasmin's case is a process of self-begetting. In a sense, Yasmin's writing eschews what Benjamin Whorf observes: "we dissect nature along lines laid down by our native languages,"[9] reminding one of Joyce's Stephen Dedalus who complains to Irish Nationalist Davin "When the soul of a man is born in this country, there are nets flung at it to hold it back from flight. You talk to me of nationality, language and religion. I shall try to fly by those nets."[10]

In sum, *Women Dancing on Rooftops* is an exercise in extraterritoriality, unhoused and wandering across nations and cultures, a daring tight rope act without nets to be *pandictic* (to say everything when a particular language permits us only to say something) perhaps in search of silence and truth!

NOTES

1. Keynote Address, XIV International Conference on Canadian Studies, University of Pondicherry, 5-7 January 1998, Pondicherry.
2. Ralph Turner, "Sponsored and Contest Mobility and the School System," *American Sociological Review*, 25 (6), pp. 855-67.
3. S. Sri, "Multiple Solitudes: Multicultural Voices in the Canadian Literary Landscape, XIV International Conference on Canadian Studies, University of Pondicherry, 5-7 January 1998, Pondicherry

4. C.D. Narasimhaiah and C.N. Srinath, ed., *The Literary Criterion*, Vol. XXIX, No. 3, 1994, p. 66.
5. Doris et al. "Multiculturalism and Integration," *Immigration and Refugee Policy: Australia and Canada Compared*, ed. H. Adelman et al (Toronto: Univ. of Toronto, 1994), p. 402.
6. Lorne Foster, *Turnstile Immigration: Multiculturalism, Social Order and Social Justice in Canada* (Toronto: Thompson Educational Publishing, 1998), p. 130.
7. Eva Hofman, *Lost in Translation: A Life in a New Language* (New York: Penguin, 1990), p. 29.
8. Yasmin Ladha, *Women Dancing On Rooftops: Bring Your Belly Close* (Toronto: TSAR, 1997), p. 5.
9. Benjamin Whorf, "Language, Thought and Reality: Selected Writings," John B. Carroll, ed. (Cambridge, Mass: MIT Press, 1956), p. 213.
10. James Joyce, *A Portrait of the Artist as a Young Man* (New York: Viking,1956), p. 203

Afro-Canadian Poetry and Womanism

NEERJA CHAND
R.L.A. College, University of Delhi

Womanism has been defined by Chikwenye Okonjo Ogunyemi as a philosophy that celebrates black roots, the ideals of black life, while giving a balanced presentation of black womandom. According to Ogunyemi, womanism also concerns itself as much with the black sexual power tussle as with the world power structure that subjugates blacks and aims at a dynamism of wholeness and self-healing that one sees in the positive integrative endings of womanist narratives.[1] In a similar vain, American Black Feminist poet and critic Alice Walker refers to the "feminist of color" who is committed to the survival and wholeness of entire people, male and female . . . (but who) loves herself, regardless.[2] A womanist is not a separatist but a universalist for she is committed to the survival and wholeness of entire people, male and female. A deep preoccupation and concern for the entire humanity, male and female, non-black and black, is therefore the distinguishing mark of womanism which is deeply and firmly entrenched in its African roots.

Afro-Canadian poets like Claire Harris, Dionne Brand and Marlene Nourbese Philips represent what Arun Prabha Mukherjee terms as "Oppositinal Aesthetics."[3] Writings from a hyphenated space, the poetry of these women poets draws its vigour and sustenance not from the tenets of western feminism but from the ideas and ideology of womanism. Claire Harris, who is one of the best black womanist poets writing in Canada today, is a native of Port of Spain, Trinidad. Harris started writing in Nigeria in 1975 and continues to do so to this day from Calgary, Canada. Her poems are mainly—though not only—about women, centering around their friendships, loyalties, pain and suffering and also about their healing—both physical, mental or/and spiritual, on an individual as well as on a societal or national level, not with a feminist but a humanist agenda. However, despite a subterranean turbulence, these poems are calm and exude an extraordinary serenity, grace and dignity and include men. The dynamic wholeness of Claire Harris's proactive (rather than reactive) emancipatory agenda is clearly articulated in an interview with Janice Williamson: "I want my writing to rehabilitate the Black person, her beauty, her smile, her walk, her genius . . . his too. I also want to explore the reality of Canadian society . . . which I must free to include me."[4]

Personal becomes political and one woman's story becomes the story of a family, a movement, a people in a poem from the volume *Fables from the Women's Quarters.*[5] *Where the Sky is a Pitiful Tent* focusses on a native woman's Sisyphus like unique resilience and innate capacity to heal and be whole again in the face of calamitous, adverse or hostile circumstances.

Where the Sky is a Pitiful Tent is a short narrative in eight sections, the speaker is a native woman in Guatemala, the wife of a guerilla. Within the short scope of an eight-section poem, the poet tells us the story of a family, a movement, a people. Each section occupies only one page. The poem is in first person and narrated by a woman who is a wife and a mother to begin with and becomes an active participant in the freedom struggle after the death of her husband and son.

Claire Harris uses a unique narrative technique here. There are two narratives, the mother's (in the poem) and the daughter's (in the footnotes). Every page of the poem concludes with a few lines from a testimony made by the daughter, a famous Guatemalan guerilla Rigoberta Manchu, who, in the footnotes, tells the story of her parents' struggle and their eventual destruction. In this unique technique of using a counter narrative, the fictional story in the poem gets appropriately grounded in reality and the poetic voice gains an added dimension and intensity in counterpoint with the factual statement of the daughter's narrative.

In the woman's narrative, we see a man (her husband) who is totally committed to the cause he has embraced, getting more and more deeply entrenched and finally meeting a violent death through torture. Initially, the woman is timid, so "porous with fear" as she says "even the rustle of ants in the grass flows through me." She is reluctant to let her husband go. She offers prayers at the ancient tribal well when she senses his inevitable death drawing closer. But by the time the death actually approaches, she has acquired enough strength and courage to take on and complete his unfinished task. In this poem, both man and woman have a commonality of goal and complement and "continue" being with each other even after death, due to their national/political commitment and shared ideology.

But the poem is more than a story of a man and a woman pitched together against hostile circumstances and a common enemy. In a typical womanist vein, Claire Harris chooses to write the story of a people who live in mud huts on the mountainside, eking out a subsistence existence. Powerful landlords forcibly seize their fields and their protests are crushed by military brutality. Soldiers terrorise the population by torturing and mutilating anyone they choose to accuse of being a guerilla and by lynching them in public in the market place and forcing the villagers to watch the execution. The people abandon their villages and hide in the mountains while more and more of them join the guerillas in their liberation movement.

As in all womanist writings, the woman's experience here is not an isolated or separatist phenomenon. She shares it with her people. Her relationship with her man is very important. The man and woman are indispensable to each other in this life. She articulates the intensity of her physical need for him. She suffers when he withdraws into himself and becomes unresponsive to her pleadings. As she witnesses his mangled corpse, she is overwhelmed by the memory of him dancing the wedding dance. His horrendous death creates an inevitable distance between them which she bridges, not by reverting back to a traditional, patriarchally defined role of ,passivity and subservience, but by becoming one with the country and the political ideology he had sacrificed his life for. The passionate love for the land and its people, the brutality of the oppressors, the heroism of the struggle in "this surreal country," its corn, its salt, its "bullet laden air," its "fields that sprout skulls"—become for her, them now. In his death the man and wife become more inseparable than ever before.

After her 14-year-old brother is burnt to death and her parents are brutally killed by the army, in a gesture of healing of the self and the people, it is the daughter who continues the struggle. Rigoberta Manchu reports:

> Our only way of commemorating the spilled blood of our parents was to go on fighting and following the path they had followed. . . . Their death gave us hope, because it is not just that the blood of all those people be erased forever. It is our duty on this earth to revive it. . . . I fight so they will recognise me. . . . If I have taken advantage of this chance to tell the story of my life it is because I know that my people cannot tell their stories. But they are no different from mine.

In 1975, during a leave of absence from her job as a high school teacher in Calgary, Harris visited Nigeria and began to write for publication. About this trip Harris says:

> I did not go to Africa looking for my *roots.* These are very deeply embedded in the black earth of the West Indies. But my much-maligned ancestors came from Africa. I wanted to stand where they might have stood. I did.[6]

Seen in Stormlight, also from the volume *Fables from the Women's Quarters*, recalls a Nigerian experience in a very interesting manner. Using a cinematic technique in which scenes flash in and out of focus in the manner of a jerky flickering of very bad movies, Harris finds herself in a culture which is almost alien to her. In her words: "the more doors opened paradoxically the more closed the society became." Her Nigerian experience turned out to be, as she says, the great adventure of her life and jolted her into writing.

The poem *Seen in Stormlight* was written in the months preceding the coup that deposed General Gowon and captures the taste of the onset of a storm in the thickening air of the universities (which were closed twice in the ten months that she was there), as well as in the streets and market places. Harris says in the footnotes: An African thunderstorm is an awesome layered thing. It closes over the earth like a gigantic calabash and human beings become seeds to be rattled at will like chac-chacs.

> Lagos raptures
> Fragments storm in the stormwind
> And splinters huge. . . .
> Lagos its men masks
> Frozen in greed-fear
> Or simply there
> Trapped in the life
> A city like Ifa Kola flung
> To await reading. (45)

Ifa Kola is a nut used by the Yoruba priests to prophesy the future. The nuts can be thrown in innumerable computations, all of which have a specific meaning. In this dismal uncertainty of circumstance and spectacle of unmitigated sorrow, not surprisingly it is women and children who provide some relief and healing through their innocent "dream smiles" and dreams of a new race, dreams of ease and grace.

> And children curve dream smiles
> Or else cry
> At the hyena gnawing inside
> Women suckling life in struggle
> Dream earth a new race
> In spite of thunder—
> Or else dream ease and grace (51)

Black Sisyphus is the title of the third poem in Claire Harris's third book of poetry *Travelling to find a Remedy* (1987)[7] a multiple winner of The Writer's Guild of Alberta Award and the First Alberta Culture Poetry Prize. The speaker recalls a childhood memory with her father:

> His fingers kneading my six year old hands
> As if they would refashion them (30)

The Black Sisyphus is a powerful poem about the poet-daughter-speaker's father's experiences in Trinidad. He is portrayed as a father who "enjoyed with life/he could not be/convinced that being human was not enough." He is a tough and dignified black figure who "would not be cast out again" from this "island garden" i.e. Trinidad which was created by his forefathers "from a wilderness of loss." Transtromer's lines quoted "From an African Diary"

> The road from one way of life to another is hard
> Those who are ahead have a long way to go (30)

speak for all immigrations and all exiles in all times and spaces. The nascent immigrants with their raw, haunting traumas as well as the ones who left their homelands a long time ago. Perhaps there is no difference because both do not belong. In her article *Poets in Limbo* Claire Harris writes that even after more than two hundred years in Canada, Blacks as a group are still seen as newcomers. Harris refers to the marginalisation of the blacks in Canada as "a blatant ethnocentricity (which) condemns people of colour to the sidelines: eternal immigrants forever poised on the verge of *not belonging*."[8]

A Grammar of the Heart from the volume *The Conception of Winter* (1989)[9] is a poem about the life journey of the poet-daughter-narrator's mother from the age of 8 to her death in a Calgary hospital. The entire journey pictures her as a female version of *The Black Sisyphus*—an epitome of dignity, resilience and grace under pressure.

> When she was eight death wheeling over her house a great flight of corbeaux of darkness snatched sisters a brother now deathbeds have become her womb from her first husband's at twenty she birthed grief in black veils and in honey then her father died she drew from the hollow of that death the modern breadwinner & so fashionable she laughed often was young her mother died she shed the daughter became wife once more and finally if death knocked again she wouldn't answer (54)

Her refusal to submit to the dark forces of death and disaster, her quiet gaiety, gentle cheerfulness point towards a dynamism of wholeness and self-healing, so much an integral part of her African roots and womanism.

> She was a woman who thought herself unwatched
> Her heart secret around the first grief
> she moved through her life as if she wasn't there.

And still

> I remember how she filled the house with such quiet gaiety.
> She was so gentle we rose each morning at five to be almost alone
> with her...
> and how cool she could be
> how adamant in the face of certain griefs. (58)

This discussion would be incomplete if we did not look at *Policeman Cleared in Jaywalking Case*, Claire Harris's most well known poem. Published in the volume *Fables from the Women's Quarters,* this poem epitomises Claire Harris's concern for and preoccupation with her black roots in a racially charged Canada, her quiet and subdued rage in an outrageous situation and her shattered vision of a dynamic wholeness in Canada that is both black and white but unable to blend beautifully.

Jaywalking is a long poem about a 15-year-old black girl who was arrested by the Calgary police and strip-searched for the crime of jaywalking. The poem begins with a quotation from the *Edmonton Journal*, the headline of which also forms the title of the poem. The pro-police reporting is followed by an inventory of the items that the newspaper and Alberta law enforcement appeal board conveniently forgot to consider. The suppressed rage of the poet-speaker is evident right from the opening lines of the poem:

> Look you, child, I signify. (40)

To signify, Harris tells us, indicates, in a black community, an act of acknowledgement of sharing, of identifying with. In an acknowledgement of three hundred years of shared history of the blacks, Harris finds herself in total empathy/identification with the 15-year-old child, who is both "black and female." She fondly remembers the grace and dignity of the black world where as a 15-year-old child she herself was caught in a similar situation—jaywalking. The warmth and concern of the "black faces anxious around her" who helped her in rising to her own feet, the grin of the face of the small boy carrying her books and the black policeman—a father figure, reprimanding her fondly and releasing her with a smile "with sympathy sent on in the warm green morning" are all presented in sharp contrast with the callousness of the white Canadian world.

> Where somebody's black girl child
> jaywalking to school is stripped spread searched

and

> pale hands soiling the black flesh (40)

The poem ends on a note of rage and fear. The scathing critique in the concluding lines is addressed directly to Canada with its dehumanising devices. "acid rain that shrivels trees," its "clinging fires that shrivel skins," its "law that shrivels children" and its inevitable sweet seductions.

> And I fear your naked fear of all that's different. . . .
> Your dreams of power your foolish innocence. . . .
> Even I fear the ease you make of living this stolen land all its
> graceful seductions (41)

In a candid moment of self-analysis, the poet-speaker discovers that the enemy is as much outside as within her. If she does not heal herself on an individual level and become whole inside, she can be very easily sucked in, "drowned" because she is vulnerable to the sickness of a sick society where she, as a black woman is considered the 'other.' "And I fear myself the rage alive in me." The poem concludes like this:

> but I fear most myself how easy to drown in your world dead believe myself living who stands 'other' and vulnerable to your soul's disease
> Look you child, I signify. (41)

In an essay "Between the Rock and a Hard Place," Clare Harris reiterates this dilemma and compares her writing space in Canada to "life in a Blizzard." She says: "It is hard not to be blown off one's feet in a snow-storm, hard not to be blinded by all that white stuff, difficult to prevent oneself from changing direction with the wind."[10]

Womanism, as we said in the beginning, is a philosophy that celebrates black roots and the ideals of black life. While giving a balanced presentation of black women, Claire Harris celebrates their black roots and the ideals propagated by black life. While doing so, she also hits hard at the world power structures that subjugate blacks and women as second class citizens and aims at a dynamic wholeness and healing from both within and without, on an individual as well as on a societal level. Throughout her oeuvre, Claire Harris's larger concerns and preoccupations, her emancipatory agenda, remain "to rehabilitate the Black person, her beauty, her smile, her walk, her genius . . . his too" and to "explore the reality of Canadian society" which she must constantly analyse, dissect and cauterise in order to free it from a variety of "solipsistic exclusions constructed around the word 'Canadian,'" to heal its "soul's disease" and sickness, to make it dynamic and whole, so that eventually it can include her. This is certainly a womanist agenda and goes much beyond feminism.

NOTES

1. Chikwenye Okonjo Ogunyemi, "Womanism: The Dynamics of the Contemporary Black Female Novel in English," *Signs*, 11: 1 (1985), pp. 63-80.
2. Alice Walker, *Living by the Word: Selected Writings (1973-1987)* (New York: Harcourt Brace Jovanovich, 1982).
3. Alice Walker, *In Search of Our Mother's Gardens* (New York: Harcourt Brace Jovanovich, 1983), pp. xi-xii
4. Arun Prabha Mukherjee, *Oppositinal Aesthetics: Readings from a Hyphenated Space* (Toronto, Canada: TSAR, 1994).
5. Janice Williamson, *Sounding Differences: Conversations with Seventeen Canadian Women Writers* (Toronto: University of Toronto Press 1993). Interview with Claire Harris "dreams of a new naming," pp. 115-305.
6. Claire Harris, *Fables from the Women's Quarters* (Toronto: William Wallace, 1984), p. 43.

7. Claire Harris, *Travelling to find a Remedy* (Fiddlehead Poetry Books and Goose Lane. Fredericton, New Brunswick, Canada, 1986).
8. Claire Harris, "Poets in Limbo," *A Mazing Space: Writing Canadian Women Writing*, ed. Shirlly Neuman and Smaro Kamboureli (Edmonton: Longspoon/ NeWest Press, 1986), pp. 115-25.
9. Claire Harris, *The Conception of Winter* (Stratford, Ontario: William Wallace, 1989).
10. Claire Harris, "Between the Rock and a Hard Place," *The Literary Criterion: Aspects of Contemporary Canadian Literature*, Vol. XXXII, Nos. 1 & 2, 1997.

Spiritual Globalization: A Study of Uma Parameswaran's "On the Shores of the Irish Sea"

V. MEENAKUMARI
A.P.A. College for Women, Palani

The transformation of the world into a global village bears testimony to the scientific and technological accomplishment and well-established trade and commerce. Globalization is the highest form of modernity in human history and is an interlocking phenomenon of a dynamic nature. The power of capital is such today that a financially led globalized capitalism is structurally evolving with the tremendous support of advances in tendentious information technology. The universe is compressed into a compact disc by a multi-layered set of networks. In fact, globalization becomes imperative in the present economic scenario to attain complacency in food, fuel and other essential products. Yet, totality in globalization seems to be far-fetched phenomena since the powerful magic accompanying the dynamics of globalization creates pseudo-gods which claim submission and demand sacrifice. This malefic milieu leads to technological terrorism as well as environmental invasion. Ninan Koshky observes in his *The Imperial Thrust of Modernity* that "globalization promotes inequality, unrest, conflict, economic inequality is greening: more conflicts and civil wars are emerging." The extirpation of these clogs is possible only when people have a free access to spiritual globalization.

Spiritual globalization is seeking divinity in everything and holding all elements, animate and inanimate things as incarnation of God. *Advaita* preached by Adishankara emphasizes non-duality that is *Sarvam Brahmamayam.* The theory of non-duality elucidates the truth that God and things created by Him are one and the same. In the world of Adishankara, true wisdom is seeking God in every atom, from ants to elephants and also in all controversies. Brahman is not an object but is the very subjective core, the essence in each individual.

> Pratyage karasam poornamanantam Sarvatomukham
> Ehamevadhvayam Brahma neha nanasti Kinchit
>
> Viveka Choodamani 467

The following lines quite explicitly state this idea.

> Esha devo vishvakarma mahatma sada Jananam hirdaye sannivishishta
> Hirdya, manisha manasa viklubdhaye ya etad viduramrithaste bhavanti (Svetachva tharo Upanishad 4-17)

Non-duality, the principle idea of Adishankara is clearly pictured in Emerson's poem "Brahma." He says that Brahma is the doubt and the doubter, darkness and light, reality and illusion. In the *Bhagavad-Gita*, Lord Krishna says that he is the Self, seated in the hearts of all beings. He is the beginning, the middle and also the end of all beings.

> aham atma gudakesa sarvabhutaayasthitah
> ahamadishiha madhyamcha bhutanamanta eva cha
>
> (The *Gita*, Ch.10 Sloka 20)

Uma Parameswaran, who is an Indo-Canadian poet and who expresses Canadian experiences in Indian images, captures the same idea of Non-Duality in her poem "An Invocation Dance for Lata." In the state of equipoise, her mind is held steadfast in contemplation of the Supreme and she realizes the presence of the Supreme Self in cold and heat, pleasure and pain, honour and dishonour. She observes that all opposites converge in the universal, divine mother. For her, mother Ambike is the "Goddess as lovely as the dawn and as frightening as moonless night." She is a wide sea of compassion and also a wielder of sword. She is the giver of grief and also the sole comfort. She is the creator and destroyer bringing worlds into a being and in time dissolving them into nothingness. The continued dance of the world of plurality to the rhythm of change and death is maintained in the "presence" of the Self. The poetess gets an awakening at the

Spirit, the Supreme Power functions through matter through all controversies:

Non-duality elicits the fact of divinity prevailing in the five elements—air, water, fire and earth, which are the progenitors of life. The congregation of these elements results in the creation of life. Tamil poet Manickavasaka casts light on the view of God being air, earth, light, reality and illusion. Daitrio Upanishad enunciates the same theory of God existing in all elements, which can be observed in the following lines:

> Tasmadhva etasmadatman Aakasha sambhutah
> Aakashadvayuh vayorani aknerapaha
> Adbhaya Prithvi prithviya aushadhy
> Aushdhiyoannam annatpurushah (Daitrio Upanishad 2-1)

Uma Parameswaran who is a celebrant of non-duality worships the progenitors of life in her poem "On the Shores of the Irish Sea."

> Earth, air, fire, water,
> Progenitors of all life
> Inspire, exhort, goad, needle,
> Nag us night and day
> I pray. (12)

The poetess in "On the Shores of the Irish Sea" makes a quest for fire, which is the giver and taker of life. She walks farther, flies higher, dives deeper to find the fire, which is the creator of life and which is now but ember in empty pyres waiting for the bodies that lie scattered on ocean floor due to air crash.

Non-duality finds the perfect niche for its complement in the people considering all places as their own and all people as their consanguinity. In "On the Shores of the Irish Sea," Uma Parameswaran, standing on the Irish seashore, laments for the three hundred Canadian hearts stopped by the Indian flight 182. Her poetic sensibility overwhelms her humane feelings melting away the national, geographical and cultural barriers. This catastrophe etches a permanent niche in the heart of the poetess and she has been mourning for the death of the Canadians for fifteen long winters and fifteen short summers. The spiritual globalization is attained when the poetess holds all the dead as her brethren, glowing forever in history and hearts. She lights camphor markers in her heart, builds stupa, gnomon, pyramid and obelisk in her mind and sings dirges to the dead in her soul. The poetess' sense of belongingness to everywhere gives her an unalloyed joy and unfettered freedom to see her own Narmada and Cauvery in the rivers of Canada. She transplants India in Canada by bringing Ganga to Assiniboine, by building temples on the Canadian seashores and by seeing the flute player dancing on the waters of La Salle.

The great access of timelessness or eternity is accorded a warm welcome by the people with a poised mind. There is an acute awareness in Uma Parameswaran on the ephemerality of earthly time when she says that she is mourning for "ever-young dead" with "slowly-aging eyes." The phrase "every-young dead" is indicative of the world of eternity to which Death takes one after death. It also echoes John Donne's "one short sleepe past, we wake eternally" (Death Be Not Proud). Just as sleep is not the end of life, but only a refreshing pause between two spans of activity, so too death is not an end, but only a restful pause in the unmanifested condition that comes between two successive manifested existences in different embodiments," observes Swami Chinmayananda. The phrase "slowly-aging eyes" poignantly affirms the transitoriness of earthly life.

Uma Parameswaran's poem "On the Shores of the Irish Sea" develops the Greek idea that the movement of time is circular. The poetess makes a smooth sail from the present to the past and from the immediate past to the remote past. She again sails forward from the remote past to the immediate past and finally to the present. The poem "On the Shores of the Irish Sea" opens with the poetess standing on the Irish seashores on June 24, 2000, the 15th anniversary of the air crash of AI Flight 182, bewailing the death of the unfortunate victims. Her mental journey moves back to the days of the past on which she has come and settled in Canada. The poetess' words

> Remember now and forever
> the date etched in caves of memory
> where there and here come together

to make us who we be

is explicit of the fact that her mind is the place where there is a perfect blend of the past and the present. In the *Gita*, in the 'Visvarupa,' the Lord expresses Himself as the world phenomena, a conception of oneness arises in which not only space shrinks but even Time becomes an object of observation. Arjuna has seen in that picture the past merging with the present and moving forward to mingle with the entire future. T.S. Eliot's view that the past lives in the present is clear in the lines "where there and here come together to make us who we be."

Uma Parameswaran dives deep into the abyss of the past and brings the dark day of ignominy to the surface where Komagatamaru was driven into the open sea on July 23, 1914 in Canada. She then flies higher to the sky to observe the great loss that occurred on June 23, 1985 when Flight 182 hurtled through the sky into the Irish Sea, stopping three hundred Canadian hearts. The poetess now lands on June 23, 2000 and expresses her sorrow for not bringing the criminals, who have killed many innocent hearts, to light because of "an inquiry that drags its feet." Uma Parameswaran takes the reader to the memories that are sunnier ones. One such memory is of November 2, 1949 with Jawaharlal Nehru standing on the Pacific shore thanking the Gadars for their part in the freedom struggle. The poetess' mental voyage ends on the shores of the Irish Sea. She lights camphor in her heart for those hearts which stopped due to the aircrash. The victory of Uma Parameswaran in viewing the whole world as her own and all human beings as her brethren may be hailed as 'strategic win' in attaining spiritual globalization.

It has been necessary for the people to equip their minds in accordance to the ideology of spiritual globalization to achieve universal peace. Equal vision is the hallmark of globalization. The perfected cannot make distinctions based upon likes and dislikes. In and through all forms and situations, he sees the expression of the same dynamic Truth which he experiences as his own Self. For instance, Kaniyan Poongundranar, a Tamil poet, through his words sows the seeds of non-duality in the minds of the readers. Uma Parameswaran's Kanishka poems "On the Shores of the Irish Sea" and "An Invocation Dance for Lata" not only manifest non-duality but also carve a niche for the world in the arena of spiritual globalization.

Bibliography

Uma Parameswaran. *Sisters at the Well.* New Delhi: India log, 2002.

Ninan Koshy. *Globalization—The Imperial Thrust of Modernity.* Mumbai: Vikas Adhyayan Kendra, 2002.

The South-East Asian Diaspora in Canada Uma Parameswaran's *Sons Must Die*

N. KALAAMANI
Bharathidasan University, Tiruchirappalli

> The earth is full of Indians, you know that we get everywhere. We become tinkers in Australia and our heads end up in Idi Amin's fridge. Columbus was right: maybe the world's made up of the Indies East, West, North, Damn it You should be proud of us, our enterprise, the way we push against frontiers. Only thing is we are not Indian like you. You better get used to us.

These are the words of Chamcha, a character in Salman Rushdie's novel *The Satanic Verses*. This is an echo of the Indian Diaspora in Canada or United States or Australia or anywhere around the world. Expatriates, exiles or emigrant settlers who find themselves displaced from one country or culture and aspire to accept the new identity of the alien land into which they have moved into constitute the Diasporic Community.

What surfaces in diasporic experience is the underlying trauma in this act of displacement. The strategic concern underlying this diasporic writing is the search for home. Is their home this new country or the memories of the land they have left behind or whether expatriation is a virtual snapping of the immigrants' ties with the mother country? Whether he makes mental visits home to refurnish his emotional and cultural loss?

An exploration into this phenomenon made Rushdie observe that there can never he a complete breaking away for the expatriate from his home country. In an essay written in 1993, Rushdie says: "Exiles or emigrants or expatriates are humbled by some sense of loss, some way to reclaim to look back even at the risk of being mutated into pillars of salt." Himself an expatriate writer, he precisely analyzes how "if we do look back we must also do in the knowledge which gives rise to profound uncertainties that our physical alienation from India almost inevitably means that we will not be capable of reclaiming precisely the thing that was lost."

This is true in case of many writers, who come back for their home country at recurrent intervals to recover the 'lost patia' but often return disillusioned recognizing that home is no longer what it used to be, what far away in some foreign land they had loved and cherished in their memories.

Whilst this is so, some writers opt for this permanent exile abroad, and yet continue to draw their cultural and aesthetic sustenance and substance from their Indian past as in the case of Bharati Mukherjee, Uma Parameswaran, Rohinton Mistry, Chitra Divakaruni and many others. The act of displacement activates the diaspora writers to their frequent mental visits home through dreams and literature, so much so that their homeland reappears to them as a series of objects or fragments of narratives. It is thus that the writers retain their contact with their original home reliving her through their memory/dreams. Uma Parameswaran, talking about this experience, observes how "though the landscape around us was spruce and pine, the landscape of memory was filled with jasmine and mango."

Diasporic writers, in the words of William Safron, "being dispersed from a certain original centre or two or more peripheral regions, retain a collective memory, vision or myth about their homeland—its physical location, history and achievements. They for one reason or other continue to relate personally or vicariously to that homeland. . . . And their ethno-communal consciousness and solidarity are significantly defined by the existence of such relationship."

As a result of this whether the writer "straddles two cultures" or "falls between two stools" to echo Rushdie, there is always the dual feeling of the sense of wonder and adventure at the sight of the new landscape and simultaneously the nostalgia for the world left behind. The ensuing conflict between these two mental frames are well observed by these lines of Vijayasree, who finds the tensions patterning themselves into art experience in an expatriate writer: "The experiencing of inhabiting two geographical and cultural spaces simultaneously is wrought with subtle and involved tensions which get polarized into patterns such as dislocation versus relocation, domicile versus diasporic consciousness, dispossession versus integration, heritage versus hybridity and exile versus involvement."

However, the writers of the diaspora remain the voice of the marginals though coloured with a vibrant emotion; and their stories are those that depict the struggle to negotiate into a new space and culture. They draw their strength from their home country whilst assimilating in a new milieu. A good illustration is Uma Parameswaran's literary works wherein she unifies an essential Canadian sensibility with that of her Indian historic past. Like every expatriate writer, she attempts to "grab the best of two worlds," to use her own phrase: Most of her one-act plays recall an Indian past, with its mythology, legends and the gods and goddesses. Her early play *Meera* written in 1971 is a script that deals with the episodes linking Meera's life with that of Lord Krishna, affirming the power of faith and the spiritual space. *Sita's Promise* is an attempt to link the epic India with modern Canada through myth and dance, dealing with the forest exile of Rama, Sita and Lakshmana. *Dear Deedi, My Sister*, composed in the 1980s, deals with the women issues.

Uma Parameswaran's *Sons Must Die* was written much earlier, in 1962. Its main evocation was the Indo-Pakistan war of 1947-1948. The idealism and romanticism of war was shred to pieces when the author had the first-hand experience of meeting several families in India who lost their sons. Many young women lost their brothers, as some lost their young husbands.

Sons Must Die depicts the horrors of war and is set in the backdrop of Kashmir. Here, three women from different parts of India—a Tamil Brahmin, wrapped in Kanjivaran silk, Zohra Begum a Muslim mother wearing a salwar kameez suit with gold embroidery on the blue velvet and Prem Behn, a Punjabi mother—meet in Kashmir in search of their sons. The three mothers have lost their sons while fighting for Kashmir.

The play opens with the description of the beauty of Kashmir which had lured rulers of various cultures and nations:

> Kashmir! Valley beloved of the Great!
> Many have been the wars fought here
> These two thousand years.
> Fratricidal wars for all wars are fratricidal,
> No hollow platitude all men ARE brothers
> Many were the hands that held your sceptre
> Varied the faiths of your rulers.

The whole history of rulers is traced and her power over people is thus established. She was an enchantress who could lure people and also be the valley beloved of the Gods. But "is this enchantress worth sons' lives," asks the author, as one by one the mother's come and bemoan the death of their sons.

Meenakshi cries out, "My son, my son, where are you?" But as he is not alive, he cannot respond. Her tears eclipse the beauty of the land when she exclaims:

> I know nothing but that I love my son
> And he a wanderer wrecked perhaps.
> Fighting for a region we need not have
> Though ours by right it may be

As she slumps down crying, Zohra Begum appeals in the same valley, she too looking out for her son. She is proud that she has sent her two sons and their father to the warfield who went there willingly. Though the mother is crestfallen, she does not fall to weeping but sorrowfully proclaims: "O Allah, send us not such mournful punishment." Last of all comes the Punjabi mother Prem Behn, who sees her son, a young lad in perfect health, who becomes a victim of the onslaught. Happy to see his mother, he pitifully cries out that he does not want to die, asks his mother to prevent his death, his implorations to his mother are pitiful:

> I am too young to be dead
> I refuse
> I want to live,
> Feel the blood of youth coursing
> Through my veins,

> To race over the fields, to swim across the Sutlej,
> To see spring's first spring
> To join harvest songs and dances.

His yearning for life on the death-bed in the battlefield is agonizing. He is twenty years old and is too young to die. The disillusionment is appalling. He had loved India and the beautiful Kashmir but they have killed him: and yet the mother who has been fed on the romanticism of war, says: "Go Kishore, Go," saying "Few die in so noble a cause." The chorus and the other characters foreground the atrocity of war. The poet, the dacoit, the British nun and the Indian sadhu provide perspectives on the horrors of war.

The poet is the first to see the ravages: he witnesses the green splendour of the valley transformed into a stream of blood and wailing mothers whose sons must die. Whereas the poet is disillusioned with humanity to see the beauty metamorphosed into bloodshed, a nun appears there and she is closely followed by a dacoit. The nun is a European, in the attire of the Order of St. Joseph, murmuring the prayer with her fingers rolling the rosary. Engrossed in her prayer, she is startled on seeing Zohra wondering whether she is a Pakistani. Seeing her fright, the chorus assure her that there is nothing to fear:

> Come, come, not all tez wearers are Pakistanis
> Nor all Pakistanis ravagers.

and tell her "You are safe here." But the nun who has witnessed the evils of war exclaims that the imprint on the human heart is deep. As if in answer to her fears comes the dacoit.

> Dacoit: Ha! Where is she whose purse is heavy with gold?
> Chorus: Barbarian! Would you waylay a woman?
> Dacoit: Sure I would, if she has gold.
> Chorus: Attack a servant of God?
> Dacoit: God? Who is that? And where is he?

The episode of the dacoit is satirical of the institution of religion Hindus or Christians or Muslims. The God that came out of the pillar and the God of the Immaculate Conception are laughed at by the dacoit:

> There is no God. And her God.
> Ha! Virgin Mary, Immaculate Conception
> I too am a God.
> For I doubt my mother ever married.

It is at this moment that a Sadhu, clad in leopard skin enters. He has a brass jug in one hand and a trishul in the other, looking like Shiva. The dacoit is puzzled and exclaims whether it was a World Conference of Religions shaping out here.

The Sadhu's words to the dacoit are paradoxical. Yet they communicate the central message of the play. He observes that he too has often wondered if there was a God. Waiting, fasting, praying and mortifying himself in icy caves, "hoping to come face to face with him." But he did not come. But "then I saw a mother and her babe" and knew that it was here that God lived:

> I looked on the mother
> And her babe I felt something shooting this
> Flooding my mind with Light.
> And it is,
> . . . there I saw what perhaps is God
> See the mothers that are.
> They give birth to sons,
> Are proud and jealous for them.
> But when the sons leave
> What can the mother do?
> Except that God knows what is to be.

The sons leave the mother and combat for their survival in an alien land.

The land may be beautiful, but what is it to a mother—the sons she had guarded zealously have left her shores. Is this the price of expatriation? The play is open-ended. If there is one question that troubles the mind after reading the play, it is: should sons die? There are two sides to the issue. Sons leave their mothers (or mother country) Diaspora studies have pivoted the experience of the sons. But what about the mother? What price does she pay?

The Miranda-Caliban Complex in Margaret Laurence's Fiction

V. BHARATHI HARISHANKAR
University of Madras

The nature of any "dominance" is that it, like the margins it defines, is a social construct, a fabrication of language and institutional design. Margins have a way of speaking back from the edges of power, of resisting those who occupy a centre by having laid claim to the terms that declare that they do occupy a centre. If they are not recognised for the creativity of the differences they bring to bear on cultural perception, margins also have a way of making the centre irrelevant.[1]

> Man is human only to the extent to which he tries to impose his existence on another man in order to be recognised by him. . . . The only means of breaking this vicious circle that throws me back on myself is to restore to the other, through mediation and recognition his human reality, . . . The other has to perform the same operation. "Action from one side only would be useless, because what is to happen can only be brought about by means of both"; "they recognise themselves as mutually recognising each other."[2]

Reconstructing canonical texts through alternative readings is a method followed both by feminist and postcolonial critics. Shakespeare's *The Tempest*[3] has been subject to many such readings.[4] It is common critical practice to see the relationships between Prospero and Caliban and Prospero and Miranda as explaining colonialism and its feminine trope. Laura E. Donaldson's article "The Miranda Complex: Colonialism and the Question of Feminist Reading"[5] draws attention to the fact that the relationship between Miranda and Caliban has not been adequately explored by critics. Laura Donaldson uses this concept to show the inadequacies of white feminist readings. In particular, she criticises the readings offered by Sandra Gilbert and Susan Gubar in their book, *Madwoman in the Attic* and by Gayatri Spivak in her article "Three Women's Texts and a Critique of Imperialism." By focussing on the subtle nuances that exist in the interactive relationship between Miranda and Caliban, fresh interpretations of colonial texts become possible. This paper is an attempt to explore the problems that exist in the relationship between the 'white' female protagonists and the 'natives' in Margaret Laurence's Manawaka fiction. Her novels *The Stone Angel*, *The Fire-Dwellers* and *A Bird in the House* highlight the colonial problem and its possible solution. The culminating point may be found in *The Diviners* where the two oppressed categories come together. Thus, following the central idea of epigraphs, the paper examines the colonial dilemma and its resolution in Laurence's novels.

The Prospero-Caliban complex and the Prospero-Miranda complex work with different sets of binary oppositions: self-other, coloniser-colonised, male-female, white-black, good-evil and centre-margin. The Prospero complex enacts the oppression of both natives and women by the Western patriarch. Both Caliban and Miranda, to use Laura Donaldson's words, are "colonised and tricked" and exist only "as man's other side, his denied, abused and hidden side." (68)

Given the paradigms of the blacks in a white world and women in a man's world, it is surprising that these two marginalised categories do not 'see' each other. Further, in the relationship between the oppressed, the oppressor-oppressed roles re-appear. One reason for this situation is their mutual invisibility and their relating to each other through the common oppressor, Prospero. While Miranda sees Caliban as her father's slave and does not grant him individuality, Caliban sees her merely as a sexual object. According to Laura Donaldson, Caliban devises his "own quest for mastery through one of patriarchy's most dehumanizing and oppressive weapons—the threat of rape." (70) The entire colonial situation becomes complex because oppression exists at more than one level—sexual, racial, cultural, national, economic, social and psychological.

In Laurence's fiction, alienation of the natives is both physical and psychological. The physical aspect can be traced in the economic deprivation of the natives and the resulting social nullification. This is very well brought out in Laurence's descriptions of the miserable living conditions of the Tonnerres, the Calibans of Manawaka. Interestingly enough, all the descriptions are made from the standpoint of Miranda, i.e., the white woman. To Hagar Shipley, the Tonnerres "lived all in a swarm in a shack somewhere."[6] In Vanessa MacLeod's description, the Tonnerre's family shack is "a small square cabin made of poplar poles and chinked with mud . . . a chaos of lean-tos, wooden packing cases, warped lumber, discarded car tires [sic] ramshackle chicken coops, tangled strands of barbed wire and rusty tin cans."[7] Morag Gunn describes the shack as an assemblage of "old planks, tar paper, the lids of wooden crates, some shingles and flattened pieces of tin."[8] The final point of physical alienation occurs when Lazarus Tonnerre's body is not allowed to be buried in the town graveyard for fear of "his halfbreed bones spoiling their cemetery." In Jules' words, the small town racism has denied "the Metis, once lords of the prairies . . . burial space in their own land." (268)

The psychological alienation of the Metis results out of two distinct attitudes of the whites. One is the ethnocentric stance when the colonial woman acts like the feminine counterpart of the western patriarch. Even though Manawaka's racial hierarchy includes the Scots, Irish, Cree and Ukrainian, it rejects the Metis in *A Bird in the House* as 'neither flesh, fowl, nor good salt herring." (115) In *The Stone Angel,* Jason Currie prohibits Matt from going on a hunting expedition with Lazarus for the social disgrace involved in "gallivanting around the country with a Metis." Hagar defies her father in marrying Bram whose social value is next to nothing because he dates half-breed girls. However, she shares Jason's hatred for and prejudice against the Metis in worrying about John's friendship with the Tonnerre boys. Like Hagar, Grandmother MacLeod in *A Bird in the House* refuses to go on a holiday to Diamond Lake, if Piquette Tonnerre is to accompany them. Such an attitude imposes, what Fanon calls, "the internalization" and "epidermalisation" of the inferiority. (13)

Another stance adopted by the whites is their romantic and/or patronising attitude towards the natives. Fanon points out how a white man addressing a Negro "behaves exactly like an adult with a child and starts smirking, whispering, patronizing, cozening." (31) In *A Bird in the House*, Vanessa takes a romantic view of Piquette as "a real Indian" who "sprang from the people of Big Bear and Poundmaker, of Tecumseh, of the Iroquois." In the short story entitled "The Loons" Vanessa sees Piquette as a daughter of the forest, a kind of junior prophetess of the wilds" who will have an intimate knowledge of "where the whippoorwill made her nest, how the coyote reared her young." (119) Vanessa is disappointed when Piquette fails to respond.

The other facet of the relationship is the "doubly marginalised" native woman's delusion of social prestige involved in marrying a white man. Like Fanon's example of Mayotte Capecia, who made up her mind to love only "a white man, a blue-eyed blonde," (47) Piquette attempts to surprise "the old bitches an' biddies" of Manawaka by marrying "an English fella" with "blond wavy hair." (124) Vanessa sees behind Piquette's "defiant face . . . a terrifying hope." (124) As is usual in the colonial situation, her white husband leaves her with two children. She takes to drinking and dies when the shack catches fire.

Having identified the factors that lead to oppression, it is but natural to look for options to end the mutual invisibility. As Fanon states at the end of *Black Skin, White Masks* (231), there should be an authentic communication. Instead of superiority and inferiority, there should be an attempt to touch, feel and explain the other to oneself. In Laurence's fiction, the authentic communication takes the form of erasing the distinctions set up by the binaries. This standpoint may be traced throughout Laurence's fiction, that is, from her African writings to her Manawaka fiction. Margaret Laurence's anti-imperial stance is evident even in her early African writings. *The Prophet's Camel Bell* (1963), *This Side Jordan* (1960) and *The Tomorrow-Tamer* collection (1963) set in Somaliland and Ghana respectively provide insights into the nature of colonialism, for Laurence explores the roles of both the colonial and colonised. As Leslie Monkman rightly points out in his article "Ancestral and Contemporary Communities in *The Stone Angel*," in her Manawaka fiction, Margaret Laurence, "insists on the necessary acknowledgement of the Tonnerres and the values associated with them."[9] Through *The Diviners*, Laurence reinforces the need for reconciling conflicting systems of values. Though the process itself is complex, it is effected through a recognition of a common humanity. As Laurence forcefully states in *The Heart of a Stranger*, "Will we ever reach a point when it is no longer necessary to say Them and Us? I believe we must reach that point, or perish."[10]

Margaret Laurence adopts different methods to effect the reconciliation between the two groups. Laurence offers the Metis a superior position in portraying them as guides to the protagonists. For instance, in "The Loons," Vanessa is disappointed by Piquette's refusal to live up to her expectations of an Indian. On a later visit to Diamond Lake, after the deaths of her father and Piquette, she finds that the loons have vanished. She finally realises that Piquette was the only one who understood the "half-mocking, half-plaintive call" of the loons for survival (*A Bird in the House* 127). Also, Piquette mocks the pain of life as is shown in her brief and tragic existence. Similarly, in *The Fire Dwellers*, when the MacAindra family is nearly bent under the authority of Thor Thorlakson, Valentine Tonnerre releases them by disclosing the true identity of Thor as runny-nosed Vernon Winkler. In *The Diviners*, Jules Tonnerre goes a step further in becoming a 'shaman' to Morag Gunn and helps her to walk out of her sterile marriage. Commenting on Jules' role, Catherine Sheldrick Ross quotes Eliade who defines a shaman as a mediator between the earthly world and invisible powers: "Jules as shaman can help Morag make a breakthrough to the upper world. But equally important he can help her find her way back to the lower world represented by Christie and the Nuisance Grounds. Therefore he gives Morag access to deep sources of power that Brooke has kept repressed."[11]

It is in this novel that an alliance is forged between Laurence's Caliban (Jules) and her Miranda (Morag). To quote John Moss on their relationship: "[it is] a lasting connection between psyches and souls, occasionally complemented by sexual consummation and wordless touching, but needing no such reinforcement to endure."[12] One can better appreciate Laurence's successful portrayal of Jules by applying a psychoanalytic framework. The Jungian reading of the novel reveals Jules as the animus (or a woman's archetypal image of a man). This portrayal contrasts the common norm of projecting the white man as animus (Fanon 91).

Another way of effecting the reconciliation between the whites and natives is by comparison. Stacey understands her comparative well-being on seeing Valentine. As she states, "Even her presence is a reproach to me, for all I've got now and have been given and still manage to bitch on and on about it. . . . The debts are inherited and how could the damage ever be undone or forgiven?" (286) On seeing Val's present condition, Stacey is reminded of the once glorious past of the Metis. She also realises their alienation by the town and the society. Her first step towards positive thinking is evident in her honest assessment of herself. "She would like to go back in time, to explain that she never meant the town's invisible stabbing, but this is not possible, and it was hers, too, so she cannot edge away from it."[13]

In *The Diviners*, the reconciliation is complete in the figure of Pique, the daughter of Morag and Jules. Morag is triply marginalised being the town scavenger's ward, a woman and a writer. Like Piquette, Morag tries unsuccessfully to break the bonds by marrying an Englishman, Brooke Skelton (189). Jules also occupies the fringe of society because of his race. Defiant like his sister Piquette, Jules shows anger and contempt for the white man in his reaction to his audience. "One-man circus. Satin shirt with a lotta beadwork, and sometimes a phoney doeskin jacket with fringes and a lotta plastic porcupine quills in patterns. That's what they like." (226) However, divining into their respective Gunn/Logan and Tonnerre heritages shields both

Morag and Jules from their alienation. Their daughter Pique also begins by being angry and hateful. For instance, she accuses Morag of having a child for her own satisfaction without giving a thought either about Jules and herself or about the position of a half-breed in society. Through an acceptance of her heritages (both Gunn and Tonnerre) she moves forward by going back to Galloping Mountains to help her own people. Her return to her ancestral place is an affirmation of, what Mannoni calls, "an awareness of the world of others, a world in which others have to be respected."[14]

Though there is no extensive treatment of the Metis, the Manawaka fiction traces a development of the relationship between the protagonists and the Metis. Thus, the Metis are not merely "symbolic" presences as Marcienne Rocard[15] states but are a facet of a common humanity. Margaret Laurence gradually develops a position of "a new humanism and understanding." She embodies Fanon's plea in the opening pages of *Black Skin, White Masks*, in her belief in mankind and erases race prejudice through understanding and love (Fanon 9).

It is interesting to trace a near imperialist voice of Hagar in *The Stone Angel*, through a move towards understanding in *A Bird in the House* and *The Fire-Dwellers* to a total acceptance of the 'other' in *The Diviners*. The last novel forms the culminating point of two 'peripheries' forming a new 'center' or better still, a collapsing of boundaries. Margaret Laurence achieves this by focussing on human relationships which will ultimately effect a change in the way of thinking of a community, a nation and a race.

Works Cited

1. W.H. New, Editorial, *Canadian Literature*, Nos. 124-125 (1990), p. 8.
2. Frantz Fanon, *Black Skin, White Masks* (London: Pluto, 1952), p. 217.
3. William Shakespeare, *The Tempest*, ed. Stephen Orgel (Oxford: Oxford University Press, 1987).

4. For a list of readings, see Bill Aschcroft, Gareth Griffiths and Helen Tiffin, ed. *The Empire Writes back: Theory and Practice in Postcolonial Literature* (London and New York: Routledge, 1989), pp. 189-92.
5. Laura E. Donaldson, "The Miranda Complex: Colonialism and the Question of Feminist Reading," *Diacritics*, 18 (Fall 1988), pp. 65-75.
6. Margaret Laurence, *The Stone Angel* (Toronto: McClelland and Stewart, 1964), p. 127.
7. Margaret Laurence, *A Bird in the House* (1963; rpt. Toronto: McClelland and Stewart, 1974), p. 114.
8. Margaret Laurence, *The Diviners* (1974; rpt. New York: Bantam Books, 1975), p. 137.
9. Leslie Monkman, "Ancestral and Contemporary Communities in *The Stone Angel*," *Etudes Canadiennes*, Vol. 11 (1981), p. 42.
10. Margaret Laurence, *Heart of a Stranger* (Toronto; McClelland and Stewart, 1976).
11. Catherine Sheldrick Ross, "Female Rites of Passage in *Klee klyck*, *Surfacing* and *The Diviners*," *Atlantis*, 4.1 (1978), p. 93.
12. John Moss, "The Presbyterian Legacy: Laurence and *The Diviners*," *Sex and Violence in the Canadian Novel* (Toronto: McClelland and Stewart, 1977), p. 79.
13. O. Mannoni, *Prospero and Caliban: The Psychology of Colonization* (New York: Frederick A. Praeger, 1950), p. 108.
14. Margaret Laurence, *The Fire-Dwellers* (London: Macmillan, 1969), p. 225.
15. Marcienne Rocard, "The Metis in Margaret Laurence's Manawaka Works," *Etudes Canadiennes*, Vol. 5 (1978): 1, 113-17.
16. George Woodcock, "Priarie Writers and the Metis: Rudy Wiebe and Margaret Laurence," *Canadian Ethnic Studies*, 14.1 (1982), pp. 9-22.

Triplicating Narratives and Identities: Margaret Atwood's *The Blind Assassin*

SUBHADRA BHASKARAN
Bharathi Women's College, Chennai

Margaret Atwood's *The Blind Assassin*[1] is a mesmerizing novel with triple narratives interwoven into it. At the periphery is a fabrication which constructs the tragic life of Laura and her lover Alex Thomas, an idealistic youngman and a radical, depicted from the perspective of Laura's sister Iris. Embedded in it is a fiction of adultery recounting the surreptitious love affair of a wealthy maiden and a fugitive Marxist. The innermost layer at the centre contexualizes the incredible and astounding adventures of the blind assassin and the mute sacrificial maiden, synthesizing the uses of the devices of science fiction and the fabulous tales of Arabian adventure. The narrative of the blind assassin and the mute sacrificial maiden posits a parallel to the tale of the aristocratic woman and her illicit partner, who in turn are allegorical figures for the enticing and incomprehensible Laura and her lover, Alex. The recurring theme of predators and preys, delineated in the triple narratives, postulates the possibility that Atwood deliberately triplicates the identity of the protagonists in the multiple folds of the complex novel.

The Blind Assassin unravels a gripping tale which stretches across many decades covering crucial episodes in History like the depression, the world wars, the Spanish civil war etc. The memoir of Iris written in her old age focuses on the doomed love between Laura and Alex and their tragic deaths. A retrospective vision is provided of the calamity endured by the Chase family due to the reverberating effects of the world wars and the depression which laid siege to the global economy. The forbears of chase family came to the Canadian town of Port Ticonderoga from Pennsylvania in the 1820s and commenced building the town burnt out during the war of 1812. Chase sisters (Iris and Laura) grandfather, a benevolent and successful founder of a button factory, built the imposing Chase Mansion 'Avilion,' named after the 'Island Valley' in *Idylls of the King*. Mr. Chase, the father becomes an alcoholic after being shattered by the tragic death of his two brothers during the war. After the mother's fatal miscarriage and the war wounded father's escape to alcoholism, the chase daughters Iris and Laura are literally raised by their nursemaid, Reenie. In October 1934 trouble began brewing in the Button Factory and in December shut down was announced and the interior thunderstorm struck when the factory caught fire, apparently set by Alex Thomas, the radical labour agitator. The ill-fated love between Laura and Alex begins from this crucial moment. With the depression and with the closure of the factory, the disintegration of the Chase family begins. The Chase sisters are thrown into the fatal network of the evil duo, the brother Richard, a trickster, a ruthless industrialist and a rising right wing politician and his sister Winifred, an over-ambitious and cunning socialite, a perfect manipulator. Iris is tricked into a hollow marriage to Richard, Laura becomes Richard's victim of blackmail and seduction. Alex is relentlessly pursued by the law instigated by the wicked industrialist. The death of Alex during the war drives Laura to plunge into death. This external narrative structure provides the story of Laura and Alex, the story of Predators and Victims perceived from the point of view of Iris.

Peeling the outer narrative layer would reveal the novel within the novel. This inner novel is supposed to have been written by Laura, but in reality is authored by Iris. The Cult classic of Canadian literature procures posthumous justice to Laura, causing the downfall of Richard, thwarting his political ambitions at one stroke. The inner novel is about an illicit love between a young frustrated aristocratic woman and a left wing sympathizer. The Marxist always on the move to escape capture ultimately leaves his ladylove to participate in the Spanish civil war and later the Second World War. In utter misery, the disillusioned woman exclaims: "drowned now the tree as well, the sky, the wind, the clouds. All she has left is the picture. Also the story of it." (518) This fiction of adultery, the story of victims pursued by predators recounts the tragic romance of Laura and Alex from the perspective of Laura herself. From this direct recounting is launched the indirect narration of Iris filling up the gaps in the narration of the future lives of the lovers.

The innermost narrative layer constitutes the tale recounted by the Marxist to his mistress about a young slave boy, the blind assassin, having turned blind weaving the finest carpets. The young boy trained as an assassin is expected to kill the king, by killing and taking the place of a young mute girl, a victim with her tongue cut out and kept prepared for the next day's ritual of sacrifice. The blind assassin falls in love with the mute sacrificial maiden, rescues her from the temple and from the city before the city is destroyed by its enemies. But the termination of the story is thus: "The dead women réally are dead. Not only that, the wolves really are wolves, and the dead women can whistle them up at will. Our romantic leads are wolf meat before you can say Jack Robinson." The narrative of blind assassin and the mute maiden is an allegorical representation of the doomed love and life of Laura and Alex, the story of wolfs, predators and victims.

Like the blind assassin who is employed for political crime and who falls in love with his first victim, the deaf maiden, Alex employed by the radicals to burn down the button factory of the Chase family falls in love with Laura. Laura, in her anxiety to secure the safety of Alex, yields to Richard who offers a false promise to Laura that he would protect Alex from the law. She becomes a victim of Richard's seduction and is forced to keep her tongue within and not breathe a word about Richard's manipulative deeds to the outside world. Nothing else would be more appropriate than the allegoric presentation of the deaf sacrificial maiden to portray Laura's helpless situation. The three narratives juxtapose different perspectives of the fatal romance of the pair Laura and Alex. The triple focalization foregrounds the antithesis between a romanticized affair and a dismal reality of the destiny of lovers. The varying modes of focalization pass from the external consciousness to an internal consciousness creating an illusion of synchronic effect. The third person detached narrative of the love of Laura and Alex through the narration of Iris is alternated by first person involved narrative of the romance by the young couple representing Laura and Alex. The effect of the triple narrative is felt in providing an added dimension to the story.

The third person narrative, a kind of flashback, a replay of pre-recorded version provides dramatic vividness to the depiction. In the outer layer, the narrative strategy adopted is to provide an objective introspection, by making the impersonal narrator unfolding the details bit by bit. Due to the measure of detachment characterizing the voice of the narrator, there is evident a mastery of the incident rather than the feeling of being carried away by it. The shift in the centre of consciousness is effected when the first narrative is through Iris and the second one through a couple representing Laura and Alex. The story of Laura and Alex is triplicated in the narrative through three different techniques. Outer narrative has Iris venturing into the stream of consciousness of Alex and Laura and offers a fabrication of their tragic lives from an external point of view. The second narrative has a naturalistic depiction of the doomed lives of Laura and Alex from a direct personal viewpoint. The third narrative is an allegorical representation. of the sorrowful lives of Laura and Alex expressed through the allegoric blind assassin and the mute maiden. Iris is like a narrator in fairy tales, moving but technically detached. The voice of central consciousness is very distant from the subject narrated. Impersonality of the narrator is acquired due to her, maturity of age and experience. Detachment is a technical choice and bitterness is another element that tinges the narration at various points. One of the innovative aspects of her fictional style is that the description of betrayal, bitterness and death have apparent nature of aloofness. The innovative and experimental craft of narration makes the book a product of elaborate and extremely sophisticated planning.

The problem a narrator who elaborates on the doomed affair of the lovers is normally beset with, is objectification of the tale and that is solved by Iris by resorting to detachment. The stance in reality should be inherently strident and overtly emotional as the victim happens to be her own sister. The triple perspective, one provided by the indirect third person narrator and the other by the direct personal account and the third symbolic portrayal prove to be resourceful and satisfying. This is achieved through a deft, clever manoeuvring of the narrative strategies.

The narration of Iris oscillates between the two temporal planes, her past revolving around the lives of Laura and Alex and her present as an 83-year-old woman suffering from a heart condition but stoically weathering the physical and emotional ailments, almost inviting comparison with Hagar Shipley of *The Stone Angel*. Transition from one temporal unit to another, from past to present and vice versa is accomplished successfully through the narration from different perspectives. This narrative strategy helps in recreating the experience in its temporal entirety. The novel has a structure implying different levels of reading or interpretation.

The allegorical version of the story of Lauras and Alexes, of perpetrators and victims attributes to the novel a fairy tale quality. In the words of Shashi Deshpande, "actually, there is a fairy tale quality to their story. Its bare bones spell out a stereotyped romantic tale-all the cliched figures and symbols are here; the doomed romantic heroine, her older sacrificing, sister, the faithful retainer, the idealistic poor hero, and the two villainous figures. The sharp separation of the innocent from the wicked gives this novel a simplistically moral tone, but in the hands of a writer like Atwood, it becomes a disturbing many hued complex story told through a skilful intermeshing of three narratives."[2] The narrative technique used here is the spiral method of narration. As Robert Penn Warren describes "the author takes the reader over and over the same events from a different altitude as it were, and a different style."[3] The multiplicity of vantagepoints, the intersecting narratives present a fairly comprehensive vision of the experience in its entirety.

The three epigraphs used by the author substantiate her deliberate triplicating the narratives. The first one taken from the translated version of *Shah of Shahs* written by Ryszard Kapuseinski describes the City of Kerman where, under the order of Monarch Agha Mohammed Khan, the adults are beheaded and children are blinded and left to wander in the countryside, ultimately either dying or singing songs about the extermination of the citizen of Kerman, an epigraph meaningfully chosen for the third allegorical narrative. The second epigraph extracted from the inscription on a Carthaginian Funerary urn reads: "I swam, the sea was boundless, I saw no more, Tanit was merciless, my prayers were answered. O you who drown in love, remember me."

It is interesting to note that the epigraph can be connected to the aristocratic maiden's concluding statement in the inner layer of narrative, "Drowned now the tree, as well, the sky, the wind, the clouds." The third epigraph consists of a line "The word is a flame burning in a dark glass" from *Deep Hollow Creek* written by Sheila Watson suggesting the narrative of Iris where she is trying to throw light on the unfathomable mysteries regarding Laura and Alex.

The artistic self-reflexivity of this postmodern metafiction leads to the gradual blurring of the boundaries between the different literary genres. Iris's memoir is blended with newspaper accounts of private events like Laura's death, the subsequent inquest, Richard's death etc. and historical events like the Munich Accord, the anarchy unleashed by the Stalin-backed communists in Spain, the civil conflict in Spain etc. published in *The Tornoto Star*, *The Globe and Mail*, *The Mail* and *Empire* and the *Mayfair*. The documentary materials are juxtaposed throughout with Iris's narration, besides the intersection of various genres like memoir, romance, a fabulous fairy tale and a science fiction. Through these articles, the reader is fed with the historical and personal events as well as the inevitably subjective nature of the story telling itself. In The *Blind Assassin* the tragic lives are embodied in fictional form. Atwood delineates in the novel the Canadian culture and conjures up specially the lives of the people of high social standing, introducing the rich, eccentric Chase family and tracing the reverberating effects of the First World War on the Chase family members.

NOTES

1. Margaret Atwood, *The Blind Assassin* (New York: Bloomsbury, 2000).
2. Shashi Deshpande, "In a different mould," *The Hindu*, 5 Nov. 2000.
3. Robert Pen Warren, "William Faulkner," *Forms of Modern Fiction*, ed. William Van O'Connor (Minneapolis: The University of Minnesota Press, 1948), p. 142.

Individual's Relation with Society and Environment: A Study of Robertson Davies' *World of Wonders*

SHOBHINI GUPTA
Ch. Charan Singh University, Meerut

A major theme in Robertson Davies' fiction is transformation. *World of Wonders* is known as a sandwich between *Fifth Business* and *The Manticore*. It presents Mangus Eisengrim's side of things. It is an encouraging tale. The Mangian world-view, propounded by Spengler and explained by Liesl, is the foundation and structuring principle of *World of Wonders* and of the trilogy, in general. This view had its origin in the middle ages. Boy Staunton and Liesl Vitzliputzli represent the two aspects. In *World of Wonders*, there are, as Magnus Eisengrim says, "double words for everything." (212) Like many of Davies' texts, *World of Wonders* is an intricate structure or dialogue wherein Davies continually creates situations, images and narrative structures that are doubled. This doubling is in two ways: in terms of narrative content and narrative structure. In the content phase, the focus is on the circus and theatre sections of the novel, examining images of doubling and considering the role of the uncanny and the grotesque as important preoccupations of the novel. In the narrative phase, the dialogism and double voicing are examined.

We know that this is the third novel in Davies' the Deptford trilogy. While it is not necessary to read the novels in this trilogy in sequence, doing so makes each story more complete and interesting and clarifies the relationships between some of the characters. This novel tells the life story of the unfortunate boy introduced in *Fifth Business*, who was spirited away from his Canadian home by one of the members of a travelling sideshow.

The quest is one of the indispensable structures of romance. It is clear that Davies writes romances and not realistic novels. His characters are reduced to their essences and all unnecessary details are eliminated. The theme is self-identity. It is interesting that in the books of the Deptford Trilogy, the second most important romance theme, love, does not hold a pre-eminent place.

Magnus Eisengrim follows the path of the romantic hero. Magnus relates the story in preparation for a film role; he is to play the great illusionist, Robert Houdin. He, Ramsay and Liesl line together at her estate, Sorgenfrei in Switzerland. Magnus explains how he came to be there while Ramsay writes it all down in academic penance for the fanciful history. In the final section, Ramsay completes the account, telling again of Boy Staunton and of fateful stone that brought about Eisengrim's premature birth as Paul Dempster.

Paul's progress occurs in stages, and at each stage he participates in an illusion. As a boy, he is raped and abducted by Willard the Wizard and he joins Willard's travelling carnival: he works inside a dummy that tells fortunes. Later, he becomes the stand-in for Sir John Tresize, a swashbuckling old actor past coping with exotic feats of daring. He moves on to Switzerland, where he repairs a badly damaged collection of mechanical toys—illusion again—and there he meets Liesl; they force each other to make love and he becomes Magnus Eisengrim. As *World of Wonders* begins, he is to be Robert Houdin. He has already been Paul Dempster, Cass, Jules Legrand and Mungo Fetch, and always the animator of illusion.

In *Fifth Business*, saints have a peculiarly Protestant representation. They are aspects in a psychological, specifically Jungian narrative, not a spiritual one. *World of Wonders* thrives on a similar anomaly. Purporting to plead for the necessity of wonder, it in fact rather effectively displays the sordid machinery behind the things we wonder at. Davies is clearly more concerned with the procedures of creation than he is with cause or effect. He describes events preceding Magnus' metamorphosis into the greatest illusionist in the world, but he shows us nothing of his talent, none of his illusions. In *World of Wonders*, Davies has created a portrait of the artist from a Jungian perspective. He shows not the sources of personality but the variety of its parts. When these parts come together, individuation is achieved. After the mutual rape with Liesl at Sorgenfrei, Magnus the artist has been reborn. How he actually comes to be great is unimportant.

The novel begins with a frame story; at Sorgenfrei, the BBC is shooting the life of the famous magician Robert Houdin. Magnus had always been very secretive about his life and Ramsay was avid to understand the real person behind the one he had invented. His desire was to be immortalized as a historian biographer. The frame story takes place in two separate locales, Sorgenfrei and London, where they are viewing the rushes and filming close-ups, and is itself divided into three parts, mirroring important passages and stages of the illusionist's life. After dinner, each evening, the group gathers to hear *World of Wonders*; the title has a triple meaning, taking its name from Magnus' life story, Mangian way, and the circus that marks the beginning of his quest. As a child, Paul had obeyed his father, once inside the grounds, he is drawn to the magician Willard the Wizard. Taking advantage of the boy's interest, Willard brutally sodomizes and then kidnaps him, forcing him to work in the circus, and enslaving him sexually until he is reduced to a perfect non-entity, the invisible and anonymous gaffer in the foul-smelling, dark and claustrophobic automaton, Abdullah. Magnus calls it a descent into hell and this lasts for seven years, until he and Willard leave Canada for Europe to escape trouble with the law. There, Paul takes his revenge. Willard consents to become a geek through Paul's coercion, a bestial savage who eats live animals on stage. Paul furthermore cruelly prolongs Willard's unbearable suffering from morphine addiction by withholding a merciful death. When he finally does allow him to die, the second part of his life, and of the book itself begins.

Magnus goes to England after Willard's death. Because of a happy likeness in appearance, he falls into Sir John Tresize's theatre company as a double in a play for the aging Sir John. There, as Mungo Fetch, the last in a series of names that had included Paul Dempster, Cass Fletcher and Jules Le Grand, he forms a deep, Platonic attachment to Lady Tresize, which has a profoundly civilizing effect on him, and that initiates the upward thrust of the romance cycle. He also observes and absorbs everything about the theatre group, developing a true affection for both of the Tresizes, and perfecting those crafts of illusion, and magic that are so much a part of the theatre. In contrast to his devotion and identification with Sir John, there is another new addition to the group, the playwright Roland Ingestree, who will eventually betray the aging actor. Through Magnus' story, his duplicity will eventually be unmasked. After the deaths of the Tresizes, Magnus works with clocks and mechanics, an expertise gained through his work with Willard and Abdullah. In that capacity, he meets Liesl, he is sent to Sorgenfrei to repair her grandfather's collection of rare toys.

The frame story takes over again as Ramsay, Magnus and Liesl are in bed together. They discuss the Mangian worldview, good and evil, artistic greatness, and the final mystery about the death of Boy Staunton. Magnus reveals that Boy had told him how unhappy he was and how he had intuited the man's wish to die. Before being dropped off at his hotel, he had given Boy the stone he had stolen from Ramsay's room. Thus, he had functioned as the man who granted his inmost wish, providing him with an excuse for suicide. The stone of the snowball story ends where it had begun.

The art theme is prevalent in *World of Wonders* and appears full-blown in the Cornish Trilogy. The dichotomy between egotist and egoist as well as the differences between Magnus and the man whom he is playing in the movie, Robert Houdin informs the discussion of what constitutes a great artist. Magnus is the spokesman for Davies' point of view. The true artist is one who has examined and understood his inner self. He is completely centred on what he wants and needs, is above the bourgeois crowd in his values and sense of self.

Cecelia Coulas suggests that the novel is really about the process of creating fiction and the reader's role in the process; she cites the multiple doublings of people and texts and the highly aesthetic vocabulary. Other themes related to art include the substantial section on the theatre. It is arguably enough to classify Davies as a genuine meta-fictionist.

It seems that *World of Wonders* is permeated with this duplicity; readers are also implicated in Paul's ambiguous response. As with the power of real life freak shows, *World of Wonders* compels attraction and repulsion from its viewers: we want to see, but we know we shouldn't want to. We vicariously participate in Paul's satisfaction in breaking taboos. When this force of attraction and repulsion gets faced with the grotesque or the bizarre that is at the centre of the novel's power. This is the same power that made freak shows of all stripes so popular, and that continues in different manifestations.

There are many types of doubles in the carnivalesque first section of the novel, as is obvious in a character like Andro the Hermaphrodite, who ritualistically neutralizes the opposition of male and female in his act where he wraps himself in his own arms and we see "a beautiful woman in the arms of a half-naked muscular man, whirling rhythmically around the stage in a rapturous embrace." (29) Another interesting double is Rango, the missing link, who serves as Heinie's double or shadow, a primitive second self who can behave in ways even more uncivilized than his master. But Rango is more than just a buffoon. This leads to a tragi-comic situation where Joe, who looks like a man has seen a ghost. Rango proves to be not only Heinie's double, but the double of the circus itself, as his death brings the shadow of death to Sonny, Gus and Abdullah.

Abdullah, the hideous papier-mâché automaton is one of the most engaging Doubles of this first section. Abdullah can be seen as Paul's Double, or Paul as Abdullah's, as he describes himself as the soul of Abdullah. Abdullah is the vessel in which Paul is kidnapped and the dungeon in which he is kept for seven years. Abdullah offers a perhaps perverse but nonetheless meaningful and exciting occupation. It also offers ironically enough, a means of escape from an equally stifling and confining life in Deptford. For Paul, this was a life of unmitigated shame as the son of a 'hoor' who in his mind was also the cause of his mother's ruin. If Abdullah is a coffin, it is one that offers the possibility of being born again. Abdullah repeats one of the main paradoxes of the novel, to ascend one must descend to become a master; one must first be a slave. The automaton belongs to a double world; he is responsible both for Paul's most dreadful imprisonment and for his most liberating step toward self-actualization.

Abdullah is shown as doubled not only from the inside but also from the outside. Paul's first description of Willard is very instructive in relation to Lind's comment on the double obsession of Bible and magic.

Willard is an inverted angel who represents a majesty of everything that has been unrealized and excluded from Paul's first home and first self. Willard is Paul's second self, an uncanny figure who is the processor of breathtaking secrets, but whose secrets are strangely familiar since they represent the most powerful and forbidden desires of the first self. For good and ill, Paul will become not only like Willard, he will become Willard's double, and thus move a step further toward becoming himself.

The shifting relationship between Paul and Willard is extremely complicated. Paul is completely reliant on Willard with a complete dependence of a child, but Willard is also reliant on Paul. Abdullah is more than a trick.

As Willard declines in illness, Cass rises in power, until Cass becomes his literal double, appearing on stage as Willard, and yet Willard's decline does not free Cass from his psychic bond. From the time when they flee Canada, the master/slave relationship becomes inverted, though they still remain inseparable psychic doubles. Jules, who is just a transformation of Willard into wild man, geek and shame of the Old South, is a neat mirror image inversion of Willard's transformation of Paul into Cass Fletcher. Yet, one has the sense that more than just a spirit of revenge prompts Jules' actions, particularly in his refusal to help Willard die, one sense that the symbiotic double relationship is still in effect and that Jules needs Willard as much as Willard needs Jules. Throughout, they remain preoccupied with each other's experience. Even after Willard's death, the Wizard remains a key feature in the makeup of Magnus' soul.

In another section, Paul enters the theatre-world, which seems at first to situate another inversion, in the form of a reversal of fortune. We soon discover that this world is in every way doubled and we are duped if we think that Paul has evaded the duplicitous life. He escapes from the shadow of Willard as Cecilia Coulas notes, only to 'emerge under the shadow of Irving,' (107) where he found jiggling and is inducted into the theatre-world. His role as Sir John's double bears a striking resemblance to his acting as Willard's Double. Once again, neither can exist without the other. Sir John needs Paul, but this need is doubled: it contains both poles of opposition and affinity. On the other side, it is explained that Paul is repugnant to Sir John.

In Jungian terms, Paul is Sir John's shadow. Though he is repulsive, he is also absolutely necessary, as he most desires youth. Paul is dependent on Sir John for his very existence. He cultivates the skill of being Nobody that he learned inside Abdullah, and fills what Milady calls his 'tabula rasa' with Sir John's very being. (168) As Ingestree first suggests and Magnus later confirms, Paul climbs into the body and soul of Sir John: "When I knew you," says Ingestree to Magnus, "You were inside Sir John, inside his body and inside his manner and voice and everything about him that a clever double could imitate." (227)

At first, Magnus doesn't very much like Ingestree's suggestion that he was trying to eat Sir John, but in the last section of the novel he admits his "wolfishness, his hunger not just to be like him but to be him—to possess him, to make him mine." (377) This relationship follows the same pattern; as Paul, now Mungo Fetch, ascends, Sir John descends, until in the final scene before Sir John's death, even his wife mistakes Fetch for John. Though, in one scene the Double kills his twin, there remains a sneaky duplicity in the fact that both Willard and Sir John live on as significant factors in the soul of Magnus Eisengrim. We find that doubling figures in the form as much as in the content of *World of Wonders*. Obviously, Magnus' autobiographical text is doubled by Lind's film-like text. From the very beginning we learn that the impetus for the telling of Magnus' story is that it will provide the sub-text or the shadow text for Robert Houdin's life, a life that is full of "false modesty, exaggerated humility greasy bourgeois assertions of respectability." (18) Certainly, the story of Magnus provides an ideal shadow text for Houdin's "gigantic whitewash job." (16) Magnus has no modesty or humanity and the world he takes us through mirrors the bland and cozy respectability about which Ingestree complains.

Lastly, we feel that doubling effect is essential to the novel's dialogical nature. Magnus tries to dominate us and the text with his monologue, but the other voices in the text provide resistance to such domination. *World of Wonders* is a novel of constant debates. Throughout the text, we experience ongoing debates between feeling and thinking, education and experience, reason and wonder, morality and textuality, simplicity and difficulty, the grotesque and the sublime and God and the Devil. Finally, the novel engenders a debate between the communicative practices of monologue and dialogue.

Bibliography

Bakhtin, Mikhail. *Rabelais and His World*, trans. Helene Iswolsky. Bloomington: Indiana University Press, 1984.

Balchandran, K. *Essays on Canadian Literature*, Prakash, Bareilly, 2001.

Ed. Bossire, Kamille R. La. and Linda M. Morra, *Robertson Davies: A Mingling of Contraries*. University of Ottawa Press, 2001.

Coulas, Cecilia. "What is Known and Long Familiar: The Uncanny Effect in *World of Wonders*," *Studies in Canadian Literature*, 15 (1990).

Davies, Robertson. *World of Wonders*. Harmondsworth: Penguin, 1977.

Godard, Barbara. "*World of Wonders*; Robertson Davies' Carnival," *Essays on Canadian Writing*, 30 (1985), 239-86.

Keith, W.J. *A Sense of Style, Studies in the Art of Fiction in English-Speaking Canada*, ECW Press, 1989.

King, Bruce. *New English Literatures, Cultural Nationalism in a Changing World*, Macmillan Press, London, 1980.

Mass, John. *Reader's Guide to the Canadian Novel*, 2nd ed., McClelland and Stewart, The Canadian Publishers, Toronto, 1987.

Nigh, Lynne Diamond. *Robertson Davies, Life, Works and Criticism*, York Press, Ontario, 1997.

Woman as a Victim of Marriage: Erika Ritter's *Automatic Pilot*

S. RAMASWAMY
Bangalore University

Mary Jane Edwards, writing about women's writing in Canada says:

> From the beginning of Canadian Literature in English, many women have written poetry, fiction, and drama, including Frances Brooke, the author of *The History of Emily Montague* (1769), the work usually called the first Canadian novel. Most have written from a recognizably female point of view in that they have created main characters who are women, and they have explored subjects of particular interest to women. Some of them have used their creative writing to develop specifically feminist ideas. A high proportion of them have been remarkably successful. One woman who exemplified all these traits was Lucy Maud Montgomery, the author of *Anne of Green Gables* (1908), the work which Mavis Gallant echoed in the title of her collection of short stories, *My Heart is Broken* (1964), and which the liberated Sarah Porlock gave away with regret in Marian Engel's *No Clouds of Glory* (1968). It was Marian Engel who suggested that one reason why women frequently tried to earn their living by writing was that it was the cheapest of the arts and could be done at home.[1]

Margaret Atwood, in her seminal work *Survival*, speaks of 'Victim Positions'. This is a suitable framework to analyse woman as victim in Erika Ritter's plays, especially her *Automatic Pilot*.[2] Erika Ritter was a student of McGill University, Montreal, and graduated in drama in 1968. Later on, she was a 'writer-in-residence' at Concordia University, again at Montreal. Her first play *A Visitor from Charleston* was staged in 1974. Her second play *The Splits* was a popular success both at Toronto Free Theatre and Actors' Theatre at Louisville in 1978. This was followed by her third play, *Automatic Pilot* which opened in January 1980 at Toronto's Adelaide Court, and reopened in the summer for an extended run, subsequently playing in seven regional theatres from Thundur Bay to Victoria. It was so successful that when the play won the Chalmes Award for 1980, Ritter split the $ 5000 cash prize with director William Lane, explaining that 'Marriage is a comparatively trivial undertaking beside finding a good director'. This is a characteristic statement by Ritter because all her plays centre round marriage—particularly the failure in marriage. She gives an apparently comic twist to her plays. Nevertheless, she deals seriously with the woman as a victim of marriage. The woman is victimised by her husband's inadequacies. There is a certain element of duality, resulting in a dilemma: 'To marry or not to marry, that is the question! The choice is a difficult one because in marriage—even in a bad marriage—there is a sense of security. But in single solitude, however much the person may love independence, it is a painful path to follow. More often than not, there is not only insecurity but confusing codes of sexual behaviour, especially when the woman is a career woman with a job. Whether she is a writer or a performer, certain complications set in. In *Automatic Pilot*, this marital problem is discussed, though in a comic context. Another 'feminist' playwright from Canada, Ann-Marie MacDonald, it may be remembered, has turned Shakespeare's Desdemona and Juliet into feminists in her comic re-working of *Othello* and *Romeo and Juliet*.

In Erika Ritter's first play *A Visitor from Charleston*, Eva the main character experiences emotional disturbances in her life because of an actor ex-boyfriend and a 'would-be' novelist, an ex-husband. In her second play *The Splits*, Megan, who is a scriptwriter, tries to 'Split' from all dependencies which diminish her as a human being. The problem is with her ex-husband who exploits her and the producers who want to alter her serious drama. Her fourth play *The Passing Scene*, produced in the Tarragon theatre in 1982, deals with the shaky marriage of a pair of journalists. Thus, it is seen from the above discussion that the central theme of Erika Ritter in her plays is the breakdown of marriage and the woman, who is the protaganist, is seen as the 'victim'. A word about the title 'Automatic Pilot'. The syndrome refers to the switch that is pulled whenever she can't face reality head-on.

The play has only four characters—Charlie 30, Alan her husband, who is also 30 and her two lovers Gene who is 23 and Nick who is 35. There is an in-built contrast between the two lovers. Nick is a macho man whereas Gene is delicate. Her husband Alan moves in a twilight zone—a complex homosexual-heterosexual character. The marital problem of Charlie is more complicated than the problems of other women of Ritter. If it is difficult to live with a man who leaves her for another woman, it is even more difficult if he leaves for another man. It is a double affront to her womanhood and in her state of mind to prove to herself that she is a proper woman, she takes on lovers who appreciate her for what she is—an attractive woman. The play in Two Acts has 8 scenes in Act I, and 5 scenes in Act 2. The 'time' of the play is the absolute present as the action takes place in the 1960s 70s and 80s. The place is Toronto. Many scenes are laid in the club called 'Canada Goose'. The language of the play is absolutely uninhibited as many four-letter words are used quite freely. It is a bit surprising, at least for the present writer, that a woman playwright is doing this. However, why not? In this twenty-first century, we have gone beyond postmodernism, postcolonialism and perhaps post-feminism and post women's lib. The language of the play is also 'quite liberated'. Drama has to use the spoken language reflecting the characters that are being portrayed. Here, Charlie uses the language of a modern North American, whether of the U.S. or Canada. It is perhaps significant that Charlie is a woman in the play though generally the name is associated with a man. She is full of paradoxes psychologically and as a performer on the stage she wears on male clothing to perform a self-deprecating comedy routine that presents her as unfeminine and unattractive as a transvestite. On the other hand, in her need to revenge her husband's homosexual choice, she becomes almost schizophrenially a nymphomaniac. Charlie seems able to operate only in the extreme. She is either monogamous or promiscuous. She seems to entertain a need to destroy herself and her boyfriend, Nick helps her in this and in keeping with the outspokeness of the language of the play, he is described 'a bastard but refreshingly honest about it'. At the risk of being risque, the following remark of Charlie, talking about being in bed with men may be quoted:

> A session with your average older man is like a screening of *The Sorrow and the Pity*. Only longer and sadder. You nod off two or three times and wake up, and he's STILL at it. 'I almost came that time', he says. Eventually, you start trying to outfox him, right? 'You came' you tell him. 'You definitely came. It's just been so long you've forgotten what it's like. But that was it. Trust me. Now, can we get some sleep?'
>
> But the real bitch about younger men is how goddaman earnest they are. One roll in the hay, and they're ready to move in—provided you're willing to help them with the algebra. (376)

The technical aspect of the play indeed is very interesting in so far as there are long speeches given to Charlie, making this a kind of 'one woman play'. The 'one woman play' is a type of 'Monologue' which is a unique stage performance which has been particularly the forte of actresses like Cecelia Loftus in England, Beatrice Herford and Ruth Draper of the United States and Beverley Simon in Canada. One of the most promising actresses who writes her own plays is Connie Clark in Yale whose performances were witnessed by the present writer, followed by a discussion of her art. Since *Automatic Pilot* is gynocentric in nature, the three men in the play are marginalized. If John Osborne's *Look back in Anger* was described as 'a one-man play', this play could be described as 'a one-woman play'. In fact, the play opens with Charlie speaking to the audience directly, being almost a stage manager (a sort of a 'Sutradhara' in Sanskrit drama). This technique has been adapted by Tennessee Williams in his *The Glass Menagerie* where Tom is both a character in the play as well as the chorus commentator outside the play. Just a few lines from the beginning of the play may be quoted here to indicate the 'mise en scene':

> Lights come up on the area of the stage designated as *The Canada Goose*, a comedy club, suggested by a mike on a stand and a spotlight. Charlie, dressed simply in a blouse and jeans, and without her glasses, stands nervously at the mike, speaking awkwardly into it without daring to remove it from the stand.
>
> Charlie to the Audience: I decided to try my luck as New Talent tonight, because at my age, it's an accomplishment to appear as new anything. . . . Actually, I'm accustomed to making a fool of myself. In real life, I'm the head writer for a soap opera. (353)

Throughout the play, there is a change of place and time, though we do return to the 'Canada Goose' later on. The passage of time is indicated in the various scenes in Stage Directions like 'A couple of weeks later'; 'A few days later'; 'Two days later'; 'A few hours later'; 'A day or two later'; 'Four weeks later'; 'The next morning'; 'Some weeks later' etc. The stage direction also indicates Charlie's state of mind. For example, 'Lights come up Charlie on the phone in her apartment. There are a couple of empty wine bottles beside her and she has a glass in her hand. She is drunk, but not inarticulate. A bouquet of roses is bundled conspicuously in a wastebasket'. (365) The next scene is 'A few hours later. Lights up in Charlie's apartment. The scene is unchanged except for an added empty bottle or two'. (366) The play ends with another long speech by Charlie, similar to the one with which the play started. It is relevant to invoke Mary Jane Edwards again by way of summing up women's writing in Canada.

> Contemporary Canadian women have continued the traditions of their predeccessors. During the 1970s, women were especially prominent in fiction, as the names of Margaret Atwood, Marian Engel, Mavis Gallant, Margaret Gibson, Margaret Laurence, and Alice Munro suggest. With few exceptions, the chief characters in the poems, novels, and plays of contemporary women writers were women . . . Many Canadian women dealt with subjects, sometimes with a specifically feminist stance, that were of particular importance to them and their sisters . . . Above all, Canadian women writers continued to be remarkably successful, as the career of Margaret Atwood showed most dramatically in the 1970s.[3]

NOTES

1. Erika Ritter, *Automatic Pilot, Modern Canadian Plays* (rev. ed.) ed. Jerry Wasserman (Talon Books, Vancouver, 1986), pp. 351-77.
2. Paul Denham and Mary Jane Edwards, "Introduction," *Canadian Literature in the 70s* (Holt, Rinehart and Winston, Toronto, 1980), p. xix.
3. *Ibid.* pp. xix-xx.

Motherhood in Margaret Laurence's *The Stone Angel* and Kamala Markandaya's *Nectar in a Sieve*: A Comparative Study

ANILA JOSEPH
Vimala College, Thrissur

Canadian literature has developed an identity and authenticity of its own over the years. Canadian fiction of the recent years has seen the emergence of a number of women writers like Margaret Atwood, Margaret Laurence, Alice Munro and Susanna Moodie. Indian writing in English has grown voluminously over the years and is fast gaining interest. In the post-Independence era, women writers like Anita Desai, Bharati Mukherjee, Nayantara Sahgal and Kamala Markandaya seem to dominate Indian fiction. It is interesting to observe that these Canadian and Indian women writers project their women characters as being independent, intelligent and assertive.

This article makes an attempt to compare the concept of motherhood in Margaret Laurence's *The Stone Angel* and Kamala Markandaya's *Nectar in a Sieve* as represented by Hagar Shipley and Rukmani respectively. The similarity in the works of these writers is intriguing. Laurence's heroine fails as wife and mother, nevertheless she survives with dignity and pride. Markandaya's heroine on the other hand succeeds as wife and mother and leads a life of pride and dignity. The problems experienced by two women, housewives of two different cultures, and their achievements provoke such a comparison. Both Canada and India are part of the Commonwealth and have been under British rule for a very long period. Hence the influence of British culture and literature on these novelists is considerable. Their writings throw a light on the societies to which they belong.

In both Margaret Laurence's *The Stone Angel* and Kamala Markandaya's *Nectar in a Sieve*, the narrator-protagonists are two (aged) widows. Hagar in *The Stone Angel* is a ninety-year old widow whereas Rukmani in *Nectar in a Sieve* is a much younger widow. Hagar possesses a determination and pride which is rarely found in a woman. This uncompromising pride helps to see her through a stormy marriage. In Hagar. Laurence gives us the picture of a wonderful woman who is able to attain self-understanding towards the end of her life and thus learns to accept herself. Rukmani on the other hand is an ordinary woman, torn between traditional values and modernism, but with an unlimited power of endurance. In the case of Rukmani pride supports her because though she is assertive, she is submissive. Here Markandaya gives us a remarkable woman who is able to negate her own personality and emerge successful. So we have two mothers, who in spite of several similarities are contrasting characters. Adrienne Rich remarks:

> all human life on the planet is born of woman. Because young human beings depend upon nurture for a much longer period than other mammals, and because of the division of labour long established in human groups, where women not only bear and suckle but are assigned almost total responsibility for children, most of us know both love and disappointment power and tenderness in the person of a woman (10)

The childhood experiences of Hagar and Rukmani are entirely different because Hagar's mother died at her birth whereas Rukmani has been nurtured and nourished by motherly love. This basic difference has played a major role in the formation of these two individuals as women and mothers. The title of the novel *The Stone Angel* is significant for its impact on Hagar. At ninety Hagar sees "this first, largest and certainly the costliest" (3) tombstone marking her mother's grave, the only connection she has with her mother.

Both these women, especially Hagar, have not been happy in their married lives and hence they do not suffer from intense grief when their husbands die. Hagar's marriage to Bram was an impulsive one, devoid of love or understanding and they were already separated at the time of Bram's death. Rukmani on the other hand loved and respected Nathan but her roots were in her children. She received fortitude from her children after Nathan's death. Moreover Rukmani is proud of her husband's property and the house he has built for her while Hagar dislikes everything related to her husband.

Rukmani is able to rebuild social relationships after Nathan's death and create a new identity as the mother of Puli, the leper boy she adopts, while Hagar is able to be a mother to Sandra Wong, and has a moving relationship with her as she would with a daughter only when she nears death. The absence of a daughter might have stood in the way of Hagar's maturity as a woman which she now achieves through Sandra. Hagar was against going to an old age home. Rukmani, after her husband's death, returns to the village and takes up her responsibilities. Hagar seems to be seeking emancipation from the clutches of her family and society while Rukmani is content with her lot.

Nectar in a Sieve commences after Rukmani returns to the village with Puli. She is the protagonist as well as the narrator. A simple peasant woman, her portrayal of life in a primitive Indian village includes the ravages of nature. She is the daughter of the headman of the village and is married to Nathan, a poor-tenant, who is much below her in social status. Rukmani being a woman of endurance adjusts well to her married life. She gives birth to a girl whom she calls Ira. This is slightly disappointing in the Indian context even to a mother like Rukmani because a male child is preferred as the first-born and she says, "I turned away and, despite myself, tears came, tears of weakness and disappointment; for what woman wants a girl for her first born." (14) As though to compensate this, with the help of Kenny, the English doctor, she bears six sons in a row. The coming of the tannery upsets the rhythm of life in the village and in Rukmani's family. They wage a perpetual fight against hunger and poverty to which are added the disasters from external forces.

Rukmani's daughter Ira is married at the age of fourteen but is forced to return to the home of her parents because she is unable to bear her husband a child. Ironically, at this time,

Rukmani is expecting her youngest child, Kuti. Ira bears no rivalry towards her mother which can be traced back to the tolerant culture in which they live as well as the perfect understanding between the mother and daughter. Due to drought, crops fail and the family is on the verge of starvation. To this, Rukmani has to witness the death of one son and two other sons leaving the land for positions she distrusts. Once again the family is caught in the grips of drought. The youngest child Kuti falls ill and Ira turns to prostitution for the purpose of saving her younger brother. Ira takes on the role of a mother. But Kuti dies and Ira later gives birth to an albino child whose father is British. Nathan is evicted from the land by the Zamindar and they decide to go to their son who is in the city. Unable to find him they live on charity and petty jobs. A leper boy Puli helps them. Nathan dies and Rukmani returns to the village with Puli whom she takes care of and cures. This is the endearing story of Rukmani as she narrates it. Kamala Markandaya idealizes motherhood through Rukmani. She is the ideal housewife in the traditional sense, but forced to face the modern predicaments, "she also rises against the social forces confronting her, remaining within the sanctity of her home" (Geetha, 12)

The Stone Angel is the first novel by Laurence written with Canadian background. Hagar's narrative alternates between the past and the present. Her marriage to Bram is an impulsive one devoid of love. She is not happy at the birth of her first son Marvin as she felt he was too much a Shipley. Ironically she has to stay with this son in her old age. Hagar remains aloof from the family till her second son John is born whom she considered to be her own son, since he was like her father. Again her pride makes her leave her husband with her younger son. Bram's reaction on hearing about her plan to leave is "if you're going go." (142) She pleads that she is leaving for the sake of John, "It's for you, for your sake. Don't you know that." (140) But John betrays her trust by deserting her to join his father who is sick. She realizes that John is ashamed of her job as housekeeper, but she suppresses it. Again his decision to marry Arlene, the daughter of Lottie whom Hagar always detested, hurts her. She drifts apart from this beloved son and his death is a fatal blow. The shock is too much and here too her pride proved to be stronger than maternal feelings. "I wouldn't cry in front of strangers, whatever it cost me." (242) Rukmani too had to witness the death of her son Raja. She suffers a mother's agony: "The sorrow within me is not for this body which has suffered and in suffering has let slip the spirit, but for you, my son." (90) And when the officials from the tannery warn her not to make claims of compensation her answer revèals the pain that only a mother can feel: "what compensation is there for death." (91) It is beyond her comprehension. All she can understand is that her son is dead.

Hagar Shipley, the narrator's voice, dominates the text as she examines and reconstructs her own life story. In a retrospective vein, she recounts her suffering and isolation because she feels the need for self-understanding as she feels "choked with it now, the incommunicable years, everything that happened and was spoken or not spoken." (296) She tries to unify memories of the past experiences and the present so as to attain an insight. Rukmani on the other hand is born with a capacity for adjustment and so is able to make her home a pleasant one. She experiences no isolation and does not feel the need for a self-examination. As the central character and protagonist, she narrates rural India as seen through her eyes, especially the picture of an Indian village. Unlike Hagar, who loves only one of her sons, Rukmani loves all her children and readily becomes a mother to Puli. Nurturing is part and parcel of Indian motherhood. Kamala Markandaya idealizes motherhood through her.

This motherliness is found in Hagar only when she nears death. It is lacking throughout her life. This is probably because she has never known a mother's love as her mother died at her birth. Now nearing her death she realizes her failure, especially her inability to be a mother to her dying brother. There we see a contrast between Hagar and Ira.

Rukmani's daughter, Ira, turns to prostitution to save her brother who was dying. This maternal instinct she learns from her mother. She cannot suffer to see her brother starve and nurturing is the primary function of a mother. Here she is a symbol of endurance and sacrifice and given the similar situation scores much higher than Hagar in spite of her moral degradation in society's view. Realizing this failure, Hagar softens in old age and she is gentle to her granddaughter. She accepts gracefully the gift of perfume offered by Tina "on my dressing-table is a bottle of *eau de cologne*, given me by Tina. . . . I dab a little on my wrists." (33) This signals a new stage in her life. Her pride dissolves and she realizes that her stubbornness will no longer be sufficient to suppress all the emotions she has refused to allow herself. Her gentle feeling towards Tina is the first sign of change, one that brings her closer to the mother and the values represented by that figure. "The woman who has felt 'unmothered' may seek mothers all her life" (Rich, 242) and this is what Hagar has been doing till now. But with the new attitude she develops a new outlook. She exhibits an increasing ability to receive mothering love and offer love in return. In effect, Margaret Laurence is also glorifying motherhood.

Hagar has never been able to perform those functions that transform "a woman from childhood to womanhood in an emotional and psychological sense, such as the mothering gestures she is asked to give her dying brother, or an act of responsive love to her husband. This inability to respond to the need of the male for her feminine nature, is, ironically, rooted in the mother-daughter relationship." (Buss, 15)

The mother's nurturing influence is very essential in a child's early life. If this nurturing and protection is absent from a girl's life, she fails to become a truly adult woman capable of offering love to those around her. So emotionally Hagar is in a child-like state waiting to be born through the mother's love.

Her first experience of this is Doris who is more a mother than daughter-in-law. Her strong pride begins to crack as her helplessness grows and she becomes more dependent on Doris Then its Mrs. Steiner, the Jewish mother at the old folks home. To Mrs. Steiner's question "Do you get used to life?" she admits "I never got used to a blessed thing" (104) and for the first time realized the need to get used to some of the things in life. The experience at Shadow Point enhances this. Hagar relates to

Murray Lees as if he is a woman. At this point: "he serves a symbolically poetic role in Hagar's life as he is the catalyst by which she is released from her guilt into a more blessed state. He offers Hagar a communion of wine and crackers which unlocks her grief and guilt from her past lack of motherliness." (Buss, 18) While narrating the story of John's death to Lees, she weeps a mother's grief which she never did at the time of the real death.

The hospital becomes for her a symbol of womanhood and the nurse is a conventional symbol of the mother as nurturer. The three ladies she meets there also represent a new view of womanhood for Hagar, a state into which she is now moving. She finds Elva's ability to respond to each individual's need marvelous and this makes her lie to Marvin, "You've been good to me, always. A better son than John." (304) This was something she should have admitted long ago. Doris and Marvin take good care of her but she refuses to acknowledge it. Again Mrs. Dobereiner's attempts to find happiness in life so that she can be released from pain appeals to Hagar and they sing together in enjoyment. The greatest influence is Mrs. Reilly who is able to retain her maternal sense in her moment of need and therefore relate it positively to her daughter. This helps Hagar to develop a touching relationship with Sandra Wong. Sandra becomes her daughter and this mothering act completes her maturity as a mother. The greatest maternal act that Hagar performs is when she gets up from her bed in her infirmity to help Sandra relieve her bladder. This is one of the greatest mothering acts besides nurturing. These small incidents show the change in Hagar. She is now able to give and receive love with her symbolic daughter, admit fear and give blessing to her son. Here we have the motherhood of Hagar complete.

Rukmani in *Nectar in a Sieve* has been a source of perennial love and success to her family. This is seen right from the beginning in the way she tends her garden. She nurtures it like a child watching the plants grow and bear fruit. This is symbolic of her nature. It shows how she is eagerly waiting to mother the children she will beget. She bears the brunt of all that happens to her family. Kamala Markandaya has pictured her as the breadwinner through her hard physical labour when they turn to stone-breaking in the city. She is an embodiment of motherhood. Even when her peaceful life is shattered, with the coming of the tannery and the outrages of nature, "the binding influence of Rukmani helps them to survive the ordeal." (Geetha, 13) As Uma Parameswaran says, it "is the story of the faceless peasant who stands silhouetted in the unending twilight of Indian agrarian bankruptcy" (233). Her spirit of endurance does not break down at any point. Her surrender and independence to her husband and children are remarkable. This gives her the strength to go on undeterred even when her husband cannot support her and the older children leave home. (In the case of Hagar the reverse happens. It is she who is running away from her family).

The mother-daughter relationship absent in *The Stone Angel* is very strong in *Nectar in a Sieve*. In spite of the setbacks suffered by Rukmani, she cares and supports Ira at every stage. Ira too, like her mother, is a symbol of endurance. She is a silent hard-working girl helping her mother as she can. Again she proves the mother in her when she takes care of her younger brother who is ill and dying due to starvation. She sells her body to nurture him, but he dies ultimately and Ira is left with the illegitimate child she gave birth to. Rukmani is traumatized by the incident, yet she remains the mother who protects and nurtures her young.

Unlike Hagar, Rukmani believes that life is for living and therefore accepts the inevitable rather than evade it. This helps her to cope with the vagaries of life. Her children too get nourishment from their mother's ability to rebuild rather than crumble in the face of calamity. In her encounters with the challenges of life, she is able to transform these challenges into finer values and thus make life worth living. Hagar runs away from situations that are challenging and hence finds that she is always isolated. Rukmani mellows with maturity and becomes more dynamic. She does not become hardened and turns out to be the centre point of her family. In fact she is the mother figure that unites the whole structure of the novel. She is the symbol of endurance, the archetypal Mother Earth from which all can draw sustenance.

She is admirable as the mother of six children whose courageous spirit remains undaunted even when threatened from all quarters. She is a good wife and a great mother whose only ambition is the welfare of her children. The most trying situation for her as a mother is when Kenny decides to employ her son Selvam in his hospital. It is a difficult situation for her as people consider it as a favour from Kenny for their clandestine relationship. Here "Rukmani is vindicated not by any social code but by her son's faith in her" (Indra, 71). This is one of the proudest and most rewarding experiences for a mother.

Rukmani "proves that within the traditional role, she can accommodate her other roles as a human being; and not through alienation and self-laceration, but through expansion and communion a deeper self-knowledge can be attained" (Indra, 71). Hagar also attains this self-knowledge, but through different means. This could to a large extent be attributed to the differences in the image of woman as conceived by the East and West. As Swami Vivekananda has pointed out "the ideal of womanhood in India is motherhood, that marvellous, unselfish, all suffering, ever forgiving mother." "In the west woman is wife." (10). So to be a mother is the greatest blessing in the Indian tradition as women are looked upon by society from this point of view.

By portraying the mother as the main protagonist, Margaret Laurence and Kamala Markandaya have effectively delineated the role of the mother in their novels *The Stone Angel* and *Nectar in a Sieve*. Though these two women differ in their role as mothers, they have a lot in common. Both possess strength of character, vigour, vitality, heroic impulse and remarkable integrity. They are survivors in the very sense of the word because they remain heroic and upright to the very end. A survivor is one who can combat with adverse situations and overcome it courageously. The spirit of survival teaches them endurance without which everything boils down to mere reconciliation and passivity. It is because of this quality which is inherent in Hagar that she is able to achieve motherhood towards the end of her life. Both these mothers are shaped by the environment in which they live. They are powerful, authoritative beings, who fight for their existence in a positive manner and hence survive with dignity. It is surprising that in spite of these similarities in character, they differ in their role as mothers.

Margaret Laurence and Kamala Markandaya are pioneers in their respective literary worlds. The experiences of these novelists have gone into these writings and so comparison becomes worthwhile. The retrospective technique used by the novelists through which the past and present are intermingled reveals the formation, growth and maturity of these mothers. Characterization of the protagonist is given utmost importance and they emerge as fully developed individuals. At the same time they remain within the womanly faculties because a mother's fulfillment and survival is from the strong bonding that she has with her children. Woman's strength matures through her cultural and emotional feelings and in this respect both these novels are wonderful treatises on the strength of woman.

Margaret Laurence and Kamala Markandaya have a similar colonial past. It is an interesting coincidence that *The Stone Angel* is Laurence's first Canadian novel and *Nectar in a Sieve* too is Markandaya's first novel. What makes the study exciting is the fact that two women writers of two different countries with different cultural background should have so much similarity in their writing. Probably this goes to prove that mothers' experiences may differ from society to society at the social level but remain universal at the emotional and psychic level.

Bibliography

Helen M. Buss, "Mother and Daughter Relationship in the Manawaka Works of Margaret Laurence," *English Literary Studies*, 1985.

P.S. Chauhan, "Kamala Markandaya: Sense and Sensibility," *The Literary Criterion*, 12.2-3 (1976) 134-47.

P. Geetha, "Feminism in the Novels of Kamala Markandaya." *Indian Women Novelists*, ed. R.K. Dhawan. New Delhi. Prestige, 1993. 18 Vols. Vol. 2. 9-21

C.T. Indra, "The True Voice of Endurance: A Study of Rukmani in Markandaya's Nectar in a Sieve." *Feminism and Recent Fiction in English*. New Delhi: Prestige, 1991. 64-71.

Margaret P. Joseph, *Kamala Markandaya*. New Delhi: Arnold Heinemann, 1980.

Margaret Laurence, *The Stone Angel*. McClelland and Stewart, 1964.

Kamala Markandaya, *Nectar in a Sieve* (New York: The John Day Company. 1954).

Kamala Markandaya. Writers of the Indian Diaspora Series. 2000.

N. Ramachandran Nair and M. Snehaprabha, ed., *Canadian Studies: New Perspectives* (New Delhi: Creative)

Pandey, Sudhakar, ed. *Perspectives on Canadian Fiction*. Prestige. New Delhi, 1994.

Uma Parameswaran, "India for the Western Reader: A Study of Kamala Markandaya's Novels," *Texas Quarterly*, 11.2. (1968) 231-47

Adrienne Rich, *Of Woman Born: Motherhood as Experience and Institution* (W.W. Norton, New York: 1976).

Christian Riegel, ed., *Challenging Territory: The Writings of Margaret Laurence*. Alberta, The University of Alberta Press, 1997.

M.F. Salat, *The Canadian Novel: A Search for Identity*. New World Literature Series, 68. B.R., New Delhi, 1993.

Meena Shirwadkar, *Image of Woman in the Indo-Anglian Novel*. New Delhi: Sterling, 1979.

Swami Vivekananda, *Women of India*. Ramakrishna Math, Madras, 1900.

George Woodcock, ed., *A Place to Stand On--Essays by and about Margaret Laurence*. Vol. IV. Western Canadian Literary Documents Series.

Trial and Liberation in Global Context: A Comparative Study of Sharon Pollock's *Blood Relations* and Vijay Tendulkar's *Silence! The Court is in Session*

R. VEDAVALLI
Bharathi Women's College, Chennai

A society which has enslaved half of the humanity just on the difference of sex, the algebraic sum of chromosomes cannot claim itself as civilized or progressed. Simon de Beauvoir's statement that 'one is not born a woman but becomes one' expresses in a nutshell the cause for woman's subordination. During 1970s and 80s, 'Feminism' was broadly defined as a politic emerging from a common experience of women all over the world. Sexuality was the major cause of oppression and patriarchy is perpetuated through family and heterosexual relations. This led to the rejection of marriage, heterosexuality and the family by the radical feminists. The demands of the suffocating patriarchal system on women as mothers, wives and daughters have led to rebellious thinking and attempts to break away from the patriarchal institutions like marriage and family.

The social status and condition of women in Canada and India remain identical in many ways. In the later part of the 20th century, women in Canada and India took their courage from modern education and the resultant economic independence and began to question the established conventions of patriarchal society. Thanks to the process of modernization and globalization and the complex phenomenon of interaction with the existing patriarchy. Feminist literature, writings by women and writings about women, reflects this phenomenon and voices the voiceless. The present paper attempts to study how the playwrights Sharon Pollock and Vijay Tendulkar have delineated their women characters in their attempt to make women visible and audible. Their plays *Blood Relations*[1] and *Silence! The Court is in Session*[2] question the imposition of patriarchal values and its restrictive norms on women. They expose the sociological and psychological factors that sustain the gender inequality and suggest ways to change them.

Sharon Pollock, a committed artist, deals with the historical and sociological problems. Pollock considers theatre as an instrument of moral enquiry and firmly believes that a play should provide meaningful discussions about issues that concern humanity. Her plays *Walsh* (1973) and *Komagata Maru Incident* are docudramas that deal with historical events in social and political fields, in an attempt to give correct history. Her next play *One Tiger to a Hill* urges prison reforms and condemns institutional complacency and public apathy. It is *Blood Relations* which changes Pollock's identity from a social playwright to that of a feminist and her other plays *Generations*, *Whiskey Six* and *Doc* endorse this label. However, Pollock objects to the ideological labels like social playwright or feminist. In an interview, she affirms "Of course, it says something about women today. It says something about me today, things that I have felt."[3]

Blood Relations deals with private life, the politics of family. It is based on the real life incident of the famous axe murder case. Lizzie Borden, a new England spinster was charged of the murder of her father and stepmother in the year 1892, and later acquitted of the crime. What fascinates is the ambiguity surrounding the murder, "who did this?" as often questioned by Lizzie's actress friend and Emma, Lizzie's sister.

The action of the play takes place in Fall River, near Boston. It is a re-enactment of the crucial events of the murder of 1892 except the murder. The scenes move back and forth from 1892 to 1902. The play is set as a play within the play. It all started as a game by the actress to get the truth out of Lizzie. It is agreed that the actress is to play the role of Miss Lizzie Borden and Lizzie to do the role of Bridget, the Irish maid in the household of Mr. Bordens, who later testified in the trials. She has to do the role in order to paint the background to the actress.

The events of both 1892 and 1902 are juxtaposed throughout. Through this technique, the past, the present and (by implication) the future are all made to bear on one another. The first act presents the day before the murder while the scenes on the day of the murder are presented in the second act, that begins with the departure of Emma, Lizzie's sister for the weekend. Lizzie, the 34-year-old, strong-willed, rebellious, Victorian spinster feels the very atmosphere of her house, stifling and suffocating with no air of freedom. She dreams of living in her own farmhouse or in the beautiful small house on the hill with a view.

> Lizzie: I know it. . . . I want out of all this. . . . I hate this house, I hate. . . . I want out. Try to understand how I feel. . . . Why can't I do something? . . . Eh? I mean . . . I could . . . I could go into your office . . . learn how to keep books? (598)

Mr. Borden, Lizzie's father is a symbol of Victorian patriarchy. He is very rigid and traditional. After the death of Lizzie's mother, he has taken Abigail as his second wife. Lizzie hates the very sight of her and her father's surrender to her. Further, when she comes to know that her father is going to transfer their farm on Abigail's name at the instigation of Abigail's brother Harry, Lizzie gets infuriated. She cannot tolerate Harry. But Mr. Borden accepts to transfer the farm as he believes that Harry, being the only male member of the family, will look after his children and wife after his death.

Emma also lives under similar conditions but she is very docile. Lizzie vehemently opposes the act of her father as she knew that it will come under the management of Harry. She claims her right in her father's property and wants to be left alone to lead her life. She finds fault with Emma for not joining with her in the struggle.

> I've a legal right to one-third because I am his flesh and blood. (601)
>
> I thought you could talk to him, really talk to him, make him understand that we're people, *individual people*, and we have to live separate lives, and his will should make it possible for us to do that. And the farm can't go to Harry. (613)

She also rejects the idea of her father to get her married to Johnny MacLeod, a widower with three children.

> You want me living my life by the Farmers' Almanac; having everyone over for Christmas dinner; waiting up for my husband; and *serving at socials*. (596)
> He's looking for a housekeeper and it isn't going to be me! (597)

She is such a strong-willed person, that she can't be forced to do what she doesn't want to do.

> No! There's something you don't understand, Papa. You can't make me do one thing that I don't want to do. I' m going to keep on doing just what I want when I want—like always! (600)

Mr. Borden also is well aware of this quality of Miss Lizzie, The argument over the issue of farm between Lizzie and Mr. Borden makes him very angry. In an angry mood Borden takes an axe and kills the pigeons, the pets of Lizzie. She is shocked at the sight of the innocent birds dying and feels pity and remorse.

> He killed my birds! He took the axe and he killed them! Emma, I ran out and held them in my hands, I felt their hearts throbbing and pumping and the blood gushed out of their necks, it was all over my hands, don't you care about that? (613)

Lizzie hates her father for this act and considers her stepmother to be the cause for all this. She kills her stepmother finally and in her opinion it is an act of cleansing the house of the evil, destroying the evil to protect the good.

After the murder, Lizzie plans to go away from the house to make her father believe that Mrs. Borden was killed by some burglars. But before she could leave, her father returns home. Lizzie behaves like a very good girl, makes him believe that she will be obedient, gets a kiss from him (perhaps the farewell kiss) and hums him to sleep. The actress Lizzie raises the hatchet to kill Mr. Borden and the play within the play ends with a block out.

Emma, from the day of the murder till the replay of the action of the murder in 1902, goes on asking "Did Lizzie commit the murder?." Lizzie answers Emma: "Did you never stop and think that if I did, then you were guilty too." (634) Then the actress says, "Lizzie, you did." But Lizzie answers "I didn't. You did." The play ends there and the question "who did this?" remains unanswered.

The play has deeper levels of meaning. Lizzie's answer to Emma 'you were guilty too' signifies that if Lizzie is guilty, Emma is also guilty because it is Emma who brought up Lizzie like a mother and moulded her. Emma stands for the society which has failed in its duty. On the day of the murder, in the morning, Lizzie pleaded with Emma not to go out but to speak to their father. Emma went out for a weekend trip in order to escape from the grim situation in the house. She failed to act at the right time and so is a coward. It is the society which didn't care for Lizzie, her feelings and rightful desires, that has led her to commit the murder. It is the society that has to be blamed for making Lizzie turn to violence. In the play within the play, the actress raising her hatchet to kill her father goes to prove that given the situation any woman would have done the same, and the society is responsible for the murder.

Killing of the pigeons symbolizes the destruction of innocence and beauty, the inherent feminine qualities. The tyrant male, in order to perpetuate patriarchy, has killed the woman and her freedom. Lizzie's killing of her father and stepmother is only an act of *Samhara,* destroying the evil to save the innocent and meek. When time requires, a woman becomes 'Kali,' destroys the evil and paves the way for the perpetuation of the good. So, in the scales of *dharma*, Lizzie is not guilty of murder and is finally liberated, symbolically from the clutches of patriarchy.

Vijay Tendulkar, the famous avant-grade Marathi angry young man, in his plays voices his anguish at the prevailing social conditions and the role modern man has to play. Like Sharon Pollock, Tendulkar also bases his dramas on real life experiences, incidents, news items etc. As he himself has remarked, "the basic urge has always been to let out my concerns vis-à-vis 'my' reality: the human condition as I perceive it."

In the play *Silence! The Court is in Session*, Tendulkar questions the imposition of patriarchal values on women and its restrictive norms. In the play, Leela Benare, a member of a theatre group which comes to perform at a village is involved in a mock-trial cunningly planned by her co-actors. But it turns out to be a real trial of her private life and Benare is accused of infanticide, immorality and unwed motherhood. Benare's defence of herself in the form of a monologue (a reminder of Nora's declaration of independence) exposes the hypocrisy and double standards of the society that failed to respect her natural feelings and the men who used her body only as a commodity.

First, at the age of fourteen, when Benare did not even know what sex is, she is exploited by her maternal uncle in the name of love.

> Why, I was hardly fourteen! I didn't even know what sin was. . . . I insisted on marriage. So I could live my beautiful lovely dream openly. Like everyone else! But all of them—my mother too—were against it. And my brave man turned tail and ran. Such a rage—I felt such a rage against him then—I felt like smashing his face in public and spitting on it! (117)

The position, responsibility and respectability attached to maternal uncle is very high in Indian culture. If a child's father dies unfortunately, it is the maternal uncle who takes up the responsibility of looking after his sister and her child. But here it is the maternal uncle who has ruined Benare's life. Benare tries to commit suicide by jumping from the parapet. But she does not die. Being stung once, she is very careful. Yet the biological impulse would not leave her. Now she has crossed thirty. She falls in love with Prof. Damle out of admiration for his intellect.

> This love is intelligent. It is love for an unusual intellect. It isn't love at all—it's worship! But it was the same mistake. I offered up my body on the altar of my worship. And my intellectual god took the offering—and went his way. He didn't want my mind, or my devotion—he didn't care about them! (118)

Prof. Damle who fell in love only with her body, leaves her pregnant and refuses to marry. The fact that she is going to be a mother makes her happy and she loves the body for the sake of the tender little bud:

> a tender little bud—of what will be a lisping, laughing, dancing little life—my son—my whole existence! I want my body now for him—for him alone. He must have a mother . . . a father to call his own—a house—to be looked after—he must have a good name. (118)

In her desire to give a good name to her child in the society, an identity in the form of a father, Benare begs her male friends one after another to marry her, putting aside her sense of shame and dignity. But now having known the secret, they mock at her and make her stand in the witness box to pass judgement. Her plight reminds one of Draupadi in the court of Kauravas. All 'Duryodhanas' stand around and laugh at Benare. But no Lord Krishna comes to her rescue.

Now, her plea to allow her to live in peace with her child falls on deaf ears. The same society which deifies motherhood, "We have acknowledged woman as the mother of mankind .Our culture enjoins us to perpetual worship of her" (79) would not allow a woman to give birth to her child because she is not married. The Judge (Kashikar), who shared the lofty idea that mother and the motherland are superior even to heaven passes the judgment that she should abort her child as no memento of her sin should remain for future generations. Though completely shaken by the judgment, Benare determines not to allow this to happen.

Both Lizzie and Benare in their battle against patriarchy end up breaking the social institutions like family and marriage. It is interesting to note that many striking similarities are there in the two plays under discussion. Both the writers have adopted similar stage techniques like play-within-the-play and role-within-the-role. The structure of the play helps the writers to maintain ambiguity. The reader is left to wonder "who did the murder?" in *Blood Relations* and does Benare abort the child or give birth to it? in the play *Silence! The Court is in Session!*

Above all, this technique allows the writers to mix the audience and performers and thereby the writers involve the society in their struggle against patriarchy. It is based on the feminist belief that the society does not exclude men and the upliftment of women could be possible only with the change in the attitude of men.

Still, the difference of culture from which the writers have come could be perceived in their attitude towards this problem. Lizzie, the product of the West, could easily throw away the shackles of marriage, family or children. She liberates herself through violent means. She could easily avoid marriage and still flirt with Dr. Patrick. But Benare's sufferings are more due to her orientation in Indian culture and the norms and double standards of Indian society. A learned lawyer like Sukatme, the protector of human rights, says *Na Stri Swatantryamarhati* i.e. a woman is not fit for independence and the reason he gives for this statement is "woman bears the grave responsibility of building up the high values of society." (115) One wonders how a slave could build up high values.

The statement of Kashikar, a learned judge, "What I say is, our society should revive the old custom of child marriage. Marry off the girls before puberty. All this promiscuity will come to a full stop" (98) mocks at the great work done by our social reformers to put an end to child marriage. The double standard is quite evident when the society forgives and forgets people like Prof. Damle and points its finger towards Benare for all the sins. Benare is not permitted to become an unwed mother lest she spoil the society. India is a land of Kunti, who could not bring up her great son Karna, though he might be the son of the Sun god. Benare is neither allowed to die, nor permitted to give birth to her child. Here, the pertinent question arises: what will be the future of women in such a stern, rigid society in an era of technological advancement where test tube babies and cloning babies have come into existence?

In the West, single parent family is an accepted norm. But in India the stigma attached to an unwed mother will not allow her to live in dignity. The result is the increasing rate of abortion, infanticide and orphan children. Government's measures to protect the orphans may give them a place to live in but not a home. It is high time that government looks into the matter to make necessary changes in the law.

With all sufferings, Benare is not violent like Lizzie because she is rooted in the Indian culture of love and motherhood. She has an aim in life to become a mother and bring up her loving child. In this era of globalization, the West has to learn this lesson from the East that motherhood will not deprive a woman of her rights but will make her complete.

NOTES

1. Sharon Pollock, *Blood Relations*, *Modern Canadian Drama*, ed. Richard Plant (Queen's University, 1984).
2. Vijay Tendulkar, *Silence! The Court is in Session*, *Five Plays* (Delhi: Oxford University Press, 1992).
3. Robert Wallace and Cynthia Zimmerman, *Conversations with English-Canadian Playwrights* (Toronto: The Watchhouse Press, 1982), p. 117.

"Lesbian Continuum": Gender Oppositionalism in Canadian Literature

D. PARAMESWARI
Madurai-Kamaraj University, Madurai

"Lesbian Continuum," according to Adrienne Rich, denotes forms of primary intimacy between and among women, including the sharing of a rich inner life, the bonding against male tyranny, the giving and receiving of practical and political support."[1] The concept defies the narrow male-oriented perception of lesbianism and helps to better comprehend female psychology.

Lesbian writers create a significant record by oppositionalising male and even female writing. They check society's perception of the lesbians. In a lesbian novel one gets to know what it means to view a budding culture from a lesbian perspective. By showing communities where lesbianism is central rather than marginal this literature suggests that society need not be based on heterosexuality alone. It stresses the need for changing conservative attitudes to gender issues, questioning gender norms, defying and deliberating on male-determined society and its values. This new genre of writing portrays a community where the conventions of the patriarchal society no longer apply and wherein a counter culture is constructed. The different versions of lesbian experience depicted here consolidate the lesbian community and encourage a bonding, physical and spiritual, among women themselves.

Psychologists have different views on lesbian relationship. Psychologists categorize all human beings into three groups, based on the predominance of sexual tendencies: heterosexuals, bisexuals and homosexuals. The heterosexuals are those people who establish normal sexual relationship with the members of the opposite sex; the bisexuals are the ones who are erotically interested in both the sexes, whereas the homosexuals are inclined more towards the members of their own sex than towards those of the other. According to Havelock Ellis,[2] most of the human beings possess all these three tendencies in different degrees and therefore develop homosexual inclination at some stage or the other in their life, though the urge may not be strong enough in many people to manifest itself in practice. Some might indulge in homosexuality due to forced separation from the opposite sex and such victims resume normal heterosexual life when brought back to the heterosexual partner. Among those who may rightly be called homosexuals, the urge may be either latent or overt. Latent homosexuals express their inverted sex impulse in their manners and attitude, whereas the overt members give vent to their impulse by choosing members of their own sex and gratifying themselves erotically. With these overt homosexuals, their perversion remains mostly permanent and unchanging and they subsequently grow immuned to the emotional and sexual allurements from the opposite sex. Thus, for Havelock Ellis, the conservative psychologist, homosexuality is a perversion and an unnatural behaviour. To Kraft-Ebing, the lesbians and lesbian manners are the products of congenital inversion, and that way unnatural. Joan Blackwood, a lesbian sociologist argues "Though it has long been recognized that there is no particular connection between 'morality' and 'naturalness' many critics persist in believing that "whatever is unnatural is immoral."[3]

Numerous psychological factors contribute to homosexuality. Some psychologists agree that "rearousal of oedipal fantasies has been . . . a cause of homosexuality in some individuals. Unresolved oedipal fantasies are revived and the overwhelming guilt feelings over such incestuous desires block [normal heterosexual life]."[4] The result is homosexuality. The disturbed emotional condition of a child due to the birth of the next infant might sometimes generate this kind of sexual deviation in later years. With the addition of the new arrival in the family, the elder child who has been so far receiving all attention from its mother feels frustrated. At this time, if it meets an affectionate member of the same sex, it finds in her "a substitute mother upon whom [it] can lean with child-like dependence"[5]; the situation gradually instills homosexual impulse. Unhappy marital experience of the parents may be yet another factor contributing towards homosexuality. Their incompatible marital relationship produces a strong hatred in the child for heterosexual alliance which it finds as one involving uncomfortable interactions.[6]

Feminist psychologists have differing views on lesbianism. Adrienne Rich asserts that heterosexuality is a political strategy of patriarchy meant to promote and satisfy the sexual needs of the male. Concepts like 'the angel at home,' 'home sweet home' and sacredness of the home because of the angelic presence of the women were promoted by patriarchy. According to Nancy Chodorov, since women have women as mothers, the mother remains a primary internal object to the girl so that heterosexual relationships are on the model of non-exclusive, secondary relationship to her. Lesbianism, then, is a better alternative paradigm for heterosexuality.

Lesbian literature is a genre that defies firm categorization since there can be no single definition. Further, it is very difficult to specify as to what prominent features constitute lesbian writing. Whatever its controversial components are, there is consensus at least on two points: i) the author must be a lesbian, and ii) the central characters are lesbians. An author is not considered a lesbian writer if she has not published at least one work with overt 'queer' content. Novels with an apparent lesbian overtone but written by heterosexual women do not qualify as lesbian novels, an instance being Mary McCarthy's *The Group*. Lesbian works with distinct lesbian contents, but written by men, such as Henry James' *The Bostonians* or Compton Mackenzies' *Extraordinary Women* do not come within the purview of lesbian literature. Those works by heterosexuals that portray lesbians as nothing more than foils to more significant heterosexual main characters do not form part of lesbian literary culture. Next, although the audience does not have to be exclusively lesbians, the work ought to have a particular appeal to the lesbians. Jeanette

Winterson's *Oranges Are Not the Only Fruits* attracts more number of heterosexual and less homosexual readers. Willa Cather, one of the America's premier literary artists in the early twentieth century, reflected her own lesbianism in her creation of strong women characters and in the exploration of the male homosexuality.

There has been a long history of lesbian writing. Radcliffe Hall who lived her lesbianism openly and proudly was condemned for her work, *The Well of Loneliness*. The conservative attitudes banned the book as obscure. The work opposed the treatment meted out for lesbians such as physical and verbal harassment, devaluation and indifference. It caused a loud scandal as it endorsed the view that lesbians should have a place in society and not be shunned as social pariahs. Hall's novel, however, helped several lesbians to discover that they were not alone.

Not all lesbian novelists in the later years felt comfortable talking openly about lesbianism in their writing, since blatant lesbianism could result in getting a novel banned, or discourage its publisher. These writers frequently disguise the lesbian contents of their works, a very good illustration being Virginia Woolf's *Orlando: A Biography*. It explores the gender and sexual identification in a text that revolves around the adventures of Orlando who is transformed from male to female over a few centuries. Strictly speaking, this is not a lesbian text as it neither has an overt lesbian content nor an appeal to the lesbian audience.

Marie Claire Blais, an immensely prolific presence on both the Quebec and the international French literary scene, herself a lesbian and a heterosexual, went to the United States in 1963 and lived a lesbian life with the painter, Mary Meigs and little later attempted to work out a three way relationship among herself, Meigs and Meigs's lover of fourteen years Barbara Deming. After an implicit version of the homosexual life of her gay male protagonist in *The Wolf*, Blais unequivocally turns her attention to lesbian life in *Les nuits de l'underground*, a more honest version of the lesbian passion which Blais finds at once lyrical, mystical and liberating. Her novel *L'ange de la solitude* is a visionary account of a literary commune composed of young lesbians affected by the death, at twenty, of one of their members. Blais remains enormously productive despite the reluctance among her readers and critics to accept the gay and lesbian contents of her fiction. Although gay and lesbian Quebecois literature has only a forty-year history, it has flourished and seems destined to merge into mainstream Quebecois literature.

Nicole Brossard, a feminist and lesbian, a Quebecoise writer and editor, is radical in her approach to gender, sexuality and literary creation. Brossard's native Montreal figures in her work as a site of writing and renewal. She was born into a prestigious family that included a Supreme Court judge and into a repressive culture controlled by the Catholic Church. She credits her personal independence to a family tradition of high deals and liberal ideas and to her suffragist paternal grandmother. She reads the institution of motherhood as forced reproduction, stating that it has "killed [her] womb." She declared war against heterosexist ideas and patriarchal institutions. In 1972, she met a young gym teacher, Germaine, and the next summer they left for six weeks in Greece where they became lovers. In 1978, Brossard met Marisa, the woman of her life, and celebrated her love in *Picture Theory* where she invents border crossers and radical city dwellers; she assures that her "synchronous women will modify the horizon, using the science of energy." She contends that although woman, a projection of phallic desire and will to power, lies suspended over our heart like a threat to extinction; to intervene through writing is to create an alternative reality. As she states in *These Our Mothers*, "to write I am a woman is full of consequences."

A turning point in both women's and lesbian writing in Canada was the anthology, *Women and Words* with Betsy Warland as the collection's coordinator. Warland writes about positioning herself against the universalism of imperial male discourse in the interest of what she calls "multiversatility, transversing and transcendence."

With the forming of the Queer Nation in the late 80s in the US, the gay/lesbian community reclaimed the word 'queer' from its pejorative association. The queer culture and the queer literature were subsequently developed in vast proportions. In fact, Canadian prominent lesbian writers such as Dionne Brand, Helen Humphreys, Ann Marie MacDonald, Marion Douglas, Camilla Gibb, Jane Eaton Hamilton, Elizabeth Ruth, Linda Little, Lydia Kwa and Shani Mootoo have won mainstream Canadian lesbian awards. We have today annotated bibliography of Canadian lesbians and bisexual women, alongside a tendency to invite some of these terrific writers to read at a queer literary night or a lesbian mystery night. Such is the present socio cultural trend in Canada.

Against this background the present paper attempts to analyse a few Canadian lesbian short stories. The Toronto based activist, Judith Nichol's story, "Lesbians in Poughkeepsie" controverts the issue of the 'experience' and 'institution' of motherhood, to quote the words of Rich. One of the lesbians laments, "I have two girls and they are killing me. . . . They are breaking my heart about six times a day."[7] Andrea continues, "the other bad thing about kids is the breast feeding and the saggy tits. My girls are fifteen and seventeen and they've pretty near sucked me dry." (6) Anabella, the other companion is violent towards her son when she finds him stubborn and demanding. "Without speaking Anabella stood up, rolling the boy off her lap. He landed with a soft thud on the floor." (9) Feminist extremists like Shulamith Firestone advocate artificial reproduction since motherhood, in their view, keeps a woman in life-long slavery. Adrienne Rich; on the other hand, declares that the 'institution' of motherhood i.e., features such as rape and its aftermath, the concept of illegal, illegitimate children born out of wedlock, absence of social benefits for mothers and minimal responsibilities and maximum rights for the father are the social evils to be condemned, and not the 'experience,' i.e., the potentials of a woman to be loving, caring and affectionate towards her children. The lesbians in this story, while not being caught in the 'institution,' also repel the 'experience' or suffer from a total absence of the 'experience' of motherhood.

Nichol's story also talks about the "animated women," (1) "holding their hands together over the lip of the edge in giddy communion" at the dinner party of the local lesbians; Anabella, the dominating lesbian, describes herself as an "avid heterosexual with aesthetic appreciation for women." (2) A triangular love-relationship sets in when Anabella and Andrea feel attracted towards Maria. "How do you know each other?," (5) Andrea asks Anabella, seeing the latter talking to the former. Anabella gives a pseudo-assurance: "Do you think Maria would take me when she could have any one of you loveliness?" (5) Anabella next sincerely pleads to Maria, "Well, do you find me even slightly attractive?" and "Do you think I'm terribly masculine?" (8) The short story that reveals the aggressiveness and possessiveness of the lesbians ends with love, concern and confidence; and it refuses to accept the commonly held assumption that homosexual relationships are doomed to be fleeting: "Then, without asking Andrea reached up and pinched the skin at the nape of Maria's neck. When Andrea could not get a good angle, she stood up and moved behind Maria, brushing Maria's hair out of the way. 'You'll feel bruised tomorrow. When you wake up, you should really call me,' Andrea said." (10) She further insists, "you probably won't, but you really should." (10) The party-lesbians in the story may transform themselves into sleeping lesbians, but their sleep will lead them to a reawakening. There is faith/affirmation at the end of the story when Maria, after imagining "a sky above her with no stars and bareness below it," "feels hopeful." (10)

In Kathryn Ann's long story "Michigan" the emphasis is on the humaneness of lesbians, though there is an erotic, sexual orientation as well. The rapport between Chris and Joan who meet at the annual Michigan Woman's Festival ultimately illustrates what Adrienne Rich would call a 'spiritual bonding' in the ' lesbian continuum.' Little sex and slight misunderstanding lead a longing for each other, a final joy and communion, between Chris and Joan.

In Ingrid E. MacDonald's short story, "Catherine, Catherine" the governing theme is that of a woman putting on the guise of a male and acting as a male partner to women. The story opens with the description of the Acre where "thousands of corpses were brought, carried by horses or pushed in carts up the long steep incline, on a cobbled path, to be buried after the "plagues had had their way with the living."[8] A twenty four-year-old woman is left out by the disease that killed 35000 Londoners in one year. The girl's nailing her father's coffin with a wooden sole of her shoe is symbolic of her contempt for men. Subsequently, she walks in the direction of south, away from London and takes a new name "a name, the name, the right new name for herself" (99) with which she will act as a male and wreak vengeance on the male community. Christened as Peter because of her male attire, she protests like a jealous male when Eva "took Percy aside and freely kissed as she pleased." (100) She aspires to become "a man and not a wife." (103) She then calls herself Matthew, and thenceforth picks up more names like Percy and Cornelieus. Meanwhile, she prepares a leather membrum in imitation of the male genital organ and feels proud in her breech with the membrum wrapped around her. The new Cornelieus finds himself in the company of a young maid by name Catherine, satisfying her sexually, with the leather membrum. She often tells herself, "something in me rebelled against my womanish birth and cursed the form I was born with." (106) She laments that her life is a "tale of misery, neither man nor woman and neither able to be." (106) Meanwhile, the young maid Catherine discovers that Cornelieus is only a woman and is amazed to see "how their natures were identical in everyway." (108) She takes a knife and cuts away the membrum from her man-woman lover. In due course, the young maid is given to understand from the parish-priest that her man-woman lover is Catherine and now there are two Catherines, involved in emotional and physical solidarity; they happily part: "We kissed and vowed that all that was intimate between us be forgotten from our memory and our joy as much as our grief be lapsed from our thoughts." (111) Such is the solidarity that the two women aspire for.

In the other lesbian story, "Etta James and Your Heart" by Ann Decter, the central theme spins round a party, a get-together. The scene of action is the winter solstice party, an annual gathering of old and good friends. The participants feel that "there is no time at all and all the time in the world, because there is nothing to do now but loving each other."[9] They are happy that as lesbians they are lucky because they do not succumb to AIDS: "Well, I'm worried that lesbians just aren't taking AIDS seriously, and I would really like to say to all the lesbians listening tonight to do some research, take precautions. You know, there are no guarantees, no guarantees at all in this life." (117) At the end of the party, the members realize what makes their life meaningful is togetherness—togetherness among women as the vital part of living.

Lesbian texts thus re-envision a different lesbian future. It highlights how the phallocentric society is limited in its view of lesbianism. In the 80s and 90s, the lesbian writers have written detective stories, mysteries and romances that focus on lesbians and lesbian culture. In all these texts the pivotal point is what it means to negotiate the division between heterosexual life and the homosexual. Though there are difficulties for these writers for getting publishers, they persist in their attempt to write and publish. They portray communities where lesbianism is central rather than marginal. The lesbian literature constructs a gender oppositionalism on the premise that society need not be assessed in terms of heterosexuality and lesbianism need not be viewed as something immoral, unnatural and erotic, for it ultimately pleads for an emotional and spiritual bonding between women, a 'lesbian continuum.'

NOTES

1. Adrienne Rich, "Compulsory Heterosexuality and Lesbian Existence." Elizabeth Abel and Amily K. Abel, ed., *The Signs Reader: Women, Gender and Scholarship* (1983), pp. 156-57.
2. Havelock Ellis, "The Study of Sexual Inversion," *The Psychology of Sex. A Student's Manual* (London, 1933).

3. Joan Blackwood, "Aristotle, Sex and a Three-Legged Dog: The Naturalness of Lesbian Sex," Sharon Dale Stone, ed., *Lesbians in Canada* (Toronto, 1990), p. 155.
4. Walter J. Coville, Tomothy W. Costello and Fabian L. Rouke, *Abnormal Psychology* (New York: Barnes and Noble, 1970), p. 171.
5. D.L. West, *Homosexuality* (Middlesex: Penguin, 1974), p. 208.
6. Louis P. Thorpe, *The Psychology of Mental Health* (New York: Ronald, 1960), p. 263.
7. Judith Nichols, "Lesbians in Poughkeepsie," *Blithe House Quarterly* (1997-2004), p. 6.
8. Ingrid E. MacDonald, "Catherine, Catherine," *Dykewords: An Anthology of Lesbian Writing*, ed. The Lesbian Writing and Publishing Collective (Toronto: Women's Press, 1990), p. 97.
9. Ann Decter, "Etta James and Your Heart," *Dykewords*, p. 119.

Globalisation, Consumerism and Gender Roles

ANURADHA BHOITE
University of Pune

Almost in all human societies, barring a few, gender is a significant factor which determines person's higher or lower position in social hierarchy. Though different societies have undergone various stages of social and economic evolution, the sex-linked statuses have remained more or less the same. In modern times, the globalization of the economy and its attendant awe-inspiring consumerism are just turning topsy-turvy the societal values of different societies. The question arises: what is the position and role of woman in this fast-changing society, rampant with mindless consumerism? Whether technological developments and production forces with their focus and consumer economy in postmodernity are sidetracking all human values? Whether consumerism is becoming a mono-God, devouring or belittling other aspects of society or rather the values such as equality, freedom and liberty?

It is commonly believed that men earn and women consume. So modern consumerism spread over the globe, targets women by various mechanisms. In the present paper, I wish to examine how far consumerism is utilizing traditional norms of inequality and dependence status of women for commercial purposes.

Canada is a developed state while India is still a third world country. The comparison of gender role in these two countries will shed some light on the age-long differential statuses of men and women in the present times in the context of globalization and consumerism.

Consumption consumption is not new to human society. If we go by the literal meaning of the term consumption, it means to use, to destroy, to exhaust economic objects for individual gratification or for personal satisfaction. To possess, to hoard, to accumulate, to squander the objects of consumption may be basic human nature. But societal imperatives operate on selective basis, in this field too. Though man has dreamt of homogenous society, actually for the functioning of the society, there are different layers or strata in society. They are hierarchically arranged. Once this hierarchical structure of higher and lower status is built up in the society, it becomes more or less permanent feature, very difficult to break or bring down. Because higher ups enjoy various privileges and through them they dominate lower classes for maintaining their privileges. In the hierarchically-arranged structure of the society, the people who occupy higher rung of the social ladder, try to keep their higher position intact vis-à-vis people belonging to lower strata, by different strategies and mechanisms. Because of the inter-relatedness between economic and social domination, the higher ups show their social superiority by conspicuous consumption. They start possessing the products which will be out of reach for the common man. In pre-modern society scarce objects were symbols of social and cultural superiority. What is significant in modern times is at one end, abundance of goods due to amazing technological progress and at the other end, large masses are just the passive spectators, especially in the third world country, lacking the necessary purchasing power.

Generally it is said that postmodern neo-capitalism is creating needs or excess needs for the consumption of products. In this context, I am to state that this economic phenomenon is not new to human society. In olden days also the traders, manufacturers of scarce goods tried to lure the kings, the tribal lords, Zamindars or people belonging to privileged sector of the society for purchasing the goods which were luxuries or excesses. The festival processions, the diamond-studded jewellery, the decorative palaces, the super-fine clothes, the elaborate marriage ceremonies, the milk abhishekas, the tulas (weighing ceremony of privileged few) of royal families and other privileged people, were just nothing but squandering of wealth or conspicuous consumption in front of poor masses who were mute spectators.

The same thing is happening in modern times. The post-modern society of the present day, based on capitalistic mode of production and consumption, is just dividing the rift between the haves and have-nots by providing and producing newer objects for the consumption of the wealthy at the cost of the labour of the lower classes. So globalization now means intrusion of advanced capitalism into the less developed societies for capturing the higher strata into its fold, is widening the social rift.

Now let us come to the Gender roles in relation to consumerism which is a global phenomenon. But in modern times, the capitalist economy armed with advanced marketing strategies has been exploiting the existing popular social modes which have mass appeal for furtherance of its ruthless goal of getting more money without any moral concern. T.V., magazines, newspapers, street posters—all these ad items are rampant with the ad shows depicting the traditional social norms governing the male, female relationship in the society. For example, the ad of Baniyan worn by men, shows a woman with her scanty clothes coming nearer to man because he is wearing a particular brand of Baniyan and admiring him. Here the presence of woman is used just as a sex-symbol.

Another example is importance given to Miss India, Miss World, Miss Universe pageants. These are nothing but social exhibitions for mass transactions of money on the global or national level where woman's body is actually the pivot of all business. The cosmetic industries, the gyms, the beauty parlours are just nourishing, and creating wealth for the wealthy people.

To quote from the electronic text, "Even in this age of market segmentation, where men are addressed as style-conscious buyers, the association of femininity remains nearly seamless. And these terms have been mutually reinforcing consumption coded as a female pursuit, frivolous and even wasteful, a form of leisure rather than productive work. In turn, consumer identity obscures, women's important contribution to economic and political life. In such locations as "Mrs. Consumers" and "born to shop," women appear only on the receiving end of the Consumer Culture. (Kathy L. Peiss, *Journal for Mult- Media History*, Vol.

1 No. 1, Fall 1998, 1). "Erasing the difference among women and stressing those between the sexes, advertisers touted women's supposedly universal desire for beauty, their interest and natural sense of duty to the family's well being." (*Ibid.*, 3)

The image of the female consumer came into prominence in a period when American society made women's nature and appropriate roles a subject matter of intense debate. After all, women were increasingly visible in higher education, the professions and the workplace. They had won the right to vote, participated in urban reform, and volunteered for war relief work. Some scientists questioned the very existence of sex differences. In an era in which traditional roles were challenged from many quarters, the mass-market's model of the woman consumer tended to reinforce the gender divide.

In India, in the 19th century and also in the early part of 20th century, the educators and the reformers tried to uplift the image of the woman as equal partner in different aspects of life. After independence too, in the latter half of the 20th century, Indian Constitution passed different laws for creating a space for her in society as first class citizen enjoying freedom, equality and liberty. But I think this relentless consumerism in postmodern society, under the guise of globalization, in India and probably in Canada has taken her back to her traditional roles and age-old social images.

The little ray of hope lies in such attempts as Rally's adbusters, 'No buying day' in Canada. But it is difficult to predict whether such lone attempts will succeed in the face of devouring gushing onslaught of consumerism in the 21st century.

Women's Role in Development: Canada And India

N. SHAIK MOHAMED
Jamal Mohamed College, Tiruchirappalli

Introduction

The World Bank speaks of development along the lines of its own criterion as symbolised by the private car, the jet airlines, consumption and waste. The developed countries measure their development in terms of education, health and standard of living of the people. Similarly, the less developed countries try to indicate their mode of development in increasing calories of food available per head. The elites, who hold power in many states, desire to live in a luxurious style, try to allocate an excessive proportion of the national income to luxury expenditure, consequently not enough is left over for agriculture and the industries needed to modernise it.

Women can and should play a key role in the process of development. Improper development is due partly to the population explosion in which women, as the child bearers, play a primordial part. Moreover, the task of preparing meals in the home, which is such an enormous source of saving, is entirely in their hands. Again, women in their maternal role are educators, especially during early childhood. Finally, women, like men, have an essential political function to perform and must be able to speak on the matters against their development. The purpose of the present paper is briefly to review various roles women play in Canada and India.

Women as Agents of Reproduction

Women act as agents of reproduction. They are responsible for the unprecedented catastrophe commonly known as the population explosion. The most obvious correlations with reduced fertility are wealth, standard of living, and, in particular, education. Educated women have far fewer children than illiterate ones. It is true in Canada that the average size of the family ranges from two to three. The female literacy rate (99%) in Canada is also definitely higher than India. Therefore, the accelerated literacy rate in Canada has been helping largely to keep the family size as small as possible. Moreover the total fertility rate in Canada is 1.9 percent (1990) and 3.87 in India. This suggests that women in India are more prone to child bearing. Again, the birth rate in Canada is 14.6 per 1000 where in India it is 29.7 per 1000, which is almost double. All these indicate that the women in Canada have been less active in reproduction of human beings than their counterpart, the Indian women.

Women as Farmers and Growers of Food

In a Canadian province it used to be dishonourable for women to work in the fields. The poorest, who had no choice, were degraded by the mere act of doing so, and their "virtue" called into question. Women were among the most significant supporters of industrialisation, since they were fighting for a double liberation; like their husbands, from landlords and moneylenders but also from the unending family oppression.

By contrast, if one visits an Indian village, one finds the women are still confined to the house and the farmyard. Again, only the poorest and thus most despised go to work in the fields. They are prisoners in their own homes, allowed only to thresh and husk the rice and to share in the work of transplantation, harvesting or irrigation. Thus we find two extremes in Canada and India: women play a lesser role in the agricultural field in Canada and enhanced role in India. However, if women are to play a larger part in agricultural production without being overburdened, their domestic tasks will have to be shared increasingly by men and children.

Women as Cooks and Dietitians

In Canada, wheat remains the staple diet. The crude method of cooking eliminates the parts richest in protein. Dairying is common to almost all farming areas in Canada and has become a highly specialised business in the more densely populated sections. In India, rice and wheat are considered to be the principal food items. The white rice is not only dearer than unpolished rice, but it has a much lower nutritional value, having lost most of its vitamins. The women in two countries should be relieved of their role as beasts of burden and steps be taken to make wider use of animal power. (Dumont, Rene)

Women as Mothers and Educators

Women ın Canada are considered to be good mothers as they can keep the birth rate and disease at a lower level and education of the child at a higher level. It is evident from the infant mortality rate which is 7 per thousand (1990); whereas for the same, India touches the figure of 80 per thousand. It is attributed that the high literacy rate enjoyed among the women of Canada, enables them to achieve the same. The Canadian Government also has implemented many health and wealth programmes for the betterment of the children and motherhood.

On the other hand, literacy (70%) and ignorance are the common features of Indian women as they could not adopt preventive measures to safeguard their children. In India, the children in rural areas need special attention as 99 million live in rural areas as against 19 million in urban areas. There is poor knowledge of nutrition health and hygiene among Indian mothers. The infant mortality rate in India is almost ten times that of Canada. Therefore, drastic measures are required in this respect to meet the situation.

Women as Citizens

The young (Christian) ladies in Canada are now refusing to be bought and sold like cattle and are claiming the right to choose their own mates. The women who are up in the arms about this situation are primarily those who are qualified. They have discarded veil and refuse to be shut up in the home. It is evident from a survey in Canada which shows that hardly 3% of female international managers are working for North American firms.

In India, under Article 14, women are guaranteed equality before law and Article 16 (1) and (2) provide for equality of opportunities. Thus, constitution not only treats women equal to men but also opens the way for them to participate fully in all spheres of national development.

It has been observed that with some exceptions, the role played by the women in India has been very weak due to various reasons. It is evident from the 1991 census figures, that about 6 out of 10 females are still illiterate. This position is grim in rural areas. Under the process of democratic decentralisation where enormous powers are being handed down, women may not have success in getting their share of development.

Ours is a male dominated society and this dominance is comparatively more in the rural areas. Now, conditions, one-third share in public life is to be given to women in India, which again may create tension from the male members.

Conclusion

The role of women in Canada and India differs socially, culturally and politically. Women in Canada are blessed with more education and knowledge which make them attain a certain level of development; the women in India, who are weak in structure, education and knowledge cannot meet the challenges related to their development. Despite these limitations, there is also need for attitudinal change among the male members both in India and Canada, who should give a fair chance to women in public life, education and employment opportunities. The day is not far when women's participation in grassroots democracy would show its positive effect on the democratic structure of the nation.

Works Cited

Adler, Nancy J., "*W*omen in International Management: Where are they?" *California Management Review*, Vol. XXVI, No. 4, Summer 1984, pp. 78-79.

Dumont, Rene, "Development and Mounting Famine: A role for Women," *International Labour Review*, Vol. III, No. 6, June 1975, pp. 451-58.

Singh, Mohinder, "Political Equity for Women," *Social Welfare*, Vol. 41, No. 10, January 1995, pp. 13-15.

_____, "Women in India's Development," *Social Welfare*, Vol. XI, No. 10, December 1993, pp. 19-22.

Different Strokes: Multiculturalism and Civil Society in Canada and India

SUNIL SONDHI
Rajdhani College, University of Delhi

Introduction

Although talk of civil society is in fashion both in Canada and in India, there is quite a contrast in the focus of discussion in the two countries (CIVICUS 1994). In India discussion on civil society has centred on individual rights, especially the right to participate in the political process. More and more citizens in India are demanding that their voices be heard and their interest reflected in the policy-making process which has been overwhelmingly dominated by the bureaucracy, business and special-interest groups.

In Canada, the story is more complicated in that there is a "twist" in discussion; many people attempt to address the issues of civil society without actually referring to it (Thomson 2000). Nevertheless, the focus has been to regain the ethos of community and directly or indirectly inspire moral behaviour and a sense of responsibility. Weighing in for more responsibility may mean less individual rights, which is quite a contrast to what is happening in India.

Social Entrepreneurship vs Political Participation

The "twist" in discussion of civil society in Canada stems from the fact that there is strong resistance to talk of morality and responsibility in Canadian public discourse. As a result, many forward-looking community leaders have fashioned different ways to inspire and mobilize people who believe in civil society (Bornstein 1998). One example is reference to social entrepreneurship. By calling for business and economic development, as well as the betterment of community, "social entrepreneurship" appeals to those who cherish the inherent values of civil society as manifest in the Canadian spirit throughout history, but who doubt the usefulness of and resist talk of civility, morality and social responsibility (Catford 1998).

Also, many corporate leaders are talking about corporate-community involvement and community investment, rather than philanthropy and corporate social responsibility, which are traditionally terms used in discussing the role of corporations in the community (Canon 2000). These are but two manifestations of the "twist" which illustrates how Canadians are trying to address the issues surrounding civil society without talking about morality and responsibility.

Of interest to those who are in Canada is the fact that discussion of civil society in India lacks this tension between individual rights on the one hand and morality and responsibility on the other. It is as if the Indian contribution to the global civil society debate says that *more individualism leads to more moral citizens and that more individual rights lead to more socially responsible communities*. Aside from its veracity, a common belief among those who advocate on behalf of civil society in India is that individuals in a democratic society, bestowed full rights of political participation, will exercise rights with utmost consideration for the public good, rather than utilize rights for private, sometimes selfish gains.

Civil Society and Multiculturalism in Canada

Canada's experience with diverse communities distinguishes it from most other countries. Its 30 million inhabitants reflect a cultural, ethnic and linguistic makeup found rarely elsewhere. Diversity has been a fundamental characteristic of Canada since its beginnings.

A broad framework of laws and policies supports Canada's approach to diversity. At the federal level, these include the Canadian Charter of Rights and Freedoms, the Canadian Human Rights Act, the Employment Equity Act, the Official Languages Act, the Pay Equity Act and the Multiculturalism Act. Provinces and territories also have laws, human rights commissions and programmes that promote diversity. Finally, Canada reinforces its commitment to diversity as a signatory to international conventions including, for example, the Universal Declaration of Human Rights and the International Covenant on Economic, Social and Cultural Rights.

However, making equality of opportunity meaningful in a diverse society requires more than constitutional measures and legislation. All levels of government in Canada deliver programmes that mobilize communities to promote dialogue and help people overcome barriers to their participation in society (Reiss 1999).

Canada's future depends on maintaining and strengthening its capacity to bring together peoples with many differences—even grievances—and building a peaceful society where no one's identity or cultural heritage has to be compromised. Canada's approach to diversity is based on the belief that the common good is best served when everyone is accepted and respected for who he/she is, and that this ultimately makes for a resilient, more harmonious and more creative society. This faith in the value of community recognizes that respect for cultural distinctiveness is intrinsic to an individual's sense of self-worth and identity, and a society that accommodates everyone equally and encourages achievement, participation, attachment to country and a sense of belonging.

In 1971, Canada became the first country in the world to adopt an official Multiculturalism policy. This policy provided for programmes and services to support ethnocultural associations and to help individuals overcome barriers to their full participation in Canadian society. In 1982, the multicultural character of Canada gained constitutional recognition in Section 27 of the newly adopted Canadian Charter of Rights and Freedoms. It specified that the courts were to interpret the Charter "in a manner consistent with the preservation and enhancement of the multicultural heritage of Canada." By virtue of this section of the Charter, Canada became a constitutional multicultural state.

Lessons learned through experience with multiculturalism have taught Canada that acceptance and understanding of communities make collective development possible. However, experience with diversity also shows that inequities must be acknowledged and addressed for a diverse people to move forward together. This is a slow and sometimes painful process, but it is essential if all Canadian communities are to enjoy the same sense of belonging and attachment to their country. It also serves to familiarize Canadians with the history they share and the obligations that their history confers.

As with official languages and multiculturalism, Canada has learned that constitutional measures and legislation alone are not enough to ensure equal opportunity to communities in a diverse society. To contribute fully and achieve their full potential, all communities must have a voice in society and a chance to shape the future direction of the country of which they are a part. This requires mechanisms to enable communities and groups to speak out and be heard, and to participate in national debates. It also requires programmes that help equip communities and organizations with the skills and tools they need to advance their interests.

Canada has embraced diversity, or cultural pluralism as some people refer to it, in both policy and practice. It is viewed as one of Canada's most important attributes, socially and economically (McLeod 1997). Canadians value diverse communities for enriching cultural expression and making daily life more varied and interesting. Businesses and employers recognize that diversity in the workplace promotes innovation, stimulates teamwork and creativity and helps expand markets for goods and services. As the diversity of the population expands, new links are forged with the world at a time when Canadians recognize the increasing importance of having a credible voice in international affairs and in strengthening our advantage in the global economy.

Canada's distinctiveness lies in having been a multicultural society from its earliest days. The foundation had already been laid for constructive co-existence among culturally and racially diverse communities. And the close links these communities enjoy with virtually every country on earth lead the Government of Canada to be enthusiastic about the economic potential of multiculturalism (Zadek 1997).

While its record in recognizing the rights of all its peoples is far from perfect, Canada has learned a great deal from its diverse communities. Accepting and then coming to value the differences between communities has changed and continues to change Canada, making the country a better place. However, as Canadians look to the future it is clear that new pressures will make balancing diversity and unity even more challenging (Lassiter 1997).

Canada has managed its increasing diversity and maintained unity by balancing rights and responsibilities in citizenship, and individual and collective rights in its Constitution. However, the global forces of change that affect all countries affect Canada too. The diversity of the Canadian populace is increasing faster than at any time in its history. Communication technologies—satellites, computers and the Internet—are fundamentally changing relationships, transactions and expectations in its economy and in its society. And with exports accounting for more than 40% of its GDP, Canada is affected by the evolution towards "one market, one world" as increased international trade makes the globe smaller and its peoples more interconnected and interdependent (Henton 1997).

The ethnocultural diversity of Canada's population is a major advantage when access to global markets is more important than ever to its economic prosperity. Protecting this advantage means that steps to eradicate racism are essential. Beyond the inequity, suffering and social disruption that intolerance and racism causes, Canada cannot afford to have any of its citizens marginalized.

As a knowledge-based economy in an increasingly competitive global marketplace, every mind matters (Warwick 1997). All Canadians must have the opportunity to develop and contribute to their full potential. As a consequence, the Government of Canada is working with provincial and territorial governments, the private and voluntary sectors and individual Canadians to help strengthen its institutions, build safer and more supportive communities and reinforce shared values. For example, the Government of Canada is working to make the federal public service more representative of the diverse communities it serves.

It is enhancing its multiculturalism programming, expanding its anti-racism activities and strengthening its support for other minority groups such as persons with disabilities to help more individual Canadians overcome barriers to their full participation in society.

The Government is also working to increase access to all forms of Canadian cultural expression in all media. A major effort is under way to digitize the holdings of Canada's cultural institutions and link them to form a virtual museum of Canada. These and many other efforts will help ensure that, as the world becomes smaller and Canada's connections with other countries deepen, Canada can use new technologies to strengthen its communities, to find and connect with one another, share their stories and perspectives, and work together for the common good while maintaining a strong sense of place and of pride in being Canadian.

In these and many other ways it is being ensured that change works to Canada's advantage—that its communities remain a source of strength and creativity, and that they continue to play a pivotal role in making Canada a modern, forward-looking country.

Civil Society in India: Focus on Individual Rights

Turning back to India, an overview of civil society in India shows the rise of volunteerism following the deepening of democracy and developments around the new non-profit corporation legislation. India in the 1990s has gone through a massive political and economic transformation as has never been seen before in the post-Independence era. The topic of civil society is at the core of the current debate about how to reinvigorate India politically and socially and create an unprecedented level of true democracy (Tandon 1991).

The centrality of moral or civic responsibility is, politically and socially, in direct contrast to, if not the polar opposite of, what the term connotes in India. In India, the discussion of civil society in the last decade at least, has centred on a call for *more* individual political and social rights, not less. Indeed, the word 'citizens' has earned a status of sacred canon in India's political discourse these days. The word is used for example in judging whether or not policies proposed by established political parties are good for society. With approval ratings for political parties on a constant decline, several would-be politicians today run for offices as unaffiliated candidates.

"Citizens," in this particular usage, denote individuals who act autonomously and voluntarily with a well-informed understanding of public life and civic mind. Calls for civil society in India in the 1990s are superficial at best and devoid of meaning. The press, politicians and the average person use the term civil society because it has become "politically correct" to do so, and doing so will garner the support of those who feel deeply that something has gone wrong in the country but don't know exactly what. Indeed, the word citizen is often placed at the opposite end of the spectrum from government, bureaucracy and big business. Citizen is everything that the government and business is not.

From one standpoint, citizenship's greatest strength is the power of participating in a democracy. There is nothing new in recognizing that Indian democracy endorses an individual's right to participate in the political process. These days, however, Indian people have discovered that they do not really possess the power to exert meaningful influence on the political process. This realization is definitely behind the force pushing for the legislation of the new non-profit corporation law.

Thus, essentially, the message in the civil society debate in India is "power to the people." In a way, the Indians at present, who are so disillusioned by the domestic political and economic situation, are entrusting their last hope to the abstract sense of citizens. Citizens in this sense, are moral and responsible beings, who consciously strive to act for what is good for the public. This is the crystallized notion of individuals as social beings at the core of a democratic society. Whereas Canadians are wary of uncontrolled exercise of individual rights for the maintenance of social order and a civic mind-set, people in India are saying, "we can make it work, so give us the requisite rights."

Indian bureaucrats have been on the defensive during the last few years. Traditionally they were hailed as the elite heroes who made India's post-Independence reconstruction possible. While Indian lawmakers were often viewed domestically and internationally as lacking leadership, bureaucrats on the other hand were often admired for their efficiency and effectiveness. Times have changed. These days, it is hard to open a daily newspaper and not find an article that talks about the bureaucracy's inflexibility, ineptitude, inter-ministry fighting, collusive practices with business as well as cases of embezzlement and bribery. Also heard often are complaints about legislators' inability to manifest strong enough initiatives to control, guide and chastise the bureaucracy when it is not working well.

One of the issues involving heated controversies and exchanges is in public works. People today tend to view the whole array of public works projects as an example of government kowtowing to the interests of the construction industry with little, if any, benefit accruing to local citizens who live where projects are implemented. People often see more harm than good in them, such as with dam construction projects across the nation.

Civil society, in this particular context, is a society where citizens not only can freely express their views about community development, but also can exert meaningful influence by participating in policy-making decisions (Dowell 2000). Traditional criticism of the people's initiative is to point out that local council members as well as the mayor are elected to represent the diverse views of citizens and that having the local council is sufficient means to ensure that citizens' voices are incorporated in the democratic political process. These days, this is not enough to satisfy people, especially when political representatives are under attack with allegations, and justifiable observations, that they are actually only representing the interests of those who already have access to power (Fowler 2000).

Commonalties and Differences in the Civil Society Debate in Canada and India

There is no question that maintaining a strong and healthy civil society is viewed as a necessary condition for a workable democracy. Both in Canada and in India, the level of citizens' political participation is deemed as a crucial measurement of whether civil society is healthy. The two societies differ substantially, however, in viewing their citizens as moral beings. In Canada, the prevalent understanding is that society has been focusing too much on individuals' private rights, which in effect encourages people to make light of, if not disregard, individuals as social and moral beings. Non-profit organizations in the 1990s are charged with the challenge of inspiring and mobilizing the apathetic and disillusioned for a social and implicitly moral cause using novel and innovative visions, charisma, cross-sector initiative and leadership.

In India, by way of contrast, trust in individuals as social beings remains unscrutinized by those who advocate on behalf of civil society. There is the perception that bestowing more individual rights goes hand in hand with creating a stronger civil society. Various forms of nonprofit and voluntary organizations provide means for Indian citizens to express and exercise their individual rights. This, in a sense, can be seen as a good example of the multiculturalism ethos which "recognizes both individual human dignity and the social dimension of human existence." Multiculturalists in Canada might be more at home on the other side of the globe.

Bibliography

Bornstein, David (1998). "Changing the world on a shoestring: an ambitious foundation promotes social change by finding 'social entrepreneurs,'" *Atlantic Monthly*, January, Vol. 281, No. 1, pp. 34-39.

Cannon, Carl (2000). "Charity for profit: how the new social entrepreneurs are creating good by sharing wealth," *National Journal*, June 16, pp. 1898-1904.

Catford, John (1998). "Social entrepreneurs are vital for health promotion—but they need supportive environments too," *Health Promotion International*, Vol. 13, No. 2, pp. 95-97.

Coeyman, Marjorie. (1999) "Social entrepreneurs eagerly move forward," *Christian Science Monitor*, April 27, Vol. 91, Issue 105, p. 17.

CIVICUS (1994). *Citizens: Strengthening Global Civil Society*. MacNaughton and Gunn, Washington DC

De Leeuw, Evelyne (1999). "Healthy cities: urban social entrepreneurship for health," *Health Promotion International*, Vol. 14, No. 3, pp. 261-69.

Dowell, William (2000). "Investing in social change," *Time*, July 24, Vol. 156; Issue 4, p. 55.

Fowler, Alan (2000). "NGDOs as a moment in history: beyond aid to social entrepreneurship or civic innovation?," *Third World Quarterly*, Vol. 21, No. 4, pp. 637-54.

Henton, Douglas, John Melville and Kimberly Walesh (1997). "The age of the civic entrepreneur: restoring civil society and building economic community," *National Civic Review*, Summer, Vol. 86, No. 2, pp. 149-56.

Lassiter, April (1997). "The new social architects," *Policy Review*, July/August, pp. 52-56.

McLeod, Heather (1997). "Cross over: the social entrepreneur," *Inc. Special Issue: State of Small*, Vol. 19, No. 7, pp. 100-4.

Prabhu, Ganesh N. (1999). "Social entrepreneurial leadership," *Career Development International*, Vol. 4, No. 3, pp. 140-45.

Reis, Tom (1999). *Unleashing the New Resources and Entrepreneurship for the Common Good: a Scan, Synthesis and Scenario for Action*. Battle Creek, MI: W.K. Kellogg Foundation. 27pp.

Tandon, Rajesh (1991). Civil Society, *The State and Roles of NGOs*. New Delhi. Society for Participatory Research.

Thompson, John, Geoff Alvy and Ann Lees (2000). "Social entrepreneurship—a new look at the people and the potential," *Management Decision*, Vol. 38, No. 5.

Warwick, David (1997). "Will social entrepreneurs blossom or hit bottom?," *People Management*, October 9, Vol. 3, Issue 20, p. 56.

Zadek, Simon and Stephen Thake (1997). "Send in the Social Entrepreneurs," *New Statesman*, June 20, Vol. 26, Issue 7339, p. 31.

Creative Writing

For Columbus

I

When grapes are her breasts
And apples her skin, I am at home—
I long for Italian brothers, Greek sisters,
An African father
    an Indian mother.

I long with the same longing
As the clouds coming down, the sky
About to tilt over
Like a ship in a hefty sea.

I also long for a French aunt
Who will elegantly raise her a handkerchief
In the wind, signalling an archipelago—
As I cry out, "Islands, islands!"
        (more)

II

Now it is you who I remember,
Your neck bruised, the shadow
Of an axe coming downing
    in the Tower.

You too Cortez, as Montezuma burns
Inside, his cry resounding in the night;
You with your Quetzalcoatl face,
A helmet still glinting.

Pizarro next,
And I watch the Incas in silver mines
Living out a life, buried in sand, their heads
Above the ground while the ocean once more
threatens disaster.

III

With a Crusoe mask, I listen in the distance,
Our Friday's commands,
The Spanish Empire sinking in the background—
This treasure being all I am left with,
Bible in hand, the sun whipping by,
A lopsided moon sinking lower
into the bottomless sea,

As I try to jump over it, my *paradiso,*
El Dorado, the heathen sky
Falls prostrate
at my feet.

Cyril Dabydeen (Toronto)

Poem taken from *Imaginary Origins: Selected Poems*, Peepal Tree Press, U.K., 2000.

Tsunami's Anger

The picturesque beach, serenity of the sea
is but a delusion.
When Tsunami strikes, it splits, it annihilates
pullling out leaves and trees, flooding buildings and
minarets sweeping away hordes of children—innocent,
women-pregnant, old and aged,
Wailing, mourning is unabated,
In the winking of an eye—
The poignant human drama unveils itself.

Tsunami tides,
Mightier than the Mightiest
are a riddle unto themselves.
They strike when all is ripe,
Strike when all is joy and merriment,
When waters of the paradise are a boon,
When islanders, tourists drink of bliss
The nightmare comes, comes alive.

B.R. Nagpal (Delhi)

AIDS Virus

The dark, shanty room was unlocked
The knight with red ribbon descended
upon his dame. Their cot screeched.

She did not resist unlike a whore
She was wifely,
Her delicate beads bending, vitals sagging
body swirling.
The assault wholesale was full,
She was undone.

She was speechless: She was unaware
She fell infected
AIDS Virus was devouring her
limb by limb.

She was like a ghost in daylight,
She was like fire burnt out
She was like engulfed smoke in a desert
She was tongueless, spineless, breathless.

B.R. Nagpal (Delhi)